DATE DUE

OC 2 2 '98			
FE 2 3 '99			
MR 1 8 '99			
DE 7 '00			
DE 6 '01			
JU 2 8 '02			
MY 7 '02			
AG 8 '02			
DE 9 '02			

Arab and Israeli Terrorism

ARAB AND ISRAELI TERRORISM

The Causes and Effects of Political Violence, 1936–1993

Kameel B. Nasr

McFarland & Company, Inc., Publishers
Jefferson, North Carolina, and London

British Library Cataloguing-in-Publication data are available

Library of Congress Cataloguing-in-Publication Data

Nasr, Kameel B., 1949–
    Arab and Israeli terrorism : the causes and effects of political
violence, 1936–1993 / Kameel B. Nasr.
      p. cm.
    Includes bibliographical references and index.
    ISBN 0-7864-0280-6 (library binding : 50# alkaline paper) ∞
    1. Jewish-Arab relations—1949–   2. Terrorism—Israel—
History. 3. Abu Nidal. I. Title.
DS119.7.N346 1997
956.04—dc20   96-38464
                                           CIP

Manufactured in the United States of America

*McFarland & Company, Inc., Publishers
  Box 611, Jefferson, North Carolina 28640*

May the bodies of the innocent
thrown along the road of despair
bring us closer to the palace of peace.

Contents

viii   **Contents**

Preface

Mistakes provide us an opportunity to learn, and the sadly mistaken violence proceeding from years of discord in the Middle East offers us a special chance to understand the nature of conflict, the psychology of humans and their societies, and the effectiveness of methods for dealing with dissension. Learning is a difficult task when it requires us to question our own attitudes and practices.

As a path for achieving satisfaction, comfort, economic and social well-being, the Palestinian-Israeli dispute, always active in the form of covert or low intensity war, has been rife with mistakes, stupidity, ignorance, and failure. Moreover, the terrorist war, fought by both sides, was as racist as it was political, with Arab terrorists leaving a bomb on a bus just because all the passengers were Jews, and Israelis revenge bombing a village because the residents were Arab. Any Jew, any Arab—and when it came to intentional terrorism, any Westerner—would suffice. Justice, as well as an effective way of winning the conflict, was abandoned, thrown to a bad wind that whirls back on itself to bring still greater evil.

If we are to learn, we must first collect information, trying as much as possible to remain impartial. Most of the literature on the Middle East conflict favors one side, and we read books to see if the authors' ideas match our own, tossing aside as propaganda those books which threaten our smug notion of who is right and who is wrong. As a Palestinian American, I tried very hard to maintain academic integrity, and you can judge whether I have succeeded. My investigation was entirely independent, and naturally its shortcomings are my responsibility. I conducted research in the United States, Europe, North Africa, and the Middle East, interviewing leaders and members of clandestine organizations, gunmen, government officials, crime reporters, and other knowledgeable people.

I have never seen the advantage of war, and this prejudice colors the book, for it seems to me that politically the Middle East has wasted more than half a century in conflict producing no resolution that could not have been reached decades earlier. In this respect, the book is critical of those who made policy,

1

Israeli and Arab, for they have generally shown a lack of foresight and ratio-
nality. I believe that historians will view the decades of Palestinian-Israeli
conflict as critically as we view the European religious wars of the sixteenth
and seventeenth centuries, a passing phase of bitterness, suffering, and killing.

Yet, the ability of two peoples once at war to live in harmony, as we hope
Arabs and Jews will be able to do, is also a tribute to the human spirit. If we
are wise; if we choose good leaders; if our civilization has substantively
advanced over the millennium; then we will use what we have learned to create a better world. Only in this way will the victims of terrorism be honored.

There is a story of an Arab and a Jewish merchant who met in a town
while they were both traveling to sell their goods. Upon seeing that they would
have to compete to sell the same goods in the same village, they began insulting each other. "Your mother is a whore," said the Arab, dredging up the worst
indignity. "You're impotent," retorted the Jew, and each immediately began
undercutting the price of the other in an attempt to eliminate the competi-
tion. The citizens took advantage of their dispute, playing one against the
other and collecting goods for next to nothing. At the end of the selling day,
each discovered that he did not have even enough money to return home. The
two merchants had to face either pooling their resources and returning together
or starving. But an Arab is an Arab and a Jew is a Jew, and starving was
definitely worse than being an impotent son of a whore. Both made great
noises about the price of modern living and complained about how life was
changing for the worse, but they returned together.

Introduction

Psychologists tell us that our subconscious desires are sometimes in direct conflict with our conscious intention. We profess that we want success, romance, happiness and fulfillment, yet our actions lead us to the opposite. A perceptive observer sees clearly that by our actions we avoid obtaining what we intend. The reasons for the conflict between our conscious and unconscious—what we have convinced ourselves we want and what we actually, if subconsciously, desire—lie hidden under a myriad of urges and fears; but our more basic desires are logical and real. We can notice these conflicting intentions in other people, but it takes courage and awareness to admit them to ourselves, since we negate and deny our counter-intention. This inner conflict is part of being human, but it is more pronounced in certain areas and among certain people.

We can effectively transpose the intention/counter-intention concept to international affairs, particularly the decades of conflict between Palestinians and Israelis, where we see with embarrassing clarity each side striving for the opposite of its professed desires. Both sides convinced themselves and their supporters that they wanted victory over the other side, yet their counter-intention was to maintain a state of conflict. The use of terrorism by both sides was a successful way of prolonging the conflict with a guarantee of never achieving the professed goal.

For example, the Israelis professed a desire to eliminate guerrilla or terrorist activity against their country; yet the growth of the guerrilla movements in the 1960s was a direct response to Israeli attacks against them. If Israel had not bothered with the groups—which were ineffective and merited little serious interest—they would have waned into nonexistence. Instead, every time Israel attacked them, it inspired more Palestinian recruits.[1] Thus Israel's actions, supposedly intended to eliminate terrorism, actually produced the

3

opposite result. When Israel expelled 419 Hamas supporters in 1993, the cover of the periodical *The Middle East* read, "Thanks to Israel, Hamas becomes a major player."[2] Hamas was never strong until Israel made its supporters heroes.

Similarly, Palestinians declared that they wanted their own state, but they constantly obstructed the attainment of their goal. If you read Palestinian literature and journalism you will readily notice a recurring theme of victimization: Israel bombs villages, beats prisoners, and commits every horrible act against the innocent. Palestinians lament, but this victimization is also noble, being wronged, hard done by. Palestinian actions such as attacks against Israel were not designed to win back territory—their professed goal—but to instigate counter-attacks and prolong the righteous victimization. When they became effective in a guerrilla war against Israel in 1970, Palestinians fought amongst themselves, then senselessly precipitated a civil war in Jordan that destroyed their national ambitions; then they repeated the story in Lebanon, ensuring them continued victimization.

These are harsh judgments against both sides, and few people involved in the conflict will acknowledge them, but they are necessary before we can make a meaningful assessment of terrorism's effectiveness. The stated goal is not necessarily the true goal, an observation which will help us establish a better overall understanding of the use of covert warfare.

The word terrorism was first used after the French Revolution, when a wave of *terrore* swept across the country in a cycle of retaliation and rash executions. In 1934, following the assassination of King Alexander of Yugoslavia and French foreign minister Louis Barthou at Marseilles, France proposed an international court to try terrorists.[3] After the Palestinian terrorist attack on the 1972 Munich Olympics, the subject of terrorism was raised at the United Nations, and since then there have been dozens of international conventions and proclamations, backed by an anti-terrorism intelligence network which spends $30 billion a year and in the United States alone employs 18,000 people.[4] Today we use the word terrorism to describe the activities of small politically inspired groups, but it has become an obscure concept, lacking a precise definition, associated with propaganda rather than impartial principles.

Many Israelis do not view the Stern and Irgun militias that assassinated and bombed civilians in the 1940s as terrorists, but as soldiers or commandos who often sacrificed their lives for the creation of a homeland and saved Jews from further persecution. The Palestinians look at the gunmen who invaded Israel in equally romantic terms, claiming that the real terrorists were Israeli soldiers who bombed villages. We do not tend to think of an army as terrorists, and we do not include financial, sexual, or social terrorism. Commandos, guerrillas, terrorists—the names are used interchangeably—are different from criminals since they purportedly seek political change, not financial gain.[5] The line between warfare and terror is blurry; nevertheless, certain distinct actions are designed to terrify a civilian population. Clearly, blowing up a hotel or civil airplane or placing a car bomb in a market is an act of terrorism, but terrorism experts would likely hold differing opinions about blowing up a military compound or bombing a military airport, operations which better fall under the category of warfare. Radio Moscow referred to the Afghan Mujahadeen who shot down military aircraft as terrorist. The Voice of America labeled the Shiite radicals who blew up the United States Marine compound at Beirut airport as terrorists. But those people thought of themselves as soldiers fighting a war against other soldiers.

Moreover, terrorism, like war, does not spring from a vacuum but has distinct political causes, and it is unfair to discuss the Irgun's terrorism against the British without considering the plight of Jews in Europe, or to discuss Palestinian plane hijackings without considering Israel's treatment of Palestinian civilians. To offer a list of terrorist actions without examining the historical and political context in which they occur is academically fraudulent.

Let us for now use a broad approach to discuss the incidents of violence in the Middle East, grappling with their underlying causes and their net results. Let us not allow our judgment to be obscured by a mental image of the Middle East as a cauldron of irrationality in which people, often guided by religious fanaticism, act passionately and erratically. This image is false. Actions, especially actions by groups, usually have a basis in some sort of logic.[6] We can often poke wide holes through the logic, and subconscious desires may oppose the conscious intention, but this work assumes that there are underlying reasons for acts of violence and disregards the "crazed" hypothesis that receives too much currency in Hollywood.[7]

We want to examine the overall impact that terror has had on the Middle East conflict, for both proponents and adversaries of terrorism. From there, perhaps we will be able to conclude whether bombings, assassination, the taking of hostages, and other attacks on civilians advanced or hurt the terrorists' cause. Finally, we want to see which measures are effective against terrorism or political violence.

Historians have examined the roots of the Middle East dispute beginning with the biblical story of the walls of Jericho and continuing to the rise of Islam in the seventh century. When the First Crusade arrived in Palestine in 1099, it initiated a friction between East and West, Islam and Christianity, a simmering conflict that continues to the present. Religious tensions have played a large role in the area's power struggle, although it can be argued that ethnicity or nationalism rather than religion fueled the fighting.

For purposes of our discussion, the Palestine-Israel conflict began at the end of the nineteenth century with the advent of the Zionist movement among European Jewry. Following a wave of pernicious Russian pogroms in 1881, many Jews fled to Western Europe and the United States, and some went to Palestine and formed farming settlements.[8] They did not have an easy time, and most left, but the movement to re-create a Jewish state received new impetus when the energetic journalist Theodore Herzl popularized Zionism with the publication of an 1896 tract, *The Jewish State*. The establishment of a Jewish state was being discussed by Jewish intellectuals by the time Herzl attended the 1895 trial of French army captain Alfred Dreyfus, who was framed for treason in proceedings that were accompanied by a vile outpouring of anti–Semitism, later exposed by Emile Zola. The trial convinced Herzl, as Amos Elon put it, "to do something for the Jews," and although Zionism was not his invention, Herzl successfully championed its cause.[9] The movement became official during the first Zionist Congress in Basel, Switzerland, a year later, in which Herzl became the head. The Congress committed themselves to settling in the historic land of Zion and to re-creating a Jewish state.

A monarchist and antiliberal, Herzl was so fired with the need for a Jewish state that his passion overrode any other considerations. In a preview of strange alliances, he sided with the tsar's interior minister, Count Konstantinovich von Plehve, a confirmed anti–Semite responsible for the Kishinev pogrom (April 6–8, 1903). Herzl visited the count shortly after the pogrom, urging that they work together to get Jews out of Russia.[10] Herzl believed that anti–Semitism was natural because the Jews were landless. Anti-Semitism, he said, would in fact help the Zionist dream. He knew nothing of Palestine which at the time had a population of less than half a million[11], adopting the commonly held nineteenth-century notion that European civilization was beneficial to native populations. The Zionist movement was at first solely political, utopian, but news and rumors about Jewish intentions spread quickly.

Palestine then belonged to the crumbling Ottoman Empire, but toward the end of World War I the British and French made plans to exercise control over the Middle East.[12] In 1917 Lord Allenby issued a proclamation on behalf of Britain and France to promote Arab independence in exchange for Arab cooperation against the Turks. (This story is detailed by others, including Lawrence of Arabia.[13]) In the same year the British foreign secretary issued the Balfour Declaration, which announced that Palestine would become a homeland for Jews. Arthur Balfour and Lloyd George, the British prime minister who gave the agreement his personal support, were partly inspired by biblical injunctions.[14] Much critical analysis has been applied to Balfour's one-paragraph declaration and its origins, by everyone from Palestinians who called it a piece of imperial arrogance[15] to Israelis who considered it a compassionate and courageous gift to an oppressed people.[16] No one, however, doubts its importance, since it declared British support for the Zionist movement.

For Jews it represented a dream, while for the Arabs living in Palestine — what the Balfour Declaration called the "existing non–Jewish communities" — it posed a major threat. From the earliest days, Zionist leaders discussed removing the current population.[17] Palestinian writers such as Wadi al-Bustani began to expound on the prospect of mass Jewish immigration, especially after the

British took control of Palestine, becoming the government and security force.[18] Tensions increased. It did not take a wild-eyed prophet to predict that blood would spill between Palestinians and the growing number of Jewish immigrants intent on making Zionism a reality.

That blood began to flow in Jerusalem in 1920 shortly after the Balfour Declaration was made public in Palestine, in a rare year when the holy days of Passover, Easter, and Ramadan converged. During the Muslim Nabi Musa (Moses) procession, speakers began denouncing Zionism, Jewish immigration, and land acquisition, and Zionists began heckling the marchers. The police foolishly changed the route of the march to pass through the Jewish Quarter. Chaos, violence, and mayhem broke out. Arab rioters raped two women, and at least nine people were killed.[19] Ironically, the inhabitants of the Jewish Quarter who received the brunt of Arab hatred were anti–Zionist.

The best description of that April afternoon was a riot, and the intensity of the emotions caught everyone, including Arab and Jewish leaders, by surprise. The radical groups that would later steer events had not yet formed, but the events of that day solidified for the world an image of hatred and fanaticism that would dog the Palestinians for decades.

More senseless riots broke out in the coastal city of Jaffa during 1921 May Day celebrations. Almost 100 people were killed, with casualties about equal between Arabs and Jews. Communist Jews were demonstrating against the Histadrut labor union located near the Arab section. Fistfights broke out between the Jewish groups, and shots were fired. Arabs heard the gunfire, and a rumor spread that the godless Bolsheviks were invading, so they rushed to the scene with clubs and knives, burning the Jewish immigration hostel and transforming the conflict into a Arab-Jew dispute. The British promised less immigration, and calm returned until 1929 in an unspoken truce between British, Jewish, and Arab leaders.[20]

In June 1920 the Histadrut, unhappy with the British administration's lack of protection, began forming its self-defense military wing, called the Haganah. This wing would become the Zionists' major fighting force, the antecedent of the Israeli army, with Vladimir Jabotinsky as its first leader.[21] Although the Arab side had no similar unifying force, Palestinian villages began creating defense units. Arabs outnumbered Jews almost nine to one then, but their anxiety regarding increased immigration and Jewish land acquisition became magnified. A British report noted that speeches and meetings of Zionist leaders were translated into Arabic and quoted in the press: "The wildest stories as to the intentions of the Jews and the fate awaiting the Arabs were circulated in the towns and villages, and were often believed by a credulous people."[22] The Jewish press also found no shortage of vociferous bravado among Arab leaders.

Battle lines had been drawn, the British having worsened the situation by promising independence to the Arabs and a state on the same land for the

Jews. The Colonial Department appointed Sir Herbert Samuel, a Zionist Jew who helped draft the Balfour Declaration, as governor to Palestine, raising Arab suspicion even though he seemed genuinely concerned for the welfare of the Arab residents, which also earned him resentment from radical Jews.[23] Fate and conflicting priorities would outrun the British power to control events in the region, and Great Britain would eventually bow out of the conflict in failure.

Chapter 1
The Arab General Strike

In Palestine we do not propose even to go through the form of
consulting the wishes of the present inhabitants of the country.
Lord Arthur Balfour

The disturbances of 1920–21 stemmed from spontaneous riots which pitted Zionists against anti–Zionists. Many of the indigenous Jews were
anti–Zionists or were put in the difficult position of siding with their European coreligious against their Arab neighbors, who became increasingly suspicious of their motives. Although most of the rest of the decade passed peacefully, thousands of Jewish immigrants were coming to Palestine, alarming the
residents and leading to the August 1929 riots, the worst violence Palestine
would see until 1948.

The 1929 disturbances had their genesis in another heated religious confrontation during the Jewish Holy Days of 1928. Territorial religious disputes,
grand and petty, have been plentiful in Jerusalem. If a priest, for example, over-
steps his territory and kneels for prayer in the Church of the Holy Sepulcher,
which is strictly divided between different denominations, it may lead to awkward fistfights between heavy old bearded priests in their weighty robes. Anyone who has been to Jerusalem has noticed the proximity of Jewish and Muslim holy places, and given the territoriality of religion mixed with the
mounting Zionist/anti–Zionist tension, it is astonishing that violence did not
begin sooner.

The issue in 1928 was a table and screen put in front of the Wailing Wall.
An Orthodox rabbi had placed the table for ritual equipment and erected the
screen to separate men and women for Yom Kippur services. Muslims argued
that this violated a long-standing agreement giving them control of holy places,
and this argument gave way to rumors that the Jews were conspiring to take
over the Harem al-Sharif or Temple Mount.[1] If the screen remained, Muslims maintained, it would open the door to Jewish control over the area—not
the first time Muslims had made such a complaint. Jews argued that the

9

Muslims were limiting their religious freedom. Although violence did not immediately follow the 1928 Yom Kippur screen incident, extremist leaders, who had begun organizing on both sides after the 1920 riots, made political capital exploiting fears and vilifying the opposition.[2]

Control over the Wailing Wall remained an active and emotional issue in the press until August 15, 1929, the Jewish Fast of Tisha b'Av commemorating the destruction of the Temple, when about 1000 supporters of the Revisionist party led by Jabotinsky held a demonstration around Jerusalem demanding religious rights. They waved Zionist flags and pictures of the al-Aqsa mosque with a Star of David on top of it, and they planted a flag at the Wailing Wall. The demonstrators demanded control of the Wall, and shouted that the Harem al-Sharif should be destroyed so they could rebuild the Jewish Temple. Passions were inflamed, for Muslims view the Harem al-Sharif as their third holiest shrine. The next day, a Friday and the eve of the Prophet's birthday, Islamic clerics at al-Aqsa mosque preached fire. The day after that, an Arab stabbed a Jewish youth named Avrahm Mizrachi during a petty squabble involving a football that had been innocently kicked into a tomato garden (Mizrachi died three days later), and a Jew stabbed an Arab in revenge.[3]

The Yom Kippur screen and the football detonated the political time bomb. Rumor—a most potent force in the Palestinian-Israeli conflict—spread that the Jews were taking over the Harem al-Sharif, rumor buttressed by calls from Zionist leaders for the creation of a Jewish state and transfer of the native population. Within days Arab men from villages around the country arrived in Jerusalem with clubs and knives, and after a convenient provocation they launched a ferocious attack.

Few Palestinians had guns, and when they attacked Jewish areas, they were met by gunfire from immigrants and a few police who had anticipated such trouble. Thus the countrywide body count, at least 250 dead and hundreds wounded, was about equal between Jews and Muslims. The British authorities had been oblivious to the simmering conflict, declaring just before the fighting that Palestine was "an island of peace."[4]

In the clannish city of Hebron, Arabs went on a rampage on August 24, killing about 60 residents and injuring 50.[5] The 600 Jews who had lived there since the Middle Ages were not Zionists but religious adherents, including a few American youths who had just arrived for Torah instruction. It should be noted that many Arabs tried to stop the crowds and hid their Jewish neighbors in their homes until calm was restored.[6]

Five days later a similar massacre occurred in Safed, again against innocents. A Jewish community had come to Safed after their 1492 expulsion from Spain, and the first Jewish immigrants in the 1880s had made it their center.

The British high commissioner initially blamed the Arabs for the 1929 riots, but a commission of inquiry later pinned the blame at least as much on the provocative Revisionist march.[7] The Jewish reaction to 1929 was not to retreat or to end their dream of a homeland, but to be more determined, defend themselves better, and bring in more immigrants.

Jabotinsky became one of the foremost leaders of the Zionist movement. He was an extraordinary man, intelligent, capable in languages, untiring, courageous. Believing in the racial inferiority of the Arabs, he held that it was necessary to build an "Iron Wall" of military force around the Jewish community and drive the Arabs out of Palestine, which he defined as covering both sides of the Jordan River.[8] Jabotinsky persuaded the British to start a Jewish Legion to fight with General Allenby against the Turks, and he put together a 10,000-strong army in Palestine, but it saw no action, so he refashioned it to defend Jewish settlements, and he remained on its front line. Military force was his solution for every problem with the Arabs. He formed a brownshirt youth movement in Poland called the National Youth Organization of Betar, also called Revisionists,[9] which made armed struggle and provocation its principal doctrines. Begin and Shamir considered Jabotinsky their personal idol. During the 1920 riots the British had kept him from marching—their sole responsible action—then imprisoned him along with the Arab agitators and rapists, arousing his greatest resentment at being treated equally with Arabs.

Jabotinsky's radical group began mobilizing for guerrilla war. On the other side, the Palestinian press began portraying the British as enemies since they sponsored Zionism (a portrayal that took on added weight when the British added hundreds of Jews to their security force), and extremists within the Muslim and Christian communities took up an unorganized call to arms. The Palestinians were not nationally united; power rested in the hands of leading urban families who managed isolated defense forces.[10]

Palestinians with bushy mustaches, their heads wrapped in red and white scarfs and their thighs draped in dhoti-type peasant cloths, began raiding Jewish settlements with long Ottoman Empire hunting rifles, crouching well outside the settlements and firing indiscriminately at chickens and walls, then running. Jews in loose-fitting European pants and short sleeve shirts attacked Palestinian villages to make it known that the settlers were there to stay. It's useless to say who started the violence and who was counter-attacking. As linguist and political scientist Noam Chomsky notes, "The Cycle of 'retaliation' (by Jews) and 'terror' (by Palestinians) can be traced back, step-by-step, for many years, an exercise that will quickly reveal that the terminology belongs to the realm of propaganda, not factual description."[11]

Many of the new immigrants coming to Palestine were filled with intellectual and idealistic moral values of creating a progressive socialist state, while the Arab residents were becoming increasingly apprehensive. Palestinians claim that Jews, Christians, and Muslims had lived in harmony in Palestine before the Zionist movement. This to a large extent seems true, though more often than not each group lived separately in its own village or town quarter; petty squabbles were not uncommon, and intermarriage was rare.[12]

An influence historians rarely discuss is the circulation in Palestine of an Arabic translation of *The Protocols of the Elders of Zion*. This book, brought to Palestine by British officers under the title *The Jewish Peril*, was actually written in 1905 by members of the Russian tsar's secret police, who passed it off as a secret Jewish text showing Jews conspiring to control the world, a sneaky way to fan the flames of anti–Semitism and justify the pogroms of that year. We will see similar examples of such deception in the Middle East conflict. Philip Graves showed the book to be a fraud in 1921,[13] but it continued to be brought up. Hitler used it in *Mein Kampf*. Many Palestinians, including Palestinian leaders, read the work as if it were true, augmenting their vision of a worldwide Jewish plot. The mufti of Jerusalem mentioned it before the 1930 Shaw Commission as evidence of a Jewish conspiracy.[14] I have heard Arabs discuss it as if it were fact, and Hamas communiques in the 1990s quoted from it.[15] The book is alleged to be a record of 300 Jewish wise men that met in Basel, Switzerland, in 1897 to plot world takeover—an obvious reference to the first Zionist Congress.

Passions remained high during the early 1930s. The British cracked down on meetings and demonstrations, a policy that has rarely been able to suppress a national movement. In October 1933, Palestinians staged a large demonstration after Friday prayers in the nationalist town of Jaffa. The police intervened and killed at least 12 and wounded over 100 (a policeman was also killed), which led to other demonstrations in other cities.

The major Palestinian guerilla of this time was a cleric named Izz al-Din al-Qassam, who preached an explosive doctrine of expanding the conflict against the British since they, he declared, were conspiring with the Zionists. Born near Latakia, Syria, of simple parents, Qassam studied at the prestigious al-Azhar religious university in Cairo, then agitated for Arab independence in Syria. In the wake of French occupation, he fled to Haifa in 1921 and began forming an independence movement among the rural population, importing guns from neighboring states—the Palestinians generally had obsolete arms, at first World War I leftovers, then those abandoned during the World War II North Africa campaign. Qassam had several hundred armed men organized in small cells of three to five people around the countryside near Jenin. The British knew of him but never arrested him, although it is said that he preached with either a sword or a gun in his hand.

After the British harshly put down the 1933 Jaffa demonstration, Qassam's prestige increased, and on November 12, 1935, he and about 20 of his men went to the Yabad hills to begin the armed struggle. They met a Jewish patrol a few days later and exchanged fire. The patrol called the British, who encircled his hideout with tanks on November 17. The outgunned militia, a group of five, sought death over surrender, but instead of his movement collapsing, Qassam became a revered martyr. Thousands came to his funeral. Journalists and poets built a romantic mythology about him, inspiring other young men to become guerrillas and continue his war. At first his appeal was to the rural poor, but within days of his death the bourgeois leadership, which had been at odds with him, were obligated to render praise, and he remains a Palestinian hero, his name often given to squads of fighters.[16] Hamas called their military wing the Izz al-Din Qassam Brigade. His death was probably more inspiring than his accomplishments during the mere week he operated as a guerrilla. As an Arab newspaper said, "I have heard you preach from a platform resting on a sword. Today ... you are, by God, a greater preacher than alive you ever were."[17]

On April 15, 1936, only months after Qassam's death, alleged supporters of this first Palestinian commando stopped cars and a bus on the Tulkarm-Nablus road, robbed passengers, both Arab and Jew, and shot three Jews, two of whom died.[18] They made a political speech but acted more like thieves than revolutionaries. Jews retaliated by killing two Arabs near Petach Tikrah. Again, tension mounted. The British sided with the Jews. More rumors spread. Violence erupted in Jaffa, already tense from vociferous complaints that new immigrants were taking jobs and lowering Arab salaries. Four days later Arab committees around the country began voting for a general strike. Haj Amin al-Hussani, mufti of Jerusalem, who had become the most powerful Palestinian leader after the 1929 riots,[19] followed the trend, and on April 25 the Arab Higher Committee approved an indefinite general strike.[20]

The strike began in Jaffa and Jerusalem, then spread around the country. Palestinians shut stores, cut transportation, refused to pay taxes, closed the port at Jaffa, and stopped other essential services. The British overreacted, rushing troops to Palestine and declaring martial law. The Arabs were angry that they were punished while Jews were largely left alone. Jews were given jobs in the government, and Jewish immigrants received tax benefits. The colonial mentality made it easier for the British to blame the natives and support the European Jews, with whom they could more easily identify. In a report submitted to the League of Nations, the British claimed that they killed 1000 Arabs during the six-month strike—probably a conservative figure[21]—and imprisoned 5 percent of the male population between the ages of 18 and 40. Clearly, the strike upset the British and was a main influence for the Palestinian Intifada half a century later. Furthermore, the British armed more Jewish men, enlisting and training 6000 as supernumerary police and gradually building the force to over 14,000.[22] This would prove important since those who received such training became the nucleus of the Haganah.[23] With Arab distrust of the British rising, such measures did little to win Arab friendship. The harsh emergency regulations imposed by the British, who brought 20,000 troops to Palestine,[24] were reintroduced by Israel after statehood and during their control over the West Bank and Gaza.

Although the Arab strike was mainly nonviolent, radical groups began throwing bombs. Each side established boundaries; an Arab straying into a

Jewish area or vice versa—and it was usually easy to tell one side from the other—could be a provocation. At the same time, there was a potential of integration between the two cultures in the major cities where Jewish and Arab communities lived and shopped in close proximity. In Jerusalem and Haifa the city governments ran under a coalition. Paradoxically, we see both a coming together and a separation, and this paradox would also become an important aspect of the covert war of deception to follow.

Arab leaders from neighboring states became involved in negotiating an end to the strike, making the question of Palestine an issue throughout the Arab world. After six months of disruption, Palestinian leaders agreed to end their action, and Britain agreed to appoint another commission of inquiry that would focus on Jewish immigration. The Palestinians, tired of the strike, had nevertheless won a major, though temporary, concession through their united action, and life returned to normal for a few months.

In the fall of 1936 the British sent a young Scottish intelligence officer named Orde Wingate to Palestine. A fanatic Christian fundamentalist with a Crusader's hatred for Arabs and Islam,[25] Wingate was so fired with Zionism that he scared Zionist leaders. During the 1936 general strike he formed the Special Night Squads in northern Palestine. These squads trained Jewish militias in aggressive self-defense and penetration of Arab areas. A few British soldiers were also involved in the Night Squads.

Wingate was ruthless. His method of interrogation was to shoot a prisoner in order to free the tongues of others.[26] Becoming an embarrassment to the British, Wingate was discreetly transferred to Africa, but it is difficult to underestimate the contribution he made to the organization and training of the Jewish defense committees. His Night Squads became the inspiration for Ariel Sharon's infamous Unit 101, which, beginning in the 1950s, crossed borders and bulldozed through Arab areas in a wave of destruction and devastation.[27]

Despite their minority status, the Zionists had ingredients which made their armed conflict superior to that of the Arabs. First, they had political support in Britain, which gave them the backing of a world power.[28] Second, they were better armed and trained, and the British generally enforced the heavy punishments for weapons possession only when the possessors were Arabs, though later the radical Zionist militias would become far more dangerous for the British. Third, the Zionists had high morale and were filled with determination and a specific goal, especially as the condition of Jews in Europe was disintegrating. Fourth, they were organized and well financed, while the Arabs had minor finances and were divided by clan loyalties that produced infighting. Finally, their minority status and their location in specific settlements made it easier for them to plant bombs in Arab areas such as markets, while it was difficult for Arabs to move freely into Jewish areas.

Throughout their mandate, the British sent many commissions to Palestine to study the situation and make recommendations, but the Royal Peel Commission, arriving shortly after Arab leaders agreed to end the strike, was the most controversial. Parts of the commission's report were leaked before its release. Together with a government white paper issued at the same time, it recommended that Jewish immigration and land purchases should be drastically cut—8000 immigrants for the next six months—and that the country should be partitioned between Arab and Jewish sectors with British control over Jerusalem and strategic areas. Jews were furious over the immigration recommendations, especially with Hitler in power in Germany, but although the partition plan did not satisfy Jewish aspirations, the Jews did not reject it. The Arabs, however, categorically rejected partition, as they would reject all future compromises.[29]

Jews responded to the Peel Commission restrictions by creating the Mossad, or secret service, to facilitate illegal Jewish immigration and buy weapons.[30] Arabs reacted by revolting. The 1936 strike had been mainly civil disobedience, but beginning in 1937 an intense wave of violence swept across the country. In early September 1937 Arabs killed three Jews. The Irgun, a newly formed Jewish radical militia which would dominate Middle East terrorism until it disbanded in 1950, retaliated and killed 13 Arabs. On September 26 the British acting district commissioner for Galilee, L.Y. Andrews, and his police escort were killed by unidentified assailants outside the Anglican church in Nazareth. He was pro–Jewish, and it is generally thought that his killers were Arabs. (We will see later that masquerade became a common tactic of this war, making it unwise to jump to such conclusions.) The British arrested 106 Arab community leaders around the country, instantly setting themselves at odds with the Arabs.[31] Palestinian leaders did not directly call for a revolt, but it was impossible to stop it.

The Arab rebels torched the airport at Lydda, killed British constables, robbed banks, attacked British offices, and frequently sabotaged the Iraq Petroleum Company pipeline. Small armed bands raided Jewish settlements, but the Night Squads were more effective in their aggressive defense policy. The British had introduced draconian emergency regulations that would fry the conscience of a repressive modern dictator, punishing the Arab population collectively for challenging the British. Beginning with the 1936 strike, they blew up houses, arrested en masse, executed suspects after sham trials, imposed excessive fines, fired into crowds, and bombed from the air in order to break the strike. After the airport fire the British blew up a row of nearby houses. One of the first victims of British summary justice was 76-year-old Sheik Farhan al-Said. The British thought that he was another Qassam, and they executed him for possessing a revolver, making him a martyr and creating more anti–British feeling.[32] Under the guise of a beautification program, the British blew up 220 houses in Jaffa and partly destroyed others, making 10,000 people homeless.[33] Individual officers had wide powers; one officer ordered that 12 Arabs of Halhoul village be tied up and allowed to die of thirst.[34] The British also expelled all leaders, the entire Higher Committee, leaving the Arabs in even greater disarray. It took a generation for new leaders to emerge.

The Arabs managed to put together a militia operating in the hills of Palestine, but it was never more than 1000 fighters, almost all from the peasant class. They paid a Syrian soldier named Fawzi al-Kawukji to train the Liberation Army,[35] which was reported, probably falsely, to have received funds from fascist Germany and Italy. When he arrived in August 1936, just after martial law was declared, Kawukji proclaimed himself leader of the revolt. Another guerilla leader named Abd al-Rahim al-Haj Muhammad also commanded a group in the hills until he was killed in March 1939. From the beginning the guerrillas argued with each other.

The fighters were distinguished by wearing the *keffieh* head scarf, making them easy for the British to pick them out, so they told all Arab men to wear it, and it became a national symbol. They later told residents not to carry identity cards. The militias targeted Arabs suspected of collaboration with the British[36] and sought refuge in congested town centers where troops were often afraid to enter. In October they occupied the Old City of Jerusalem, but British troops, who with their supernumeraries outnumbered the guerrillas ten to one,[37] quickly regained control.

The British attitude created division and hatred. W.F. Abboushi writes:

> The European powers decided the future of the Arab Middle East without consulting the Arabs. This was inconsistent with the big powers' own declarations as well as the covenant of the League of Nations. The inconsistency gave the Arab nationalists an anti–Western argument. Arab bitterness increased as Arab nationalism grew more intense.[38]

Arab dictators began using that anti-Western feeling to justify their power and avoid dealing with the substantive problems in their countries.

In May 1939 another white paper reversed the government projection for partition, and the Arabs were temporarily pacified. Arab deaths during 1938 due to the revolt were put at 3,717, while 92 Jews and 69 British were killed the same year.[39] In 1939 alone the British had 6000 men in detention, 250 of whom were Jews.

What actually calmed the revolt was the tense situation in Europe. Britain, which had a third of its standing army in Palestine,[40] did not want to be entangled in a local conflict in the Middle East while facing the potential for full-scale war in Europe. They needed the alliance of Arab countries and could not afford to make Palestine a stumbling block for Arab support. When the Nazis marched across the Polish frontier and war was declared, the Arabs officially ended their revolt and were unable to generate a similar uprising until 1987.

Chapter 2

The Struggle for Statehood

In his memoir, Irgun leader Menachem Begin reminds us, "The historical and linguistic origins of the political term 'terror' prove that it cannot be applied to a revolutionary war of liberation."[1] The definition has to be accepted across the board, and Irgun members cannot logically use the word "terrorists" to describe Palestinians with guns, also struggling for statehood. We need to be careful in labeling the actions of the Irgun and other pre-statehood groups as terrorist when revolutionary may be applicable. Nevertheless, terror was no doubt a central factor in achieving statehood.

Recently Jewish and Palestinian historians have rummaged through documents, collected oral accounts, and obtained an accurate picture of what led to the mass Palestinian exodus in 1948. There is no reason to duplicate their work here except to highlight central themes. With the Palestinian leadership expelled or killed, the British effectively reduced Arab military effort to sniping, the occasional bombing, and village defense forces. However, the Zionist militias employed a vibrant military campaign. They sacrificed, rationed food, and donated money to bring Jews from around the world. Their army, the Haganah, was trained, disciplined, well armed, and filled with positive morale and dynamic determination, especially after the slaughter at the hands of the Nazis. All Haganah operations were directed by the leadership. On the negative side, they had a well-orchestrated campaign to frighten the Palestinians into leaving.[2] They created hatred between the native Jewish population and the Palestinians,[3] forcing Jewish companies to hire only Jewish workers, patronizing Jewish shops, and discouraging cooperation between the two communities.[4]

Many of the Haganah had fighting experience from World War II or training as Palestine police. Furthermore, the British in 1942 sanctioned a Jewish army called the Palmach, led by Yigal Allon, which stood ready to wage a guerrilla war against the Nazis in case Erwin Rommel was successful in crossing Egypt and the Sinai into Palestine. This group never saw action, but it gave Jewish forces more practice.[5]

Jabotinsky, constantly complaining that the Jewish Agency was weak-willed, walked out of a 1923 Zionist conference. Finally, in June 1935, his Revisionists voted to break with the World Zionist Organization.[6] He founded the Irgun in 1937, appointing David Raziel and later Menachem Begin as leader. Originally the military arm of Betar and later the focus of Revisionism, the Irgun led a decisive underground campaign of assassinations, bombings, hostage-taking, and massacres, recruiting and training an emotionally tight and disciplined force. The Irgun's first action, shortly after it was formed, was a raid against an Arab village on November 14, 1937.[7] The Irgun thought that the British were on the side of the Arabs, and after the British hanged Irgun member Ben Josef on June 29, 1938—the only Jew they executed during that period—the Irgun began actions against them.[8]

Thinking that the Irgun was too conservative, in 1939 a splinter group led by Avraham Stern split from it and formed the LEHI, an abbreviation for Fighters for the Freedom of Israel, usually called the Stern Gang. The Stern were harshly anti–British, to the point of trying to form an alliance with the Nazis. Michael Cohen observes their subtle difference in technique: "The Irgun tried to erode the morale of the British army, the Lehi tried to make Palestine a place unsafe for British personnel."[9] The British caught up with Stern in an apartment in 1942 and killed him on the spot; Yitzhak Shamir took over in 1945. The combined strength of Irgun and Stern numbered about 3000, mostly Polish Jews.[10]

The British government supported the creation of a Jewish homeland in Palestine, and we have seen how they enforced the law unequally against Arabs and Jews. Indeed, without the British presence the Arabs would have been able to stop the advance of Zionism before it gained strength.[11] Nevertheless, both Stern and Irgun targeted the British administration to persuade them to remove the restrictions from immigration and withdraw from Palestine.

They tried several times to kill the British high commissioner, Sir Harold McMichael. His closest call came in the summer of 1944, when four Irgun members stood at the side of the road and tried to shoot him and his wife while they were traveling to attend a ceremony in Jaffa.[12] Three months later, the Stern group sent two commandos on the first action conducted outside Palestine in a terror war that would be largely fought on foreign soil. Shamir organized the killing of Lord Walter Guiness Moyne, a personal friend of Winston Churchill and one of the most influential formulators of Britain's Middle East policy. The Zionists suspected that Moyne was pro–Arab and hence trying to limit Jewish immigration, the crucial issue.[13] Moyne was targeted not only because he was the colonial secretary for the Middle East, but because Shamir knew that he did not use guards, making him a soft target.[14]

The amateurish assassination set the tone for future Israeli-Palestinian fiascos. The two gunmen, who spoke almost no Arabic, came overland to Cairo carrying Moyne's address. They rented bicycles, pedaled to his house, and waited for his car. At lunchtime Moyne arrived with his driver, his military officer, and his secretary. The two gunmen rushed down the long driveway and stopped the car. Lord Moyne was about to get out when he was shot three times by one of the killers, Eliahu bet-Tsuri. The other assassin, Eliahu Hakim, senselessly killed the driver—no one in the car was armed—then both men mounted their bicycles and nervously fled the scene, drawing the attention of the guard in front of the nearby residence of Greece's King George.

Moyne's military officer ran to the police post, and the police, with the help of King George's guard, chased the bicyclists by motorcycle, catching them on the Balok Bridge over the Nile. Constable al-Amin Abdullah wounded one of the assassins after a short firefight. As soon as the neighborhood discovered what had happened, an angry crowd gathered, ready to pounce on the killers, and the police had to call reinforcements to protect their captives. The killers confessed that they were sent from Palestine and were hanged on March 22, 1945. If the killers had not been caught it would have been assumed that they were Egyptian, creating tension between the Egyptian and British governments. Churchill was furious, and it took a lot of placating from the Jewish community and Dr. Chaim Weizmann to win back British support for a Jewish homeland.[15]

(Thirty years later, after the ceasefire treaty ending the 1973 war, the bodies of the assassins were included in the 1975 prisoner exchange accord. Their coffins were laid in state in Jerusalem's Hall of Heroism, and they were given a burial in Mount Herzl martyr cemetery with full military honors.[16] Israelis and Palestinians continued honoring terrorists, glorifying and encouraging more of the same.)

Zionist foreign operations against the British continued. They sent the British embassy in Rome a parcel bomb—a crude device, but when it exploded in late 1946, it set, as the *Sunday Times* said a quarter-century later, a new precedent in the world of international terrorism.[17] The bomb was credited to Stern members Yaacov Eliav and Eli Tavin. Working from Europe between 1946 and 1947, Zionist underground leaders sent over 70 mail bombs in British government envelopes to heads of the government and soldiers who had served in Palestine.[18] In June 1947 Eliav was arrested in Belgium for his letter campaign.[19]

The most sensational action of the pre–1948 era took place at Jerusalem's King David Hotel. The operation was carefully studied and professionally executed by Begin's Irgun (and later romanticized in Begin's memoirs), but the Haganah suggested the target as revenge for the British raid on the Jewish Agency headquarters.[20] The blast was aimed at the offices of the civil administration, which used the top floors of the hotel, but an auxiliary aim was to destroy documents that the British had confiscated detailing plans to sabotage roads and railways.[21]

To penetrate the King David the Zionists masqueraded as Arabs. They drove a milk truck into the building and placed seven of the large churns, each filled with 50 kilos of TNT, next to structural columns in the lower kitchen area. A guard noticed that the "Arabs" were acting strangely, and after investigating discovered what was going on and shot two of the bombers, but he in turn was also shot. No one else in the hotel knew what was going on. Begin claims that they gave the hotel a half-hour telephone warning, but that has not been substantiated. The devastatingly powerful blast collapsed an entire wing of the hotel at its busiest time, killing almost 100 Britons, Jews, and Palestinians, and wounding another hundred. Thurston Clarke's book about the incident contains a picture showing a large bloodstain from a body that was catapulted by the explosion and smashed against the YMCA across the street.[22] The British then offered a £30,000 sterling reward for Begin's head.[23] The Haganah also blew up the Semiramis Hotel in Jerusalem, killing 20, including the Spanish consul.[24] (Coincidentally, the Abu Nidal group attacked a hotel by the same name in Damascus in September 1976.)

The Irgun and Stern began a round of hostage-taking incidents against British soldiers in order to win the release of captured comrades. At the time of the King David Hotel blast, gunmen raided the office of the NAAFI club in Tel Aviv (June 28, 1946) and took five British officers hostage.[25] The Voice of Israel radio announced five days later that they would release them only when two Irgun members who had been sentenced to death were also released. The British complied, and the officers were freed. However, in a similar action a year later, two British sergeants were taken hostage to force the release of three Irgun members who had been sentenced to hang. This time the British refused to negotiate and executed the three as scheduled. The Irgun then hanged the sergeants and booby-trapped their bodies so that they exploded when they were found.[26] Later, when the British were ready to flog two captured Irgun members, an Irgun team led by Amihai Piglin kidnapped a British officer and three soldiers on December 29, 1946 and gave them the same sentence.

There were dozens of other incidents against the British administration, but those mentioned had the greatest effect on the British public and on the morale of British soldiers. After the two sergeants were found hanged, British soldiers ran out into the streets of Tel Aviv, shooting indiscriminately, killing five and wounding fifteen, and the news triggered anti–Semitic riots in England.[27] In 1977 Piglin became Israel's anti-terrorism advisor.[28]

The Zionist military campaign against Britain succeeded: it forced the British, who had built up a force of over 100,000 troops in the small country,[29] to pull out of Palestine prematurely. The United Nations had asked the British to stay until August 1948, but seeing no reason to struggle against a swell of terrorism, the British announced that they would withdraw in May.

The Zionists also systematically targeted Palestinians. Beginning before 1940, dozens of bombs exploded in markets, busses, cinemas, and cafes. Historians have documented these incidents.[30] A few Arab militias tried to stand their ground, but they had no police or military of their own, no avenue for military training, no means to systematically fight the influx of European Jews. They had snipers, organized settlement raids, and in some towns they were able to mobilize moderate defense forces, but they were no military match for the vastly superior Haganah.

My Palestinian father relates the story of how, when he was living in Nazareth, his brother came and told him that since he was a respected man in the community he should buy a rifle to show the people in the neighborhood that they were protected. My father was a pacifist, and it took a lot of persuasion from his brother to convince him to spend what was at that time a fortune and buy a rifle on the black market. My uncle brought him the gun and told him that they had to go up on the roof and shoot it in the air in order to give the people confidence. My father is a small man, and the rifle must have been as big as he was, but with the help of my uncle he fired into the air to show the people in the neighborhood that they had nothing to worry about. It was a public relations gesture directed at the neighborhood. The gun could have done nothing to forestall the conquering Zionist armies, who by this time had heavy weapons from Czechoslovakia. But the rifle made such a terrible noise. My father threw it down in disgust, vowing never to have anything to do with arms. A few months later, he and my mother joined the mass of terrorized Palestinians who were fleeing their homes for safety in Lebanon.

When news circulated that Zionist militias had massacred the inhabitants of Deir Yassin, a quiet village walking distance from Jerusalem, Palestinians began fleeing their homes by the hundreds of thousands. The massacre was carried out not to destroy the village, which had been peaceful, but to scare other Palestinians. The villagers had made a modest living from the local rock quarry, and when a Palestinian militia had asked to use their village as a base, the villagers had refused. Although the Irgun and Stern were responsible for taking the town, they had direct support from the Haganah.[31]

A few of the inhabitants of Deir Yassin tried to defend the village with their rifles, but the Haganah provided cover fire.[32] According to Jacques de Reynier, the head of the Red Cross, who arrived a day later, the Irgun and Stern killed 254 people—everyone left in the town. Women and children were the prime victims. The victors then went around the country on trucks with loudspeakers telling people in Arabic that the same would happen to them if they did not leave. There are reliable reports that the Zionists paraded a few Deir Yassin villagers on trucks around Jerusalem, then shot them in order to terrorize the locals.[33] Palestinians who remember that time speak about girls who had been raped also paraded around naked, thighs stained with blood, on the back of a truck, causing tremendous fear, especially among the sexually subdued Arabs.[34] Historian Rosemary Sayigh says, "An atrocity particularly calculated to horrify Arab peasants was the cutting open of the womb of a nine months' pregnant woman."[35]

Details of this period are contained in other studies, Israeli and Palestinian, though much of the literature is biased. History is written by the victor; thugs and murderers become heroes and liberators; atrocities are romanticized into a heritage. In October 1987 a motion was put before the Jerusalem city council to honor the five Zionist patriots who "had fallen during the battle of Deir Yassin" by naming a square after them. The site of Deir Yassin is now part of West Jerusalem. The issue became a rallying call for patriotism: all councilmen were careful to call the five "martyrs," even though they opposed the motion. Seeing that Israel might lose face by honoring those who had taken part in a massacre, Mayor Teddy Kollek forced the matter to drop, secretly promising the families of the five that the city would name streets or institutions after them in the near future.[36]

Body counts are not the objective here; rather, we want to discover a pattern. Revolutionary movements kill civilians. Taking hostages, especially soldiers and government officials, although against the Geneva Conventions, is a common and rational tactic in war. From the ruins of the Holocaust, Jews struggled courageously, with no one else's help, to build a state. The Zionists were not only intent on a new government; they needed to expel the Palestinians, and this made terrorism a necessary weapon in their struggle.

Following the 1939 declaration, the British were restricting Jewish immigration to 75,000 per year and making moderate attempts to deport the illegal immigrants to Mauritius. The Haganah had more than 60 old ships bringing refugees to Palestine.[37] Two sank; two were bombed and sunk; another was bombed and damaged. The failure of the Allies to make any attempt to free Jews during World War II remains a shameful blot on Western history.

In November 1940, when the British had put 1900 Jewish immigrants on the ship *Patria* at the port of Haifa ready for deportation, a Haganah officer named Munya Mandor planted a mine on the ship to dramatize the need for a Jewish homeland in Palestine and "make known vehemently our anger and disgust at the scandal of the country's locked gates." The blast killed 250 of the immigrants. Suspicion fell on the Palestinians. Only in 1957 when Mandor wrote about his exploits was it confirmed as a Haganah action.[38] A year later another ship, the *Struma*, was blown up in the Black Sea. The dilapidated *Struma* was heading for Palestine full of Romanian Jews, but Lord Moyne encouraged the Turks to detain it, claiming that the Nazis were encouraging emigration to deal Britain a problem in the Arab world. The complete story of the sinking has yet to emerge, though it is generally concluded that one of the two survivors, David Stoliar, was a Haganah officer who sank the ship, killing 769 passengers.[39] The mine on a third immigrant ship, *Empire Rival*, was also planted by Haganah frogmen.[40] Arabs, Russian submarines, Turks, and Nazis were suspected, and to this day the incidents are distorted.[41] After the sinking of *Struma*, the people of Tel Aviv took to the streets in a spontaneous demonstration; the British never tried to stop another ship.

The day after the British withdrew and Israeli statehood was declared, Egypt, Jordan, Syria, Iraq, Lebanon, and Saudi Arabia sent armies into Palestine, generally staying in the Arab zone designated by the United Nations.[42] Jordan's King Abdullah, who had the largest and best-equipped Arab army— 10,000 men led by British General John Glubb—did not engage the Haganah, since the king had a secret deal (some sources claim that the Jewish Agency gave him money[43]) that would give him control of the West Bank, including Jerusalem, instead of creating a Palestinian state. The Zionists had 13 percent of their population, 40,000 men, under arms; half of these men had World War II combat experience. The Arab armies, although with a combined strength of almost the same number, were new, inexperienced, disunited, and not well equipped.[44] The Islamic Brotherhood, under the leadership of Hassan al-Bannah, led a small group of volunteers into Gaza, but essentially, no major force except the British fought the Zionists, and the British, engrossed in other international matters, had neither the soldiers nor the will to fight. When the 1948 war was over, Israel was about 30 percent larger than the 1947 United Nations plan, which the Arabs staunchly opposed.

(To jump ahead of the story, in August 1951 Haj Amin, who had escaped to Lebanon, then Iraq, and had spent most of the war years in Germany trying to recruit Muslims to help the Nazis, sent a gunman named Mustafa Ashu to kill Abdullah as revenge for dealing with the Zionists. To add significance to the event, the killing took place before Friday prayers in the al-Aqsa Mosque on the Harem al-Sharif.[45] Haj Amin set up the Arab Higher Committee in Cairo after 1948 with an advanced headquarters in Gaza, but he was constrained by the Egyptians and faded into obscurity.)

The Palestinian militias, made up of a few men like my father with old rifles, played a minor role in 1947–48, concentrating on killing the odd civilian. They were no match for the Irgun, who bombed crowded areas. Ben-Gurion tells us, "Despite continuing Arab attacks, not one of the enemy ever entered a Jewish settlement.... Not one settlement was destroyed, not one abandoned."[46]

Zionist fighters overtly intended to show themselves as cruel and destructive in order to terrify the Arabs. The Israelis sought to uphold a militant image and keep the Palestinians in a continuous state of fear. The Israeli army always displayed a savage face in an attempt to rule the Palestinians by intimidation, by the implication that they were ready to kill and torture men and to rape women. In Begin's words, "The legend of terror goes before a fighting force and wins."[47] The Israelis were given to dropping a hundred bombs, or firing a hundred shots, or arresting a hundred boys, when one or two would have been enough.

After independence, both sides again resorted to terrorism for diverse reasons. For their part, the Palestinians failed to organize a mass movement; they were disunited, under weak leadership, and unable to enlist a military force to fight a conventional war. They had no significant diplomatic support or sympathy, and turned to terrorism as a substitute.

As for Israel, though it had become a nation, its territorial aspirations were not achieved. The narrowness of the new state, in one place only 15 km wide, remained unacceptable, making 1948 only a partial victory. At Israel's creation, the founders specifically voted not to define borders. Furthermore, in order to avoid facing the Palestinian refugee problem, Israel needed to keep the status quo of conflict. If they negotiated, they would have to either let the refugees return to their homes or compensate them for their loss. What's more, the Israelis did not know how to deal with the Arab population who had not fled except by intimidation. To justify their takeover they had to dehumanize the Arabs. Another reason to maintain terrorist activity was that Israeli leaders wanted to attract Jews from around the world. Just as they needed to terrify Arabs into leaving Palestine, they staged at least one anti–Jewish terrorist action abroad to convince Jews to immigrate to safety in Israel. Finally, the dynamic pioneer spirit shared by Israel's founders needed militarism to keep it alive. In defense minister Moshe Dayan's words:

> [Israel] must see the sword as the main, if not the only, instrument with which to keep its morale high and to retain its moral tensions. Toward this end it may, no—it must—invent dangers, and to this it must adopt the method of provocation-and-revenge... And above all—let us hope for a new war with the Arab countries....[48]

The patterns set by both sides continued over the decades. On the eve of statehood, the United Nations appointed a committee to investigate the situation in Palestine, selecting a member of the Swedish royal family, Count Folke Bernadotte, as its head. The count, a quiet man who favored negotiation, supported a Jewish state, having worked for the Red Cross during World War II and saved Jews from the Nazis.[49] Bernadotte landed in Beirut and traveled between various cites until he arrived in Jerusalem. After seeing the situation firsthand, he wanted the Palestinians who fled their homes to return (as affirmed in United Nations resolution 194, December 11, 1948), making him an enemy of Israel: after fighting to drive out the Arabs they did not want to be forced to allow them back. Bernadotte thought that victory had gone to the Zionists' heads and that they now had no use for the United Nations.[50]

At one checkpoint Israeli guards stopped Count Bernadotte's two cars and noted where he was sitting. A short time later an army Jeep overtook them and stopped in the road, forcing the two United Nations cars to stop. Two men rushed out of the Jeep, ran to Bernadotte's car, took out revolvers, and shot both men in the back seat. The count received six bullets while his aide,

Colonel Serot, was hit seventeen times. The killing of Serot was a mistake; the gunmen intended to kill Aage Lundstrom, another aide, but Serot had switched seats with Lundstrom moments before. The assassins shot the radiators and tires as they fled, but the getaway driver was too anxious and took off before Bernadotte's killer reached the Jeep, forcing him to take to his heels and run over the rocky countryside, throwing his gun as he ran. None of Bernadotte's men were armed.[51]

The Fatherland Front, a name used by the Stern, took responsibility for the action in a statement to Agence France Press, and Freidman Yellin, a Stern leader, was sentenced to eight years by a Jerusalem court for the crime, though he did not do the actual shooting. Yellin was released immediately after the trial and given a seat in the Israeli parliament under the name Nathan Yellin-Mor. The gunmen, also captured, were released within hours.[52] There was, as Israeli historian Jon Kimche notes, "an absence of any public conscience about this foul deed. It was condemned, regretted and deplored because it would cast reflections on Israel, and make the work of her diplomats more difficult; not because it was wrong in itself to resort to assassination."[53]

This was the last act of terrorism by the Stern and Irgun, who merged into the country's political machinery. Bernadotte's death was unnecessary, since Arab intransigence, inability to recognize Israel, and unwillingness to compromise would have allowed Israel to escape his proposals.[54]

Before moving on, let us add another tragic incident. On October 29, 1956, just before the Suez War, Israeli soldiers imposed a curfew on Kufr Kassem village, then killed 31 men, 9 women, and 7 children as they were coming home, unaware that a curfew had been declared. The soldiers later described how they were privately congratulated by high government leaders, including Ben-Gurion. Eight soldiers were put on trial and given prison sentences of between 7 and 17 years. All served in half-free circumstances and were released within three years. In September 1960 one of the senior officers present at the massacre, Lieutenant Joubrael Dahan, who was sentenced to 15 years, was appointed "officer responsible for Arab affairs" in the Arab town of Ramle.[55]

Chapter 3

Israel's Use
of Arab Disguises

In December 1992, Israel Radio reported that an Israeli army patrol dressed as Arabs encountered a group of armed Arabs, and the two sides opened fire. It turned out that the other party was a group of Israeli Border Guards also masquerading as Arabs. Neither side knew that the other was operating in the same area, and each group thought it had encountered an armed Palestinian unit. Three Border Guards and one paratrooper were wounded in the shooting.[1]

Although the incident sounds bizarre, the confrontation illustrates an important strategy of the Israeli security services. Israelis masquerading as Arabs had become so widespread during the 1987–93 Intifada in the occupied territories that they could not keep track of each other.[2] But the use of Arab disguise was not a new phenomenon; it continued a long-standing Israeli tactic. Beginning in the 1936 general strike, it became a cornerstone of Zionist or Israeli armed forces policy either to use an Arab disguise or to recruit Arabs. This manipulative tactic proved successful for Israel's military as well as groups of Israelis not part of the government. It was an effective way of assassinating Palestinian leaders and of keeping a state of conflict, disunity, and suspicion among Arabs in general and Palestinians in particular.

In the years leading to statehood Jewish nationalists dressed as Arabs in order to penetrate Arab areas, initially to spy, but later to plant explosives in Palestinian areas. The Special Night Squads infiltrated Palestinian villages in disguise, and later Sharon's Unit 101 operated without uniform, wearing civilian clothes or Arab disguise, and they inflicted serious damage.[3]

A 1992 report in the *Independent*, echoing other studies, concluded that undercover agents in Arab disguise "infiltrated the Palestinian uprising, joined in riots, and shot dead wanted suspects." These agents dressed as Palestinians, not only with the *keffiieh* head scarves but also with false mustaches and beards.[4] The Israeli government, though at first denying that it sponsored undercover death squads, conceded that Arab masquerade was an army strategy. Israeli agents formed similar squads in South Lebanon,[5] but this tactic has over a half a century of precedents.

Journalists Ian Black and Benny Morris note that during the 1936 strike the Zionists not only paid striking Palestinians to break ranks and return to work, thus creating friction in the Arab camp, but also produced "fake Arab leaflets signed by non-existent organizations such as 'the Patriotic Drivers of Palestine.'"[6] The phony leaflets criticized Palestinian national leaders for their passivity and tried to confuse citizens, setting up a more militant alternative phantom leadership. They were meant to divide and misrepresent Palestinians by trying to appear more patriotic and militant than their real leaders.

Similarly, after the beginning of the Intifada, when the Palestinian underground leadership produced regular leaflets calling for strikes and boycotts, a group of what journalist Saleh Atta calls "Orientalists, Arabists and specialists in Palestinian affairs in the army and military government" began producing and distributing fake leaflets in the name of the Intifada leadership. Atta analyzed the forgeries: "A general characteristic of these leaflets is their radical national presentation," he observed. Similar to the leaflets produced in 1936, they attacked moderate Palestinians, calling them names such as "the symphony of the surrendering voices" and urging people to expand the Intifada into armed struggle.[7] Israeli spokespersons showed these forged leaflets to journalists to discredit the Intifada. They no doubt hoodwinked several Palestinians as well, inciting them to extremism. We begin to see that these actions aimed either to radicalize Palestinians or make them appear radical. In most cases the instigators of violent acts have remained obscure or only been discovered long after the event. In the early 1980s a group dressed in *keffiehs* raided Hebron University, throwing grenades and firing at students. It was not known until a year later, after the journalistic interest had died, that the raiders were Israeli settlers.[8]

We have seen how the King David Hotel blast was engineered using Arab disguise, and the reader who is informed about the struggle to create Israel will no doubt be able to recount other incidents where Zionist militias disguised themselves as Arabs and penetrated Arab areas. Another important bombing took place January 4, 1948 in Jaffa. Jews could not enter such nationalistic Arab areas such as Jaffa without Arab disguise. A group of Oriental Jews dressed as Arabs drove a truck of orange crates into the town center and left it on the street, blowing up the Arab National Committee headquarters, the police station, and other buildings.[9] Israeli leaders often used disguise: Golda Meir dressed as an Arab woman when she went to meet King Abdullah,[10] and Menachem Begin went disguised as an Arab or Rabbi.[11] During attacks by the Stern and Irgun militias against the British, the attackers disguised themselves in police uniform,[12] but when the only enemy became the Arabs, Israelis used Arab disguise. Palestinians too turned to disguise, recruiting British deserters during the 1948 war who were able to move freely in Jewish areas and blow up the *Palestine Post* and apartment buildings, killing 50.[13] On 11 March 1948 an Arab driver at the American consulate drove a car flying the United States flag to the Jewish Agency and blew it up.[14]

The Israeli agents working in Baghdad in 1950 certainly employed disguise. In order to persuade the 130,000 Iraqi Jewish community, who had lived in Iraq since the Babylonian Captivity, to flee empty-handed to Israel, underground agents started panic among the Jews by throwing bombs at synagogues and Jewish cafes in the name of vindictive Arabs. The attacks were quickly followed by an underground publicity campaign and American fundraising to save Iraqi Jewry from the coming pogroms. Part of the underground network was by chance captured; two Mossad agents, Shalom Saleh Shalom and Yosef Basri, were executed, and 20 others received prison sentences. Even so, the ruse worked: over 121,500 Iraqi Jews fled what they thought was persecution for safety in Israel without knowing that Israel had staged a deception campaign.[15]

The group of secret service agents inside Iraq had weapons, money, safe houses, printing equipment, and a distribution network. Israeli leaders probably at least knew of the plan: Moshe Dayan was among those who brought arms into Baghdad,[16] and Yigal Allon may have been in charge of the operation. Moreover, there is evidence of complicity within the Iraqi government to encourage the Jews to flee. Although Iraq appeared the most belligerent Arab state, outlawing Zionism and being the only country to refuse to sign the ceasefire treaty, Israelis probably struck deals with Iraqi officials who made it legal and easy for the Jews to emigrate.[17] We should add here that Israel's use of Arab collaborators, recruited either through financial incentives or through extortion, often works in tandem with Arab masquerade. This tactic is used in any conflict for information-gathering. Israel actively used Arabs to disguise controversial operations; the actual actors were Arab, but their activities were Israeli.

In the case of the Iraqi Jews, the airline selected to shuttle the frightened citizens to Israel (at first via a technical stop in Cyprus) was Mid East Air Transport,[18] which appointed Iraqi Tours as their sole representative and signed a maintenance agreement with Iraqi Airways. Iraqi leaders had a financial interest in Iraqi Tours, and Iraqi Airways was run by the son of Prime Minister Nur al-Sadi.[19] Mid East Air was registered in the United States but owned by the Israeli government. It is difficult to imagine that Iraqi leaders did not know that; months before the Iraqi exodus, Mid East Air planes were used to evacuate 49,000 Jews from Yemen.[20]

The property left behind by the fleeing Iraqi Jews, a generally prosperous community, was taken over by the government, and many Iraqi officials increased their wealth through these arrangements. Moreover, Abbas Shiblak and other researchers state that fabricated reports about the plight of Iraqi Jews were circulated in the United States and Europe.[21] Thus, we have Israeli agents operating directly under Arab disguise, almost certainly working with Arab collaborators, and a disinformation campaign about Arab violence and extremism.

This type of deception remained a constant tactic for freelance Israelis. Jumping ahead to opening day of Arab Culture Week in Haifa in May 1990, a Jewish cemetery was desecrated with defiant anti–Jewish slogans urging Arabs to kill Jews. Haifa is the only integrated city in Israel, and it turned out that the perpetrators were Jews trying to incriminate Arabs so that Jews would take revenge. The slogans showed Arab hatred and extremism, but the writing was neat and calculated, not resembling the work of a mentally sick man as the government declared.[22]

Provoking riots by sneaking into Arab villages has been a mainstay for the extremist Kach party.[23] Responding to a published letter from an angry Israeli settler, journalist Robert I. Friedman writes, "Israel radio, quoting Israel's northern district police spokesman Gideon Arbel, reported that the settlers, pretending to be marauding Arabs, had attacked Israeli settlers and hurled a firebomb on an Israeli-owned car as a pretext to launch 'counterattacks' against Arab villages."[24] When Jewish extremists killed or maimed several Arab mayors on June 2, 1980, Israelis suggested they were attacked by rival Palestinians.[25]

Those familiar with the history of the region will recall a disguise operation called the Lavon Affair. Agents in Egypt, under the direct command of Israeli leaders and disguised as Muslim fundamentalists, planted small bombs against American, British, and Egyptian civil targets. The agents had received training in Israel before they began their subversive activities in Egypt. The operation aimed to weaken the links that Egypt had been forging with the West and to create internal struggle in Egypt. The operations against the British were timed to coincide with Anglo-Egyptian negotiations concerning British evacuation from Suez, which Israel opposed, and those against American facilities were aimed at destroying the growing friendly relations between Egypt and the United States (President Gamal Abdel Nasser had not yet become the West's ogre), which included a $50 million aid program and $500 million arms deal. In a word, the bombings were designed to depict Arabs as violent enemies of the West. In the early 1950s the United States was giving modest financial support to the Muslim Brothers because of their strong anti-communist platform.[26]

Bombs of nitroglycerin surrounded by acid were put in books and placed on shelves of the United States Information Service and British libraries in Cairo and Alexandria just before closing time. The acid would burn the protection around the nitro, and soon after, the bomb would explode. Bombs were also placed in the MGM theater, various American businesses, the British consulate, and Egyptian offices. By chance during the early stage of the operation, an incendiary bomb malfunctioned and discharged a cloud of smoke from an agent's pocket as he was standing in line at an Alexandria cinema. Police arrested him, and he confessed. Since the group kept intimate contact with each other, it was easy to round them up, but their Israeli controllers fled as soon as they discovered that something had gone wrong. Avraham Seidenberg, who had been court-martialed for stealing from Israeli Arabs, was the group's supervisor.

Israeli intelligence stood ready to give the West "information" about both the Brotherhood and Egyptian terrorism against the West.[27] After the plot was uncovered, the Americans and British were understandably upset and demanded an answer. The Israeli government, at first accusing Egypt of a Nazi-inspired policy against innocents, claimed that it was a rogue operation—to the end they denied responsibility—and reports about the affair in the Israeli press were sketchy and full of hazy inference. Richard Deacon states, "The full details of the Egyptian scandal were kept from the Israeli public... The Lavon Affair was classified as top secret."[28] This indicates that despite the handful of government investigations and investigations of the investigations, Israeli leaders were either encouraging similar future activities or at least making no attempt to stop them by controlling their security establishment. The inquiries focused on who gave the order, avoiding the question of the recurring policy of subterfuge used in the operation. Some leaders forged documents linking the action to Defense Minister Lavon, thus giving the affair his name, but in the end no one was responsible, and Ben-Gurion spent his last years bitterly wrapped up in the affair.

The protagonists of the ring were honored. The six surviving members, who had remained in Egyptian prisons until they were exchanged after the 1967 war, were given ranks of lieutenant colonel or major. In a low-key ceremony Chief of Staff Dan Shomron awarded the posthumous rank of lieutenant colonel to the two executed members, Moshe Marzouk and Samuel Azzar, as well as Max Bennet. When Marcella Ninio, the only female member, was married, Golda Meir led her down the aisle, and Dayan was in attendance.

Again jumping ahead three decades, we find another similar case. Israelis were caught in London masquerading as violent Arabs, probably involved in the killing of Palestinian journalist and cartoonist Naji al-Ali. The police investigation discovered that Israeli officials based in their London embassy orchestrated Arab collaborators who were trained in Israel and were involved at least in the storing of weapons connected to the operation. Britain had just completed a £10 billion contract with Saudi Arabia and was about to restore diplomatic relations with Syria.[29] The killing, which is discussed later, looked like the work of the PLO as revenge for Naji's caricature of Arafat.[30]

Israeli officials in London had a network of agents not to gain information about the PLO, but to make the PLO look like radical, vengeful killers

and to foment conflict and dissent among Palestinians and harm their cooperation with the West. As with other activities, the entire truth has not
emerged; all the weapons, Israelis, and collaborators involved have not been
uncovered—the actual killer remains unknown—and Israel did not cooperate
with the investigation, apologizing only after diplomatic threats, again indicating a desire to continue similar activities.

The fake Baghdad panic, the Lavon Affair, the sham desecration of Jewish cemeteries, the provocative Intifada leaflets, the killing of Naji—these
covert operations either went wrong or were uncovered after the event. How
many other hoaxes have been successful? How many other assassinations of
Palestinians have taken place with Israeli involvement and been made to look
like the work of radical Palestinians? In how many other countries in which
there have been anti–Jewish movements followed by an exodus to Israel—
Morocco, Yemen, Argentina, or the Soviet Union—have the agitations come
from disguised Israeli activities? Can it be that other unsolved violent attacks
thought to have been Palestinian were actually engineered by Israel as part of
its pattern of Arab masquerade?

The sudden evacuation of the Iraqi Jewish community was engineered by
Arab masquerade. Certainly, a few thousand, the young and the poor, wanted
to leave for a possible better life, but the majority of Jews would have stayed
had it not been for the underground terror activities. As mentioned, the Iraqi
agents used in the operation were brought to Israel for training, and by their
actions we can guess that they received weapons and combat instruction.[31] We
know also that Israel brought Jews from Morocco, Yemen, Argentina, and
Ethiopia for training and sent them back to their countries. If we use the Iraqi
activities as a paradigm, then we must question the motives of the training that
other nationals received. We also know that in Morocco, Yemen, and Ethiopia,
bribes were paid to officials to encourage them to collaborate with emigration
plans. Israeli leaders claimed to have paid $500,000 in bribes to Moroccan
officials.[32]

Raviv and Melman tell us that the Mossad "established a secret infrastructure for Zionist activity in Morocco … [underground members] had to
have been in combat units, and preferably they had experience in clandestine
activities … if, as they feared, their Arab neighbors launched pogroms or other
disturbances."[33] There was a pogrom in Morocco, though it is not clear what
caused it, and there were ugly expressions of anti-Semitism in other countries.
The details of Israel's activities inside Morocco remain secret.[34] Raviv and
Melman also say that the Mossad brought "young Jewish activists from
Argentina and nearby countries to Israel to receive intensive training in self-
defense. It was a secret Mossad project."[35] Also, according to the authors,
Ethiopian Jews were brought to Israel for similar training.[36] The *Independent*
tells us that during the height of the Ethiopian civil war, Israel paid $2500 for
each of the 18,000 Ethiopian Jews to immigrate.[37]

Yet the historical truth of these immigration activities remains obscured; documents have not been released, and we should not offer innuendo as a replacement for scholarship. However, if we look at the pattern of verified Arab masquerade incidents, then we have to call into question how Zionism, which was not a popular movement in the Arab Jewish communities, quickly attracted hundreds of thousands.

Other areas of possible disguise activity need investigation. We discussed Israel's mail bomb campaigns against the British, later used against Arabs. Palestinians also sent mail bombs to Israel in December 1971, but some sent to Israeli diplomats later appeared to have been fakes. One had a leaflet announcing itself as an operation of the Palestinian terrorist group Black September. The *Sunday Times* legitimately asks, "Why put the leaflets inside letters which, hopefully, would disintegrate in the blast? And why so few letters [five]... Why was the note inserted in only one of the London letters?"[38] The suspicious campaign paralleled an Israeli letter bomb campaign operating from Belgrade.

We also need to examine assassinations where we are often given to understand that Arab leaders were killed at the hands of other Arabs. This type of deception began in 1956 when the bombs that killed Egyptian general Mustapha Hafez and colonel Salah Mustapha were said to be the work of rival Arabs. A Palestinian brought Hafez a parcel bomb across the border from Israel—there are confused reports whether the messenger was a collaborator, double agent, or unwitting courier—while the mail bomb sent to Mustapha was posted from Arab East Jerusalem.[39] Israeli sources claim that these two men were helping *fedayeen* guerrilla attacks, while Palestinians say that they were stopping cross-border raids. What is clear, however, is that the Israelis leaked reports to the press blaming Arabs for killing other Arabs.[40] As Stewart Steven says of the Mossad, "The finger which pulled the trigger had been superbly camouflaged."[41] When the Mossad killed Dr. Mahmoud Hamshari in Paris in December 1972, the pro-Israeli *l'Aurore* said that he was a victim of his own bomb,[42] and the Israeli *Yedioth Aharonoth* distributed disinformation claiming that he was the brains behind the Munich massacre.[43] Other assassinations will be examined later.

Diverse studies discuss the Mossad's covert action teams, which were charged with arranging disturbances intended to create distrust among Arab states and their leaders.[44] The Mossad was helped by the Arabs' propensity to quarrel with each other and their disregard for the common good. A CIA report on the Mossad found that one of their frequent tactics against Palestinians and Arabs was to "encourage internecine conflicts and to promise monetary rewards for secret collaboration."[45] How and where have these internecine conflicts been propagated?

The Israeli military often disguised themselves as Arabs when penetrating across their border. There are credible oral reports that during the 1967 war the Israeli tanks that swept through the West Bank were painted with Iraqi flags. Stephen Green describes one major military penetration during the War of Attrition when hundreds of Israeli soldiers in Egyptian uniforms, using Egyptian tanks (with markings intact) captured from the 1967 war, crossed the Suez and inflicted serious damage.[46]

Turning Arab against Arab was a central Israeli policy. Researchers have suspected that Israeli agents provoked shooting incidents in Amman, Jordan, before the September 1970 civil war to create a state of tension and allow for Israeli "retaliation" against guerrilla bases.[47] More obvious is Lebanon, where Israel used dirty tricks in concert with an explicit bombing campaign to foster internal conflicts. Bean Grosscup echoes other reports when he writes:

> [Menachem] Begin admits that the Israeli Air Force bombed Arab civilians, canals, bridges, and transport on a regular basis. Begin's revelation is echoed by other Israeli leaders such as former Foreign Minister Abba Eban and Chief of Staff Mordachai Gur, who admit that terrorism is a central part of Israeli military policy. Eban even defends Israeli terrorism as logical, on the ground that it can move innocent parties who have been victimized by terrorism to exert pressure on their political leaders to make peace.[48]

Israel bombed bridges and civilian targets, as Jonathan Randal observes, to create maximum havoc for Lebanese civilians so they would turn against the Palestinians.[49] Israeli spokesmen said in 1993 that their bombings were "intended to create a flood of refugees."[50] Jim Muir adds that the Israelis helped fuel the Christian-Druze conflict; Noam Chomsky notes that Israeli soldiers shot into Palestinian camps from Christian areas to incite the Palestinians against the Christians, and Israeli patrols forced Christians and Muslims at gunpoint to punch one another.[51] Abundant oral reports speak of Israel's fueling the civil war by having agents in a Christian area, disguised as a militia, fire at Druze positions from the tops of buildings, while other agents fired at Christians from Muslim West Beirut. Israel's purpose has been to radicalize and divide the opposition, as is clear from its clandestine and overt activities in Lebanon. The Arab masquerade it employed sought the same effect.

Of course disguise is required and considered normal in spying and related underground operations. What we want to examine is more active disguise activities which frame the enemy and obscure historical analysis. In the examples mentioned here we can see that Israel sought to make Arabs appear as terrorists—throwing bombs at Jews and killing fellow Palestinians—and this activity goes beyond spying. The operations we have examined have for one reason or other failed; we need to ask which others may have succeeded and remain historically fraudulent. Israel held a strong capacity to fight on the battlefield, and they excelled in that area, but until the 1993 peace accord they failed to cope with the Intifada or peace negotiations or Palestinians who advocate these.

Israel worked the masquerade tactic by penetrating Palestinian organizations. Infiltrating enemy organizations is an automatic action for any sophisticated, well-financed secret service. Passive infiltration focuses on information collection, while active infiltration involves manipulation. In this area we have difficulty keeping a high standard of scholarship since most of the information comes from unsubstantiated oral sources, often with political leanings that may render that information suspect; however, if we cannot cite documentation, we can question: Did Israel penetrate Palestinian organizations, directly or in the form of collaborators, to gain information about enemy activities, or did they penetrate in order to take a controlling position? If the latter, then they would be able to steer the target group on a more militant and extremist course and divide the Palestinian movement.

In the early 1970s a group called the National Arab Youth, led by Ahmed al-Ghafour, operated internationally. Oral evidence reveals that the NAY, which was later taken over by Abu Nidal, was infiltrated by the Mossad. Infiltrating such a group would have been the first priority of the Mossad and one of the most simple tasks. It would be unrealistic to assume that the NAY was free from Israeli infiltration. Organization infiltrators aim to be more extreme, more passionate, more uncompromising, in order to advance in the group. An infiltrator is not valuable at the bottom of the heap. If a discovered *agent provocateur* achieves a controlling position, it foments suspicion and brings disrepute to the cause. In one of their many senseless operations, the NAY tried to bomb the residence of the Israeli ambassador in Nicosia (the ambassador had left his house prior to the attack); then another unit in a Land Rover stormed onto the airport and drove around an Israeli plane, shouting and firing, like Spaghetti Western Indians around a wagon train.[52]

Israel used that action to justify its mass air-sea reprisal the same night in Beirut, killing three PLO leaders. The operation had been planned for months, and Israelis, under the guise of Arabs and foreigners, had already rented cars and established a network for the raid well before the Cyprus action. As we would expect, the Israeli raiding party turned to the ruse of wearing uniforms similar to Palestinian fighters and used Arabic speakers,[53] and it is thought that the Israelis wanted to make their work look like the work of rival Palestinian factions. However, the raiding party encountered resistance at two locations and had to call for helicopters to make their escape.[54] Circumstantial evidence would indicate that Israel had known about the Nicosia action beforehand because it had infiltrated the NAY. It is also possible to assume that an infiltrator had obtained a leadership position in the group and was able to orchestrate the event so Israel could rationalize its Beirut raid. Given Israel's history of Arab disguise, we need to examine such an assumption.[55]

The NAY wreaked havoc in Europe, attacking airports in European countries most friendly to the Palestinians. In Athens they mistakenly opened fire in the airport terminal on passengers waiting for a flight to Geneva instead of Tel Aviv, killing five and wounding fifty-five.[56] They machine-gunned the Rome airport during the 1973 Christmas season and firebombed a Pan American jet,[57] a seemingly irrational act that was repeated by Abu Nidal a dozen Christmas seasons later, and while Arafat was addressing the United Nations in 1974, the NAY hijacked a plane and senselessly killed a German passenger.[58] A few days later they hijacked a KLM jet and diverted it to Nicosia, where they demanded the release of their seven comrades captured before the Israel's Beirut raid.[59] It costs a fortune to run international operations on that scale— weapons transport over borders, training, false documents, advance surveillance teams, safe houses, supervisors, etc.—and a small group such as the NAY could not have organized such activities without outside financial and logistical help. During the last hijack mentioned, the group used twelve gunmen.

How can such activities help the Palestinians win a state? Who benefits? If we look at these events in light of the long-standing Israeli disguise tactic, their authenticity must be called into question. This is not a diatribe against violence, but invading enemy territory or taking enemy hostages to negotiate the release of prisoners is a world apart from blazing a friendly European airport. Coupled with Israel's historical record of Arab masquerade designed to project Arabs as extremists, the conduct of the NAY and other proponents of meaningless violence should be reevaluated.

Israel encouraged the radicalization of its enemy, as the bombing of South Lebanon attests. It is well known that Israel helped arm various factions in Lebanon and gave support to Hamas and radicals in the occupied territories during the 1980s in order to create divisions among Palestinians.[60] We will see that Israel assassinated moderate leaders, leaving militants alone. By bombing villages and approaching the Middle East with warlike vengeance, dropping a hundred bombs when one would do, Israel instigated a policy designed to radicalize the region.[61]

Chapter 4
Birth of the Palestinian Guerrillas

Every New Year's Day during the generation of the occupation, the Palestinians in the West Bank and Gaza staged demonstrations to honor Fatah Day, commemorating the day that Fatah, the primary pillar of the Palestine national movement, surfaced in its 1965 guerrilla action against Israel, the first act of the armed struggle to liberate Palestine. Yasir Arafat, with the help of two of his close associates and a Syrian officer, organized the attack from Lebanon.[1] They spent weeks planning it, discussing it in meetings, and training 12 courageous volunteers from the Ein al-Hilweh refugee camp near Sidon who had previously crossed into Israel.

The Baath party had just taken power in Syria and lent their help to the fledgling Fatah group, who aimed to blow up a canal that was diverting water from the River Jordan, an issue which had developed into an international dispute that Arab countries were too impotent to address. Under pressure from Eisenhower after the Suez War, Israel agreed to stop building the canal. In 1963, however, the Arabs discovered that the project had been restarted, and Egypt's President Nasser, who dominated the Arab world, convened a special meeting of the Arab League to deal with the issue. Nasser got the other members to approve the creation of the Palestine Liberation Organization, but it was an impotent grouping intended merely to show people that their leaders were actively engaged in the question of Palestine, which remained the Arab world's hottest issue. As one British diplomat observed, "No one can live in the Middle East or even visit it, without realizing that Palestine is the central focus of almost every Arab's mind."[2]

It was predicted that the canal would ruin Jordan Valley agriculture, but to the relief of the Arab countries, who were not looking for another confrontation with Israel, Lebanon said it wanted no foreign troops on its soil attacking the canal from the north, so the League allocated $13 million to divert the river before it entered Israel, knowing that such a sum would be inadequate for the project. All leaders spoke eloquently; Fatah wanted to show the Arab world that unlike the old guard, they were doers, not talkers.

After a heated internal meeting just before the raid, the 20 Fatah members agreed to call the attacking group *al-Assifa* (the storm) so that members who were opposed to military action—and even at the initial stage they were a sizable number—could disassociate themselves from the venture.[3] The PLO continued to carry out military or terrorist actions by a separate body so leaders and diplomats could say that the PLO had nothing to do with the action. *Al-Assifa* became the group's guerrilla wing.

The six selected commandos had a box of dynamite and detonators, which they were going to sneak across the largely unguarded border and put next to the canal. Arafat gave them last-minute instructions on New Year's Eve, and the leaders wrote a pompous press release about the attack, "Military Communique Number One," evoking God's glory for this mighty action destined to change the course of human events. "*Al-Assifa* forces," it read, "have launched forward to announce both to the enemy and the world that we [Palestinians] have not faded away and that the armed revolution is returning for victory." The communique, full of Arabic hyperbole, was adopted by the Abu Nidal group a decade later, as was the name *al-Assifa*, without giving credit to its authors.

The leaders of this unknown cell duplicated copies of the communique on a second-hand mimeograph machine in their austere Ein al-Hilweh office; then Arafat sent two people to Beirut to hand-deliver the copies to all the newspapers, who happily carried the story on their front pages the next morning. This new *al-Assifa* group, it said, carried out a crippling attack against the canal, after which all commandos returned safely to base.

This was news to the Israeli authorities. They telephoned the canal construction crew, who were equally mystified by the news of this spectacular and daring raid. According to researcher Thomas Kiernan, one of the volunteers got scared the evening before they left and went to the Lebanese internal police, the Deuxieme Bureau (Second Office), and informed. The police rounded up the commandos and seized their dynamite. It was not until later that morning, after the Lebanese were reading the grand pronouncement in the comfort of their seaside villas, that the embarrassing reality became known: the group never left their base.[4] The Abu Nidal poster of "Military Communique Number One" and the Palestinians who demonstrate on Fatah Day do not discuss the outcome of the heroic act.

But Fatah leaders had a backup plan. Another group of five brave commandos, led by Ahmed Musa, also had ten sticks of dynamite. Arafat drove to them in his usual recklessness and put them into action that evening. Two of the five suffered from last-minute doubt about risking their lives now that the Israelis had been alerted, and they asked to be excused. The other three rode across the Jordanian border by horseback and put the TNT inside the canal, setting their detonators for the morning so they would be able to sneak back to safety before the explosion. An Israeli engineer saw the box floating in the water about midday and yanked off the detonator.[5] It probably would not have exploded. That was Fatah's magnificent beginning, the first guerrilla action to liberate Palestine, an augury for further bungling.

The roots of this guerrilla movement can be traced back to after the 1948 war, when groups of Palestinian fighters called *fedayeen* attacked Israel. They were vengeful bands of feuding Arabs, ill trained, poorly equipped, lacking a secure base, and imbued with no practical course of regaining their homeland. Operating principally in Gaza, but also in the West Bank, which Jordan annexed, they were looked upon with increased suspicion by Arab governments, though Arab leaders made tough statements about winning back Palestine. Within a couple of years the *fedayeen* had half a dozen small bands armed with rifles. In 1952 Israel claimed that there were 3742 illegal border crossings in which 60 Israelis were killed;[6] however, this includes refugees trying to visit, sometimes to collect fruit from their gardens. Generally, the first years after statehood were quiet, until Ariel Sharon was given free rein.

Sharon's ferocious attacks, almost all against civilians, had a profound psychological effect on both sides. His group was ruthless, racist, and arrogant, and they created or invented provocations in order to go into action.[7] Sharon inaugurated Unit 101 in September 1953 when it chased a group of Bedouins over the border. A month later a gang of *fedayeen* killed a mother and her two children in their sleep. Such attacks were rare since the *fedayeen* were unorganized, and the Jordanians appealed to Israel via the Joint Armistice Committee to refrain from a reprisal, vowing to find the killers. However, the Israeli cabinet approved a raid, leaving the details to Sharon.

After reading to his men graphic descriptions of the killing of the mother and children, Sharon led his Unit 101 into the West Bank village of Kibya with 600 kg of explosives. They killed 69 residents and demolished 45 houses, many blown up with the inhabitants inside. Uzi Benziman notes, "His soldiers were not bothered by the fact that they were generally attacking civilian targets because they had come to accept the Arabs, as a whole, as enemies."[8] The Israeli government, surprised by the extent of the operation, tried to say that it had nothing to do with the attack, which brought international condemnation. However, Israeli citizens applauded Sharon, especially after the gruesome murder, and he became a national hero, the Arab fighter, another case of glorifying those who kill innocents.

His troops, freed from the military discipline that epitomizes the Israeli army, masqueraded as United Nations personnel, Red Cross workers, and Arabs. Sharon's main attacks were against Gaza. In 1955 UNRWA said 275 people were killed in such raids, and Dayan admitted that only once did Arabs fire at raiding Israeli soldiers, who looted and heavily damaged property.[9] Unit 101 went into action repeatedly, provoking, aiming to deteriorate relations with neighboring countries, livening the border and creating an atmosphere for another war, which we know from Moshe Sharett's diary was being planned in 1953. Jordan, Syria, and Egypt perceived this threat and kept a tight rein on Palestinians to prevent cross-border attacks. Nasser was secretly sending letters to Ben-Gurion and negotiating through CIA officer Kermit Roosevelt, Jr., adopting a conciliatory line to achieve peace. But this changed one evening in February 1955 when Sharon's team raided the Egyptian army headquarters in Gaza. Apparently, the extent of the raid—38 killed and 44 wounded—surprised

FRC poster of a copy of "Military Communique Number One," issued by Fatah on their first raid in 1965.

Israeli leaders,[10] but it also destroyed all chance for peace for a generation. Israel said that it was responding to an Egyptian attack. Says Sharett, "Who would be foolish enough to believe that such a complicated operation could 'develop' from a casual and sudden attack on an Israeli army unit by an Egyptian unit?"[11] Alan Hart adds that during the raid a call was sent for a group of reinforcements. The Arabs sent four trucks of men that were promptly ambushed, causing the heaviest casualties of the operation. Hart claims that it was probably an Israeli masquerading as an Arab who made the call.[12]

Nasser was personally furious; the raid, using sophisticated weapons, had no provocation. Seeing that peace was impossible, he began an intensive military build up, turning to the Soviet bloc for arms (immediately making himself an enemy of the West). He also allowed the Palestinians, who held sizable demonstrations in Cairo and Gaza after the attack, to organize raids.[13] This was the birth of the movement that tried to bomb the canal in 1965. Nasser often described Sharon's raid as a major turning point.

Egyptian officers spent six months training 700 Palestinians,[14] from among whom were to rise the core group of Fatah. Nasser passed on another message via United States Quaker Elmer Jackson that he was still willing to normalize relations. Sharon answered with another Gaza raid on August 22, and Nasser allowed the *fedayeen* to attack, beginning their own cross-border killings three days later, again almost always against civilians.[15] During that summer these incursions killed or wounded 200 Israelis.[16] By 1956 raids were begun from the West Bank. Whereas before 1955 most Arabs who crossed the border were generally desperate refugees or criminals, Israel now faced commandos, trained and directed, whose effectiveness increased, although they never came close to the damage Unit 101 inflicted. Sharon says that he struck Gaza about 70 times between 1954 and 1956, "each action more difficult and complex than the last." His aim was clear: "By early 1955 the growing pressure from the paratroop raids was edging Egypt toward a crisis."[17] "Hit and run and lie to the world," Sharett complained about this philosophy.[18] Sharon's policy of provocation, misrepresentation, and aggression steered government policy, a dangerous precedent for civilian rule.[19]

Another major Sharon operation took place against Syria on December 11 and 12, 1955 when an armored column attacked near the Sea of Galilee, an attack that even the hawkish Ben-Gurion described as "too successful."[20] These incursions paved the way for the 1956 Suez War, which is said to have begun "in Chaos and ended in fiasco."[21] Ben-Gurion tells us, "We were bound to take punitive (rather than retaliatory) action" for defense, and claims that the Suez War sought to stop *fedayeen* attacks.[22] Indeed, Israel had been harassed by the *fedayeen*, whom they made Egypt promise to curb as a major ingredient to the 1957 ceasefire treaty. The Suez War was also supposed to topple Nasser, but through it he became "the undisputed hero of the Arab World."[23] Egypt stopped the *fedayeen*; the Israeli government controlled Sharon, and the region was never so quiet as the following decade.

When Israel occupied Gaza in 1956, it gave the future Palestinian activists a chance to see their enemy, and it moved them to organize resistance. Arafat, Khalil al-Wazir (Abu Jihad), Salah Kalaf (Abu Iyad), Faruq Qadumi, and Yousef Najjar would go to each others' houses and, over cups of Arabic coffee, discuss ways of winning back Palestine. Most of the group then went to Kuwait and began organizing there. At a meeting on October 10, 1959, they inaugurated Fatah. The three Arabic consonants of *Fatah* (f-t-h) are the initials read backward for "Organization to Liberate Palestine." Spelled forward the anagram has a negative meaning, but spelled backward, *Fatah*, it means "to conquer" and recalls the miraculous spread of Islam in the last millennium.

The original group consisted of two dozen with a philosophical idea of regaining their homeland, young idealists who rebelled against the passivity of the older generation[24] and were later inspired by the July 1962 FLN victory in Algeria that won independence from France through guerrilla war,[25] as well as by the liberation movements in Asia and Africa. They looked to China and North Vietnam as models. Arafat became the spokesman, and he quickly developed a dictatorial reputation which would later fuel factional fighting. The group decided to emulate the secrecy of military leaders fighting the Crusaders by using the Abu (father of) *nom de guerre*, creating for us a confusing string of Abus.

The Kuwaitis, always generous to the Palestinians, did not restrict their activities, but Kuwait was too far from Palestine. In the early 1960s the group moved to Lebanon and Jordan, pooled their resources—Arafat had a good engineering business in Kuwait, which he sold—and were able to buy light weapons and produce a 30-page monthly magazine called *Our Palestine*, edited in Kuwait by Tufiq al-Houri and printed cheaply in Beirut. As well as a propaganda tool, the modest magazine was used for fund raising. From the beginning the group invested well and turned over every stonefaced Arab leader to collect money. If Palestine had involved a contest over money instead of real estate, the Palestinians and Jews would have been locked in a more equal, if not more fierce, battle. However, the group's finances were not open, inviting corruption.

Israeli intelligence apparently knew nothing of this new group. On February 28, 1965, *al-Assifa* bombed a grain silo[26]; then, on May 25, they killed three Israelis. Israeli intelligence then overestimated the group's size, considering it a Syrian-sponsored faction. Two days later Israel retaliated, as Fatah leaders wanted and expected; but instead of piercing the heavily fortified Golan and hitting Syria, whom they publicly condemned for the attack, they raided two West Bank towns.

By mid–1965 Fatah leaders began openly meeting the Arab press, riding high on the tide of popular support. Most *al-Assifa* operations were pathetic or unsuccessful. Israel's terrain is not suited to guerrilla warfare, and few Palestinians were inclined to spend their lives for the cause. Fatah overcame that obstacle by verbally exaggerating every action and publicizing triumphs that never took place.

By the end of 1965 *al-Assifa* issued "Military Communique Number 36," which boasted of 110 cross-border operations. Israel admitted to 35 incursions and brought the subject up at the United Nations, giving the unknown group international status. The frequency of the attacks accelerated as the Fatah was bolstered, not by the minor destruction they were causing, but by the predictable Israeli reprisals. According to Abu Iyad, the Israeli army did not hit the guerrillas during their reprisals. By the June 1967 war, Fatah claimed 300 raids, at least twice the actual number, from bases in Lebanon, Syria, and Jordan.[27]

Fatah's aim was to develop a united force of *fedayeen* that would perform hit-and-run operations against Israel. They sought to involve the neighboring Arab states in the conflict, for they reasoned that since Israel publicly held the neighboring Arab countries responsible for cross-border attacks, it would

Fatah emblem used by the militant Palestinian factions.

retaliate against those countries, thus escalating the conflict. Fatah leaders knew that their *fedayeen* could not directly fight the Israeli army, but if they expanded the conflict to forcibly involve Arab countries by attacking Israel from neighboring bases, they could at least upset the current peace that had left them stateless and hopeless.[28] The Arab governments recognized the threat, censored Fatah stories in their press, and resisted being manipulated by a bunch of upstarts.

Important to the growth of the *fedayeen* was the development of a mythology that portrayed them as victims of injustice who, as in all good Arab stories, would triumph in the end. The tale of a halcyon existence destroyed in 1948 became the central focus of Palestinian life. The sentiment was translated into songs and poetry (some of which is very moving, mostly upbeat), and also into simplistic slogans that people could readily identify without analysis. Israeli leaders recognized the importance and strength of the literature: Dayan, it is said, read a poem by Radwa Tuqan and astutely exclaimed, "This is equal to 20 commandos!"[29]

Fatah looked in every corner of the world for recognition. They had relations with the radical European groups who tried to use the Palestinian cause as part of their ideology in the struggle against American imperialism and fat capitalists; however, these groups did not work with Palestinians because they cared only about their own cause and were not revolutionary enough. American Black Panthers Eldridge Cleaver and Stokely Carmichael made visits to Fatah. LSD proponent Timothy Leary also wanted to meet Arafat, but he was not invited.

American University in Beirut, seat of Arab revolutionary thinking in the late 1960s.

Arab secret services were the *fedayeen*'s greatest obstacle. Egypt arrested guerrilla leaders in Gaza in February 1966; soon after, Syria imprisoned all the Fatah members it could find, including Arafat and Abu Jihad, for over a month, forcing the guerrilla leaders to stage a hunger strike for their release. Palestinians say that the first Fatah casualty was killed not by Israeli soldiers but by a Jordanian border guard, who shot Ahmed Musa in the back after the first raid when he crossed the border back to Jordan, which was hostile to Fatah from the beginning. The story is often repeated, but its authenticity is questionable; it nevertheless illustrates the level of friction between the Palestinian organizations and Arab governments, who continually saw the guerrillas as a threat to their own power but were at the same time trying to glean political benefit from their cause. *Al-Assifa* attacks were directed more against Arab governments than against Israel.

When the Arab League launched the PLO, it nominated as its chair the eloquent Dr. Ahmed Shukeiry, a 52-year-old former Saudi representative to the United Nations, whose pugnacious language won him stature. His mouth expelled a flood of hollow words calling for Israel's destruction, but he, like other Arab leaders, firmly opposed commando actions, making him a caricature of Arab verbosity. Shukeiry was reaffirmed chairman at the first meeting of the Palestine National Council (PNC)—also nominated by the Arab League—May 28–June 2, 1964. The PNC drafted their infamous charter, revised in June 1–17, 1968, which called for Israel to be replaced by a secular state. Fatah criticized the inactivity of the Arab League in *Our Palestine*, and deliberately chose its first action against the canal as a slap in the face against the Arab states and their lackey PLO.

The other major component of the Palestine national movement formed in Beirut in the early 1950s around the picturesque American University (AUB). Since its founding in 1866 by Protestant minister Daniel Bliss, the AUB has been fertile ground for liberal, often anti–American, intellectualism. The AUB boasts that during the San Francisco conference to draft the United Nations Charter, the AUB was represented by more graduates than any other institution. George Habash and Wadi Haddad, two AUB Palestinian Christians who studied medicine and were part of a literary club called the Firm Tie, in 1954 formed the Arab National Movement (ANM). While Fatah focused on winning back Palestine, these young men were discussing left-wing politics, Marxism, the backwardness of Arab governments, and pan–Arabism, or the idea that the Arab world was one nation, which represented the mainstream political thinking among Palestinians.[30] The ANM followed Nasser, the advocate of pan–Arabism, who saw no need for a separate Palestinian state. The ANM was small, a group of intellectuals from various Arab countries who met in coffee houses and people's homes, published a newsletter, and put the Palestine-Israeli conflict in the context of capitalism, imperialism, communism, and revolutionary struggle. As the West focused on Vietnam, the Arabs were fixed on the war in Yemen, to which Nasser had committed his army. Naji Alush, a Palestinian-Lebanese writer, inspired the movement with his book *The Road to Palestine*, and the names they used, Firm Tie and ANM, alluded to a large Arab nation.

George Habash, the most charismatic of the group, became its head, and eventually he, like Ché Guevara (who met several Palestinian leaders, including Arafat), gave up his medical practice in Amman for full-time political work. Habash is accused of throwing a bomb at a synagogue in Beirut during the late 1950s. Although he denied that, his hatred of Israel crossed the line into hatred of Jews, and this racism was also transferred to his group. Habash had a bad experience in 1948, then working as a doctor in the pathetic refugee camps, affecting his attitude. Still, he and the ANM did not believe in military or guerrilla action. The ANM held that a civil strife arising from an enlightened and progressive movement was necessary to free Palestine from what they called the Zionist occupiers, so when Fatah launched its first "attack" against Israel, Habash and the ANM—as well as Nasser—did not applaud it, thinking instead about Salah al-Din eight centuries before, who overthrew corrupt Arab leaders and unified the Arabs before fighting the enemy. However, in 1964 Habash's group, too, began forming a guerrilla movement, Heroes of Return, which went into action after the 1967 war. Before and after the war Arafat and Habash met, but they could not agree to join forces. Habash instead turned the ANM and its commando groups into the Popular Front for the Liberation of Palestine (PFLP). Their slogan, "The road to liberating Palestine passes through Amman," meant that they sought to overthrow Jordan's King Hussein, establish a progressive state, and then fight and conquer Israel through guerrilla war.

The PFLP's best activity was separating and creating new movements with ideological differences. Habash was imprisoned in Syria for six months until one day his family and Haddad came to visit him and staged a tricky escape. But his lack of leadership while locked up had stirred up squabbles in the PFLP. Ahmed Jabril, an able but egotistic military leader who had formed his own mini-army in 1961 and joined the ANM in the mid–1960s, was the first to split. In sharp contrast to ANM members, Jabril had no intellectual ideology, believing only in military action. In November 1968 he took over 200 fighters, about as many as Fatah during that period, and began the PFLP–General Command, which became dependent on Syria for money and weapons. The GC made several successful attacks against Israel and is often blamed for foreign attacks, but Jabril was not involved in such adventures, which he felt had no military objective. However, two men who had left with Jabril, Abu Abbas and Talat Yaqub, broke from the GC in 1977 to form the Palestine Liberation Front (formed March 11, 1978), which was responsible for three grand failures: in summer 1980, 80 PLF men tried to raid Israel in an Aerostat, but it burned shortly after takeoff since it was painted with flammable varnish; in 1985 the PLF was in charge of the *Achille Lauro* episode, and after the Intifada a large number of PLF men tried to raid Israel in boats but were intercepted.

The second PFLP split was the work of Naif Hawathmeh, the most politically left of the group, though he felt no personal resentment for Israelis. He would be the first leading Palestinian to be interviewed by Israeli journalists and make alliances with leftist Israelis, and he was stern in his opposition to international terrorism as a means of winning back Palestine. His solution was awakening the Arab masses to revolt against their kings and reactionary rulers and uniting under a progressive, socialist banner. In February 1969 the followers of Habash and Hawathmeh were at each other's throats, literally: meetings were broken up by fistfights, then they descended into the streets of Amman in armed warfare, Arafat having to step in to mediate. Unlike the GC, Hawathmeh's new group, the Democratic Popular Front for the Liberation of Palestine (DFLP), remained autonomous.

When Israel occupied the West Bank, Fatah and the PFLP began organizing underground cells, Arafat working in Nablus to recruit young men. On December 13, 1968, the Israeli military captured one of the main leaders, Abd al-Qadir Abu Falm, and this led to the arrests of over 100 of his network, showing that the organizers were untrained in protecting undercover activity. The courts handed harsh sentences to the youths, including house demolitions and deportations, and the Arab population was neutralized. Activists operated in Gaza, but in August 1970, after the War of Attrition, Sharon took the job of taming the natives, and as usual, he excelled. Thus the guerrillas, unable to work in the occupied territories, massed themselves in Jordan. Their inability to inspire the population to action demonstrates the weakness of their leaders and the effectiveness of Israeli measures. These groups also completely failed to politicize as a fifth column the Arabs who remained in Israel after 1948. Except for isolated incidents, the Israeli Palestinians remained silent and separated from those who fled, and although Fatah and the PFLP tried many times to form cells within Israel with the intention of instigating disruptive operations against the government, they were never successful.

Using Jordan as a base, the guerrillas began attacking Israel within months of the 1967 war. On March 18, 1968, an Israeli school bus ran over a mine, killing a doctor and wounding several children. It was the last in a series of similar attacks, and Israel decided to retaliate on Fatah's base at the Karameh refugee camp across the Jordan River. According to Stephen Greene, a representative from the United States embassy informed Fatah where the attack would take place,[31] but instead of following the guerrilla rule of retreating, Fatah stayed and confronted the Israeli army. Though battle has been idealized, it is true that an entire armored column with complete command of the sky fell on the village,[32] and equally true that Arafat and those who stayed behind fought bravely, being helped by the Jordanian army. Although they suffered heavy casualties—some 125 dead—Fatah killed 25 soldiers and forced the army to turn back, a major victory to Arabs.

The Israeli action at Karameh put the hitherto obscure Fatah on the map. Volunteers began coming in droves; donations filled the vaults. Fatah, whose fighting force went from a band of 300 to an army of more than 20,000,[33] could not train or arm the number of conscripts. With them came two problems that the Palestinians were unable to handle: corruption, and a large number of collaborators or Israeli agents. There was a high drop-out rate among new fighters since the romantic vision of winning back Palestine did not correspond to the mundane activities of a basically ineffective fighting force.[34] Fatah paid its men $20-50 a month, depending on rank and family, while the PFLP could only afford half that amount. The new recruits came from a less educated group who were good at repeating slogans, but such dedication is shallow.[35] Moreover, Fatah's impact had not been exaggerated. John Laffin notes that while from June 1967 to June 1971 the *fedayeen* claimed to have killed 8619 soldiers and civilians and destroyed 351 tanks, 88 aircraft, 5331 vehicles and 312 bridges, the Beirut newspaper *al-Jarida* noted cynically that Israel does not have 312 bridges.[36]

The guerrilla groups were at their best when they fought each other. There were always splinter groups and correction movements. Before the 1970 war in Jordan the Palestinians had 20 to 40 different guerrilla bands, with

Arab governments introducing their own groups, making it difficult to organize a popular uprising,[37] especially as these organizations suffered from having too many chiefs and not being accountable to their following, a sharp contrast to the Jewish groups before 1948. It is a common phenomenon for a group fighting a strong enemy to quarrel among themselves, and they made mistake upon mistake, but the refugees, and their children, and their children's children, never gave up.

Chapter 5
"We Have Taken Over Your Flight"

As well as being a military disaster for the Arabs, the 1967 War was an emotional defeat which brought them shame, an Arab's worst degradation. Nasser's seemingly virile phrases about winning back Palestine—slogans to which Palestinians clung as desperately as a drowning man clings to the empty water around him—in the end proved impotent. Nasser's army became a military joke (Egyptian tanks have 10 gears, one forward and 9 in reverse). The depression and disappointment among Palestinians was extreme. The question of their national rights was discarded, relegated to eloquent and logical lectures at the United Nations by Third World countries.

To Americans, bogged down in the Vietnam War while their children smoked dope and revolted their society's values, Israel's victory sparked a release, a psychic triumph, the fulfillment of a dream for the perpetually tormented Jewish people. Suddenly right-wing, end-of-the-world television evangelists who were once secretly or openly anti–Semitic began molding a philosophy based on the Jews taking over Palestine so they could later be wiped out in the battle of Migido, signaling Christ's second coming. Cryptic phrases in Revelation and Daniel were uncovered and shown to apply to the present Middle East conflict, the Arabs being aligned with Satan. Americans were looking for winners, not victims, to turn their attention away from their burning cities. The image of the brave Israeli, smart, confident, righteous, was pitted against the cowardly and nasty Arab. It became easy for the Western press to vilify Arabs, especially when the Arabs turned to a stint of international terrorism, which only verified the image already cast in the media.

I remember in the United States the strong sentiment against the bloodthirsty Arab aggressors aiming to drive Israel into the sea. I recall one TV commentator making a bold speech in which he had the guts to say that among his friends were Arab Americans and that we should not condemn the whole lot of those rotten people. I felt ashamed of myself. That was the beginning of anti–Arab racism. It swelled up like a terrible infection and continued to spread after every act of Arab terrorism. The Palestinians became not a people but a problem that filled UNRWA statistics and United Nations documents. They were used as ammunition by backward Arab regimes and as target practice by incipient Israeli pilots. No one wanted to deal with refugees; the Jews had discovered that a generation earlier. This is fertile ground for terrorism.

The United States presidential campaign of 1968 brought with it a succession of candidates pledging their loyalty to the state of Israel, a tradition reaching back to Harry Truman. Robert Kennedy, like the other candidates, upheld the tradition. During his 1968 primary campaign he put on a yarmulke, walked into a synagogue, and told a cheering audience that if he was elected president he would sent 50 advanced F-4E jet fighters to Israel. (This sale, later approved by President Johnson, would radically change United States–Israeli relations.[1]) Sirhan Bishara Sirhan heard the speech. Robert Kennedy had been his hero, a champion of the poor and downtrodden, but when he heard Kennedy's promise, he snapped. In a fit of rage he decided to kill. Timing his action with the first anniversary of the 1967 war, Sirhan walked into the Los Angeles campaign headquarters and shot Robert Kennedy, revisiting tragedy on the Kennedy family and the entire nation.

Although Sirhan was a United States resident, having arrived in the country when he was 13, and although he acted alone (contrary to conspiracy theories),[2] the assassination could be called the first act of Palestinian international terrorism. The Arab world thought highly of the Kennedys—many streets were named after JFK, who had sought better relations with the Arabs—so most Arabs deplored the killing of Robert, but when news of the assassination reached Wadi Haddad, co-founder of the PFLP, he inquired about this Sirhan Sirhan. The news report he heard said that Sirhan was a Jordanian Muslim. Haddad discovered that he was from a Christian family in Jerusalem.

Haddad's conspiratorial mind began to turn: this could be the chance to publicize the Palestinian cause, he told his colleagues. Kennedy was killed by a Palestinian, not a Jordanian; a Christian, not a Muslim. He thought that if people knew that, they would begin to wonder what the problem was in Palestine. Haddad naively reasoned that people would then seek to correct the injustice so similar acts would not recur. He discussed this with other PFLP leaders, including future terrorist sponsor Ahmed al-Ghafour. They wanted to hire a lawyer for Sirhan and use the trial for propaganda.

The Popular Front sent a political officer to the United States to mount a publicity campaign for Sirhan and the cause for which he killed. Typically, however, the fellow they sent had no practical experience in dealing with the slick, image-conscious world of the American media. He wore a drab, ill-fitting suit and spoke from under a mustache with a thick accent. The Palestinian leadership's first failure was not understanding the American mind, and their second failure was being too arrogant to learn. Haddad knew the West better than others—he spoke perfect English and monitored how each event in the Palestine conflict was covered in the press—but he was trying to impress the West from an Eastern mentality. Obsessed with the effect of the assassination, he wanted the world to know that there are Christian as well as Muslim Palestinians. Sirhan was as Christian as John Wilkes Booth, who, according to Haddad, acted out of desperation.

He persuaded PFLP leaders to study a nonmilitary action in Europe to ride the wave of publicity Sirhan had created. Revolution was spreading worldwide, and the PFLP was full of anxious, romantic leftists. Soon Haddad and his assistants decided to hijack an Israeli civilian jet, El Al, in order to catch the world's headlines and advertise the Palestinian cause. They argued that El Al also transported military hardware during the 1967 war, making it a legitimate target. Haddad began studying how to hijack a plane. He insisted on being professional, using articulate and educated hijackers who would be spokespersons. He aimed to hijack the plane on the day the trial for Sirhan opened. It turned out to be the anniversary of the Egyptian Revolution.

Sirhan's trial should have never taken place. The prosecution was ready to accept a plea bargain and send Sirhan to prison, but aging judge Herbert Walker saw the prospect of a courtroom full of journalists as his last chance to cap an otherwise dull career. He rejected the agreement and demanded a full trial. Both defense and prosecution were unprepared to present their cases, and the trial was a shoddy affair. The prosecutors were unable to ask for the death sentence since they felt that Sirhan was not in his proper mind at the time, but with extra coaching from the judge the jury returned a death sentence that was subsequently overturned.

Haddad's hijack idea was not new; the first known hijacking took place in Peru in 1931. In 1954 Israeli air force planes flew alongside a Syrian civilian plane and made it land at Tel Aviv airport. They kept the passengers as hostages, hoping to bargain for the release of five Israeli soldiers caught tapping telephone lines in Syria.[3] On May Day, 1961, Antulio Ramirez started a trend when he pulled a revolver on a National Airlines flight after it took off from Miami and forced it to fly to Cuba.

Haddad discovered that hijacking planes was more complicated than it seemed. Professional hijackings involved not only smuggling arms into the country and onto the plane—that was in the days of fairly lax security measures—but the hijackers needed to know the functions of the pilot, co-pilot, navigator, and crew, the food supplies on board, the amount of fuel carried, emergency exits, and the method for taking over the flight (in fact, on the first hijack one of the gunmen took over the navigator's job). Haddad had a special zeal for such intrigues, and he attacked the project with perverted enthusiasm, approaching each future hijacking with the precision of a surgeon, developing a method for hijacking and for teaching how to hijack, a tradable asset. He wanted his hijackers to make a public statement—his reason for hijacks was headlines—and upon arrival in an Arab country, they were to turn themselves over to the authorities and answer questions to the press. They were armed, but they were not to use their arms, only threaten.

After traveling to and from several European capitals, Haddad decided on the Rome–Tel Aviv route. They had been following Sharon's travels and thought that he would be taking that flight back to Israel, but he changed his itinerary. The hijackers, who had already been trained in weapons, were given intensive PR training in their base just north of Amman. They were taught to answer questions about their cause, sitting opposite make-believe reporters and telling them in English that Palestinians could not be forgotten by the world. They played courtroom; prospective hijackers stood up before the judge and the press and delivered speeches on the history of Palestine and on the international imperialist conspiracy. Haddad himself was in Rome to give the final orders to the hijackers. They were given nonferrous guns and grenades and again exhorted not to harm any of the passengers, for that would give them negative publicity. The hijackers dressed as priests and easily passed security. It was Haddad's touch to add the priest symbolism.

For all his medical training, fanaticism, and leftist philosophy, Haddad remained a superstitious man; to him the world moved around the array of Greek Orthodox saints. He loved secrecy, intrigue. At the time of Vatican II the Roman and Eastern churches agreed that their faithful could pray in each other's churches, and one afternoon Haddad went into St. Peter's Cathedral and lit a candle for the success of the hijackings. He took another plane out of Rome before the hijackers announced to the passengers, "We are Palestinians, and we have taken over your flight." They forced the plane to Algiers, as planned, but it received little coverage, far less than the news from Vietnam. The *London Times* put the story on page five, and most papers hardly followed the hostage negotiations. America was concerned about the looming long, hot summer of racial violence and the number of people turning on, tuning in, and dropping out.

The hijackers demanded the release of 100 Palestinians in Israeli jails. All the passengers except Israelis were put on flights to Paris and Southern France. The Algerian government was incensed, believing that it was an Egyptian plot to embarrass them, but they put the Israeli passengers in a guarded hotel and negotiated for the release of the prisoners. Israel did not know what to do, issuing mixed statements and contradictory remarks. At last, thought Haddad and the PFLP leadership, we have struck Israel at their point of vulnerability; as the Vietnamese learned to fight the United States by hitting their weaknesses, so too the Palestinians had begun their guerrilla war, fighting not the way their enemy intended but catching them off guard. Even PFLP cadres who opposed the hijack were impressed. Finally, after 40 long days of negotiating, with the Italian government acting as go-between, Israel agreed to release 15 prisoners, and the Jewish passengers and plane were freed. From this incident Algeria gained the reputation of Middle East negotiator. As well as settling other hijackings, they reunified the PLO, negotiated for the release of American hostages in Tehran, and were on the brink of settling the Iran-Iraq War when the negotiating team's plane crashed in mysterious circumstances a month before Israel invaded Lebanon.[4]

El Al immediately imposed strict security, forcing Haddad's team to look for alternatives, keeping to the terrorist's rule of selecting soft targets. Instead of avoiding El Al, Jews supported the airline, and bookings increased.[5] Haddad began concocting dozens of plans for other spectaculars. A whole team set about gathering details, drawing maps, taking photos, analyzing difficulties. The PFLP executed only a small fraction of the operations, aiming for flashy actions.

Six months after the first hijack, the day after Christmas, members of the PFLP attacked an El Al jet while it was on the tarmac at Athens airport. The two gunmen walked onto the field and began shooting at it, killing a passenger and wounding a stewardess. The gunmen were arrested, tried, and given life sentences.[6] This was the first bloody attack by a Palestinian organization outside the Middle East. The Israelis struck back two days later, not at the PFLP but at the Beirut Airport, where a team of commandos helicoptered in and destroyed 13 Arab planes. Rafiel Eitan, who led the attack, claims to have dropped in for coffee in the airport bar while the destruction was raging outside. The damage was estimated at $70 million,[7] but the tab was picked up by British and American insurance companies.

The Beirut attack weakened the power of the Christian government, as Georges Corm explains: "An army that fails to defend the integrity of the national territory in fact loses all legitimacy and can no longer effectively protect the political power."[8] Since they used French helicopters, Charles de Gaulle ordered an arms embargo against Israel. Military historian Edgar O'Ballance notes, "Instead of having the anticipated effect of warning guerrillas to keep out of Lebanon, the raid had the converse effect, one of attracting Fedayeen attention in considerable volume to the country."[9] The opportunist government in Iraq rounded up 14 people, including nine Jews—one the leader of the Jewish community—and hanged them on trumped-up charges of spying, muting the uproar over the Beirut raid.[10]

In February 1969 a PFLP team including a woman guerrilla, Amira Dahbor, attacked another El Al jet in Zurich, causing a ripple of sensation throughout the Arab world.[11] Haddad chose another woman, Leila Khaled, a guerrilla who had studied at the American University in Beirut, to lead a hijacking.[12] Using a woman was not new; Haddad got the idea when nine months before a woman seized a small turboprop from Mexico and took it to Cuba. As well as fighting the Zionist-imperialist enemy, the PFLP was warring against the reactionary Arab states and their society, and involving women was part of that rebellion. Comrade Khaled and another gunman were instructed to hijack a TWA jet and take it to Damascus, let out all the passengers, then blow out the cockpit. The PFLP magazine *al-Hadaf* parachuted a photographer to document the destruction, but his camera jammed. This was the first time the Palestinians attacked a non–Israeli target, justifying it by claiming that the international community was responsible for Palestine. To their surprise, when the hijackers gave themselves up, they discovered that they were unwelcome. The incident embarrassed the Syrians, who detained the hijackers for months. However, the Syrians took advantage of the windfall, separated the Israeli passengers, and bargained them for the release of two Syrian pilots. On July 22, 1970, the PFLP hijacked an Olympic Airlines jet from Beirut and held it ransom for the release of seven Palestinian prisoners in Greece, including the ones who raided the El Al jet at the airport. Greece gave in right away.[13]

It is here that PFLP actions completely lost their purpose, no longer aiming at the enemy, but lashing out at the world. Their sense of victimization gave them license for any action, losing sight of their professed goal of liberating Palestine. The first hijackings were designed to impress the West, to advertise the Palestinian cause. Later, the PFLP aimed at an Arab audience, and that is when the West took notice. PFLP international terrorism was not restricted to airports. On January 24, 1970, a bomb was thrown at the Hapoalim Bank in London, injuring one person, and on August 17 the PFLP planted incendiary bombs in Marks and Spencer because of the owner's generous support of Israel. On May 2 gunmen broke into the Israeli embassy in Paraguay, killing one woman and wounding another.[14] They set off bombs at El Al offices in several European cities, and in the November 27, 1969, grenade attack in Athens they killed a two-year-old boy and injured fourteen.[15]

On February 21, 1970, a Swissair flight from Zurich to Tel Aviv exploded 15 minutes after taking off, killing 47 people, and another bomb exploded on an Austrian Caravelle, forcing it to turn back for an emergency landing. The PFLP immediately denied it had carried out the attacks, but airlines began banning flight mail to Israel. Although probably these actions were the work of Palestinians—many point to Ahmed Jabril—no one accepted responsibility, although someone telephoned in the name of the PFLP.[16] On March 1 the PFLP issued a believable statement saying that they were responsible for ten operations outside the Middle East, and the Swissair was not one of them.

There were a few other PFLP hijackings, and gradually they received more press coverage. The PFLP poured much of its wealth into these projects and was nearly broke until airlines began paying protection money.[17] Haddad had not initially counted on this perk. Each hijacking was timed to coincide with a particular world event, culminating in a spectacular day of hijackings, bringing planes to an abandoned British military airstrip near Zarka, Jordan, called Dawson Field just after the United States brokered a ceasefire along the Suez.[18]

Using four teams, three led by women, Haddad arranged the hijackings of Pan-American, TWA, Swissair, and El Al jets. The El Al failed, but the others succeeded. All were supposed to go to Dawson Field, but the Pan-American was a jumbo, and the fact that the runway might be too short had escaped Haddad's detailed calculations. It went to Beirut/Cairo, and a few days later a BOAC was hijacked to make up for the unsuccessful hijack and to free Khaled, who, after three plastic surgery operations, had been on the abortive El Al hijack. When the El Al returned to Britain there was a fight for Khaled, the El Al staff wanting to take her back to Israel but the British insisting that she had to stay since she committed the action over British airspace. The other hijacker, Patrick Arguelo, a Central American, was killed.

Again, these actions had nothing to do with Israel but were meant to precipitate a war in Jordan, which they did. George Habash had left for China and North Korea on September 3 and had no part with this episode, so Haddad called the tune, and everyone danced, the PLO siding with the PFLP. When in June the PFLP, led by Habash, entered the Amman Intercontinental and Philadelphia hotels and held all foreigners hostage, demanding specific concessions to the guerrillas, Hussein stepped in and defused the confrontation. However, the international hijackings, where the planes were firebombed, causing over $25 million worth of damage, was an entirely different matter (PFLP leaders did not want the planes destroyed, again demonstrating their weak leadership). Again, Jews were separated and kept as hostages, showing that for all their talk of world revolution and a secular state, the PFLP were racist. Israel arrested 440 prominent Palestinians in the West Bank and Gaza (*Ha'aretz* called the arrests counter-hostages[19]), at the same time mounting one of its largest invasions into South Lebanon. In London the Jewish Defense League (JDL) kidnapped three Egyptian embassy employees.[20]

The September 1970 hijackings created grave repercussions on the Palestinian movement. The Jordanian government took an uncompromising stand against the guerrillas, and King Hussein's elite Bedouin troops attacked the guerrilla bases, destroying ruthlessly. As mentioned, Israel used dirty tricks to help Hussein arrive at his definitive decision, so the PFLP and Israel were operating with the same intention, drawing in the entire PLO against Jordan.

The rebel fighters were located in the villages and refugee camps in northeastern Jordan, and they were counting on help from Iraq, which had made oral promises of military support to fight the monarchy. Over Iraqi radio and in person to PLO leaders, the Iraqis promised that every one of their 12,000 troops in Jordan would be under the control of the PLO. As soon as the fighting began, however, Iraq turned a deaf ear to the PLO's appeals and instead took sides with the king, allowing Jordanian troops through their lines in order to surround Palestinian bases.[21] The new PLO representative in Baghdad, Abu Nidal, had little to do with negotiations between the PLO and Iraq, the fault lying directly with the Palestinian leadership for the disaster. The failure of Iraq to honor its pledge was the first disagreement between the PLO and Iraq. One Palestinian official said that if Iraq had been straight with them from the beginning, they would have had second thoughts about their poorly armed force picking a fight with Jordanian tanks and aircraft. Although after a few months relations between the PLO and Iraq returned to a show of courtesy, bad blood continued to underscore their dialogue.[22]

The fighting created a special problem for the almost 500 passengers of the hijacked planes, since they became hostages trapped in a war zone. Keeping them away from battle was a complicated operation involving many fighters who had to be taken away from other duties to protect the passengers. They transported the hostages from the heat of the desert to the Whahdat Refugee Camp near Amman and the Intercontinental. Because of the lack of water the passengers had to dig a latrine in the garden of the plush hotel to accommodate themselves.[23]

The two spokespersons for the PFLP, poet Ghassan Kanafani and writer Bassam Abu Sharif, held a press conference justifying the hijackings and demanding that Israel release its Palestinian prisoners. The conference took place in their Amman office, a bare lightbulb hanging from the ceiling and pictures of Ché Guevara and Lenin on the walls. The hijackers also demanded the release of Sirhan Sirhan, and Ronald Reagan, then governor of California, signed a document paving the way for his release. The Nixon administration, however, stopped the deal.

The Red Cross began flying in 1000 meals a day to the hostages until King Hussein reestablished control in his country a week later and forced the Palestinians to release them.[24] Henceforth Palestinians would call that month Black September, and would give that name to the terrorist organization that would dazzle and appall the world with its international stunts against Jordanian, Israeli, and American targets.

The Black September war brought on the Palestinians' third disaster. Only Lebanon provided them refuge—a government too weak to stop them— and the PLO had evidently learned nothing from the Jordanian experience, for their own arrogance began creating the same problems for the organization in Lebanon. Moreover, President Nasser, who had changed into the PLO's protector and had been negotiating between the Jordanian government and the Palestinians, died just as he had concluded an agreement to end the Palestinian-Jordanian war, literally dropping dead minutes after hosting a conference of Arab leaders. The Palestinian movement's future remained uncertain, but the tide of nationalism had a firm hold, and though the PLO was going to suffer years of mismanagement and defeat, the movement was destined to intensify.

In a November 1970 meeting the PFLP Central Committee renounced what they called outside operations. Habash made a public announcement, vowing to attack only Israeli targets in Israel and to defend their refugee camps and villages against Israeli attacks. The PFLP stuck to this decision, conducting no more military actions outside Israel, the occupied territories, and later Lebanon. They and the other Palestinian groups continued raiding Israel, attacking both military targets and civilians. In the PNC meeting in Cairo March 1971, poet Kamal Nasser led a group of Palestinians who denounced hijackings.[25]

Wadi Haddad was not convinced, and he found himself having to leave the PFLP with a small band of radicals in 1972 after hijacking a Lufthansa jet from New Delhi to Beirut, forcing it to land in Aden. Joseph Kennedy (son of Robert) was on board, and Lufthansa paid $5 million for the release, the money being divided with South Yemen for their services. Leila Khaled made a fundraising trip to Saudi Arabia and Kuwait, who were happy to donate to the cause and keep in Haddad's good graces. At first the group's finances were open, and they refused money from such governments, remaining righteously broke, but the airline extortion and Gulf donations changed them and bent their Marxist principles. After 1970 the PFLP, operating in Lebanon and Syria, survived on the memory of the good old days as fighters in Jordan. They lived in a dream world, calling each other comrade and thinking they were working to regain their homeland.

Haddad kept his small network in Europe and established contact with German and French radicals. Using them in conjunction with the notorious Carlos, he was responsible for other spectaculars, including the December 21, 1975, attack on the OPEC meeting in Vienna, which ended up netting Carlos and Haddad $20 million.[26] His group was eventually penetrated, and two of his hijackings, which took planes to Entebbe and Mogadishu, were successfully stormed by Israeli and British commandos. After his death April 1, 1978, his organization faded away.

In 1973 airports began mandatory security procedures, thwarting most future piracy. The biggest year for hijackings was 1969, with 40 attempts. By the end of 1972, there had been 160 hijackings or attempted hijackings, the majority conducted by Cubans; 13 (my calculation) were conducted by Palestinians. That year the United States Federal Aviation Administration produced a "behavior profile" of potential hijackers, but they never made it public. Such profiles tend to be either racist or inaccurate. Thereafter, hijackings and attacks on airports became more difficult, requiring well-funded, well-organized groups. After being subject to terrorist incidents, England, France, Italy and Greece opened secret dialogues with the PLO, including small arms donations under the guise of student grants and medical aid, to keep the dirty war away from their shores and keep the oil pipeline open, since the Palestinians seemed to exercise influence in this area.[27] The PLO, suffering and benefiting from PFLP's terrorism, began opening offices in European capitals.

As for women revolutionaries, they too faded away after the initial thrill. Women had fought alongside the Prophet Mohammed,[28] and groups such as the PFLP formed women's brigades—even the misogynist Abu Nidal tried to put one together—who led a few commando raids but mostly posed for dramatic pictures in fatigues, training with rifles. They did not last; a few women, however, held important positions in the Palestinian organizations, and women played a central role in the Intifada.

From Jordan the *fedayeen* carried out hundreds of raids against Israel from their bases. There was an attack almost every day, sometimes two or three, and they were taking their toll on Israeli citizens. In 1968 Israel claimed to have intercepted 2650 *fedayeen*, while the *fedayeen* claimed to have caused over 1000 incidents.[29] In 1969 the *fedayeen* attacked Israel 500 times, but just as their cross-border terrorism was becoming effective and troublesome, Haddad precipitated a meaningless war and subsequently lost all guerrilla bases. In 1972 the Palestinians launched six raids. Before the 1970 war the PLO had visited the Chinese embassy in Damascus and arranged for a substantial donation of small weapons, which were shipped to the Iraqi port of Basra so they could be trucked to the guerrillas, who had a gun for every other fighter. The ship arrived on September 16, well after the hijackings, and weapons were stored in the PLO warehouse near Baghdad, Abu Nidal overseeing their consignment.

Most people believe that PFLP outside operations hurt more than helped their campaign. Those who participated in these terrorist activities justify them as necessary for keeping the question of Palestine alive. Leila Khaled said:

> The actions in Europe were few. The hijackings were used as a kind of struggle to put the question—who are the Palestinians?—before the world. Before we were dealt with as refugees. We yelled and screamed, but the whole world answered with more tents and did nothing.

Other members claim that if it had not been for their operations, which they considered part of the armed struggle, the Palestinian cause would have died. Historian Noah Lucas agrees with this squeaky-wheel hypothesis, adding that while the PLO terror campaign "earned it little sympathy in the world, it nevertheless succeeded in establishing the image of its cause as the quest of a victimized people for national self-determination, rather than a neglected refugee problem as it had hitherto been widely regarded."[30]

Terrorism did, however, give Palestinians the dark, fearsome image from which they have never been able to escape. Even though Palestinians virtually stopped plane hijackings by 1974, they are still known as hijackers. Golda Meir adds:

> It is not by killing and maiming children, hijacking aircraft or murdering diplomats that real movement of national liberation accomplish their aims. They must also have content, goals that will serve them long after the immediate crisis has passed.[31]

Chapter 6

Black September
vs. Mossad

> When discussing terrorism with the Israelis, Nixon startled his
> hosts by leaping from his seat and declaring that there was only
> one way to deal with terrorists. Then Chicago-gangland-style, he
> fired an imaginary submachine gun at the assembled cabinet
> members. Strange behavior, strange president.
>
> William B. Quandt[1]

When the PFLP outside operations stopped, creating a terrorism media
vacuum, the Black September commando group rushed in to fill the front
pages. Black September was not technically part of the PLO, and it is difficult
to describe the exact relation the PLO leadership had with these terrorist
operations because Black September was not a real organization but a name
used by different armed groups. The studies that describe the Black September command structure are not accurate since it changed from operation to
operation. A mixture of people loyal to Arafat, Habash, and Hawathmeh created cells of three to eight men with an outside supervisor, one cell not knowing another. PLO leaders, who before 1974 lacked central control over the various groups, set up this unit, and they helped on some operations, but they
knew nothing about others.

Black September carried out very few actions, but those they staged were
bold and bloody. Yousef Najjar and Fakhri al-Amari, who had been heads of
Fatah intelligence, were thought to have been the initial heads of Black September since they helped plan the first action. Although growing apprehensive of foreign operations, the PLO did not condemn them, thereby impli-
cating themselves. They could not come out against the Septemberists lest they
be confronted with the question, "What are you doing to liberate Palestine?"
for which they might have no answer.

The first order of business was revenge for the Black September war, and they chose to assassinate Wasfi al-Tel, the conservative Jordanian premier and defense minister whom they held responsible. PLO political chief Khaled al-Hassan, who at the time of the killing was scheduled to have a meeting at the Cairo Sheraton with Tel in order to solidify an agreement between Jordan and the PLO, claims that it was actually an internal struggle that led to Tel's assassination. According to Hassan, the Palestinian leadership wanted to reconcile with Jordan, and although a hard man, Tel was under pressure by other Arab governments to arrive at an accommodation with the PLO.

At least two groups of assassins were waiting for the premier (Abu Iyad claims that four groups cooperated on the killing)—one group inside the Sheraton and the other on the steps outside. Egyptian security may have known about the plan, but they gave Tel no protection. A friend steered Hassan away from the hotel, and when Wasfi arrived a short time later, the gunmen opened fire as soon as he got out of his car. Mundir Khalifa, the killer, walked over and put his finger into Wasfi's blood and put it to his lips, saying he got his revenge. (This phrase was interpreted to mean that Khalifa drank Tel's blood, which turned into press stories of him drinking like a vampire.) Although other agencies may have been involved in this killing, it was clearly organized by the PLO leadership, and Black September was inaugurated.

The action occurred just after the War of Attrition when Egypt and Israel were trading daily artillery fire across the Suez, and the popular mood in Egypt was strongly on the side of the Palestinian gunmen. A mob began demonstrating to free the four arrested Palestinians, and Egyptian president Anwar Sadat gave in, granting the killers bail; soon after they were quietly helped to leave the country. Most Palestinians supported the killing, giving the new terror campaign a morale boost, and dozens of young men wanted to be heroes like Tel's killers. This was followed by an unsuccessful attempt to kill Jordan's ambassador to London and a failed hijacking of a Jordanian jet. After this, Palestinian leaders such as Kamal Nasser thought it was idiocy to go after Jordan when their enemy was Israel, and Black September changed track.

In May 1972 two men and two women took control of a Sabena jet from Vienna and forced it to Tel Aviv, where it was scheduled to go, right into the lion's den. The PLO leadership arranged this hijacking but deny enlisting Haddad's expertise. The hijackers demanded the release of prisoners. The Israeli authorities shot out the plane's tires and began to negotiate, but a group of commandos disguised as mechanics with a Red Cross flag successfully stormed the plane, killing the two male terrorists and one passenger and capturing the two women, Theresa Halsa and Rima Tannous. The hijackers had time to throw their grenades, but they did not. This was the first of a few successes of Israeli counter-terrorism.[2]

Black September's biggest operation was against the 1972 Munich Olympics, planned by the flamboyant Ali Hassan Salameh (Abu Hassan) and executed by specially selected gunmen.[3] A few Palestinians had worked on the construction of the Olympic Village and thus were able to describe its layout to Abu Hassan.

The eight masked gunmen raided the Israeli Pavilion before dawn, jumping the fence with their grenades and Klashnikovs, killing weightlifter Moshe Weinberg and wounding Joseph Romano, the wrestling trainer, who bled to death. Then they burst into two of the rooms where some of the Israeli athletes were sleeping and took them hostage, demanding the release of 200 prisoners in Israeli jails. During negotiations with German authorities the gunmen allowed deadlines to pass. Chancellor Willy Brandt telephoned Prime Minister Meir and tried to persuade her to make a gesture, perhaps releasing a dozen secondary prisoners, but Meir absolutely refused, instead sending advisors.[4] Since there was no sign of the gunmen giving up without at least a partial satisfaction of their demands, bloodshed seemed inevitable.

German police could not penetrate the confined pavilion, so Chancellor Brandt told the terrorists that Israel was going to release the prisoners and transport them to Egypt, and Germany would provide a plane and crew for the gunmen to leave to an Arab country. The Palestinians reluctantly agreed to leave the compound and go to a military airport by helicopter, keeping their captives hooded, tied, and guarded.

When they arrived, two gunmen stepped out to inspect the waiting plane, returning when they discovered it had no crew. Marksmen surrounding the airfield opened fire and shot one of the Palestinians. A gunman returned the fire and killed a marksman. There was a small firefight in which the German helicopter crew tried to escape and were shot, possibly by their own marksmen. Silence descended, eventually broken by an oral demand in Arabic from the Israeli advisors, who seemed to have a deciding voice in the operation,[5] for the Palestinians to give themselves up. Again silence. An hour later the police began a ground attack using a half-dozen armored vehicles. A gunman lobbed a grenade into a helicopter and shot it while another gunman shot the hostages in the second helicopter. Three of the Palestinians survived and were imprisoned, but on October 29 three Palestinians, with the blessing of the PLO, hijacked a Lufthansa jet and demanded the release of the three. There was no reason for more blood, Brandt said, and the Germans flew their prisoners to Libya.

After the extent of the tragedy became known, the operation drew wide condemnation from nearly every part of the world.[6] To most Palestinians, however, the eight gunmen were heroes because when the time came, they were ready to carry out their threat of blowing themselves up with their hostages. Palestinians generally blamed the massacre on Israel's refusal to negotiate and German trickery. When the gunmen arrived in Libya they were given a hero's welcome.[7] King Hussein was the Arab world's sole condemning voice.

This glorification generated endless recruits for Black September, but for the world the grim picture of black-hooded terrorists standing outside the

Olympic pavilion became an image indelibly engraved on history. The 1972 Olympics were to be Germany's apology for the 1936 Berlin Games, but now they are remembered as the terrorist Olympics. Germany clamped down on Palestinians living in their country, deporting students, shutting offices, and banning organizations. When Israel bombed Lebanon in revenge raids two days later and killed between 300 and 500 people,[8] the world and the United Nations hardly made a censoring comment.[9] John Cooley notes that Munich polarized the extremism in both Arab and Israeli camps; "attention was diverted from the real issues of the Middle East conflict and focused on the new and immediate problems raised by the emergence of international political terrorism."[10]

According to Abdallah Frangi, the PLO wrote to the Olympic Committee in early 1972 requesting that Palestinian athletes be allowed to participate in the games. They received no response. They sent another letter. Again no answer. Abu Hassan then decided to stage the attack because the Olympic Committee ignored what the PLO felt was a legitimate request.[11] Frangi's research seems accurate; the PLO were scurrying in every direction for legitimacy, and perhaps the Munich bloodbath could have been avoided if the Olympic Committee had responded, perhaps saying that only recognized countries can participate or citing another official reason for refusal. Ignoring the PLO's request was the worst response.

The Japanese Red Army accelerated the cycle of Middle East violence when they attacked the Tel Aviv airport in June 1972. The raid was organized by the PFLP leadership and justified as a commando attack against Israel, not an outside operation. A PFLP official had gone to Japan and established contact with the Japanese Red Army in early 1971, and three of their members had volunteered for a suicide attack as part of their struggle against worldwide imperialism. The PFLP brought them to their base near Baalbek, Lebanon, and gave them a seven-week training course, then sent them to Rome.

A fourth Japanese man who worked for the PFLP brought them weapons in Rome, and they checked in on an Air France flight to Tel Aviv. Checked baggage was not examined at that time, and they walked through the metal detectors clean. Who would suspect two Japanese men and a woman returning to Japan via Israel? When they arrived they went to the baggage claim, collected their suitcases off the carousel, unzipped them, and immediately began firing indiscriminately while throwing shrapnel grenades. By the time the Israeli guards responded and killed two of the Japanese and wounded the third, the terrorists had killed 27 people, including 16 Catholic pilgrims from Puerto Rico and Aharon Katzir, a physicist in charge of Israel's nuclear weapons program.[12] The surviving gunman, Oko Komoto, was released in the May 1985 prisoner exchange and given a hero's welcome in Libya.[13]

A Black September atrocity matching Munich came on March 1, 1973, from a group of gunmen led by Rizig Abu Ghassan, and it also ended in tragedy. They were trying to free Abu Daoud, who had been arrested February 6 and badly tortured by the Jordanians after he was caught organizing a PLO-endorsed movement to topple King Hussein. The government tried to use him as a propaganda weapon to weaken their radical Palestinian opposition. They published a pamphlet about him and put him on TV, and most people assumed that he had made a confession. The men who fought under Abu Daoud hastily arranged an action that they thought would free their leader. "You know when you eat and sleep with your men," Abu Daoud has been quoted as saying, "they begin to treat you like a father. When they heard about me and 17 others in prison ready for execution they went mad."

They chose the Saudi Arabian embassy in Khartoum, thinking that the Saudis would be able to pressure the Jordanian monarch into freeing Abu Daoud. The embassy was hosting a party for the outgoing American chargé d'affaires, George Curtis Moore; much of Sudan's diplomatic community was present. The gunmen crashed the party, firing in the air, and took hostage everyone unable to run out the back door.

This action was bad news for the PLO leaders in Beirut, who were trying to get money out of the Saudis while building diplomatic bridges to the West. Arafat sent two messages via the Sudanese embassy in Beirut for the gunmen to release all their captives unharmed. The first message went through; the second did not. One of the gunmen, hooded and sinister, walked onto the balcony and raised his arms in defiant victory.

As well as demanding Abu Daoud's release, they passed on a list of 60 other Palestinians in Jordanian prisons, demanded the release of all women in Israeli prisons, and threw in the release of Sirhan. Jordan remained silent.[14] The king happened to be honeymooning in the United States with his new wife. Israel said it would not negotiate. American president Richard Nixon followed suit, making a badly timed statement that the United States would not negotiate just after the gunmen were promised that a negotiator was en route.[15] The White House had dispatched Undersecretary of State William Macomber but said he would observe, not negotiate. Nixon was dining with Golda Meir and Israel's United States ambassador, Yitzhak Rabin, on the night he made the announcement.[16]

The Palestinian gunmen had been well tempered and obliging to all except the two Americans. They released all women when a wife of an Arab diplomat told them it was improper for them to hold women, especially when they were demanding the release of women in Israel. The kidnappers suggested that they be allowed to fly to the United States with their captives, make a public statement, then surrender, but that was immediately turned down by the United States and Sudan.

The Khartoum action followed the December 28, 1972, Black September takeover of the Israeli embassy in Bangkok in which they demanded the release of 36 prisoners in Israeli jails. The gunmen timed their attack badly, for King Bhumipoi's only son was that day to be invested as crown prince. With the help of the Egyptian ambassador, the four terrorists gave themselves up in return for safe conduct to Cairo.[17] The Khartoum team felt that repeating such a gesture would portend poorly for the terrorist business,[18] but the Sudanese negotiators had nothing to work with, and when the Palestinians realized this, they killed Moore as well as American ambassador Cleo Noel and the Belgium chargé Guy Eid, wrongly believing he was Jewish. This senseless, racist killing probably inflicted more political harm on the Palestinian cause than any other action. Innocent diplomats who had nothing to do with the Middle East conflict were murdered in cold blood. It showed how the Palestinian mentality had degenerated, killing others to release a friend. Western diplomats distanced themselves from the Palestinians. The subsequently restrained growth of the PLO was due as much to the Palestinians as Israeli bullets.

As well as showing callous brutality, the Khartoum killings were extremely poorly timed. A week before, Israeli F-4 Phantoms had shot down a Libyan Boeing 727 traveling between Tripoli and Cairo, killing 107 passengers, including former Libyan foreign minister Salah Buassir and one American. Israel, angry at Libya's belligerence, especially the sanctuary it gave to the Munich terrorists, at first refused to apologize, blaming the crew for flying slightly off course into the occupied Sinai and asserting that the plane may have been on a suicide mission to Tel Aviv. The French pilot and navigator (who usually flew for Air France) thought they were being followed by Egyptian fighters until one of the fighters began firing at them.[19]

The Israelis crated the charred bodies and shipped them to Egypt. Hours before downing the jet, Israeli bombers had pounded Palestinian refugee camps in Lebanon and mounted a sea assault on the Nahr al-Bared refugee camp in northern Lebanon, killing a total of 106 people.[20] The Israeli government launched the attack to blacken a visit by Sadat's emissary Hafez Ismail to Washington, the first such visit since the 1967 war. Ismail was on his way to Washington to ease relations and present Sadat's peace proposal.[21]

When the Palestinians took over the Saudi embassy in Khartoum they took the heat off Israel and gave a rationale for its aggressive militarism. *Newsweek* summed it up: "As tragic as it was, the Sinai disaster was clearly not in the same league with the calculated terror and callously executed atrocity in Khartoum."[22] United States commentator Robert Pierpoint added:

> Americans have become used to thinking of Israelis as the good guys and Arabs as the bad guys.... The fact is that both sides have committed unforgivable acts of terror, both sides have killed innocents, both sides have legitimate grievances and illegitimate methods of expressing them.[23]

Palestinian leaders began seeing these terrorist actions as a grave mistake that hurt their cause. After the Khartoum disaster those involved in Black September were given other functions, thereby eliminating future organized terrorist activities outside Israel. However, whenever a terrorist action occurred, someone invariably called the press and claimed responsibility on behalf of Black September. Abu Nidal often took credit for operations in the name of Black September.

At about the same time, Black September was held responsible for attacks in the United States. In the first, March 7, 1973, two cars with unexploded bombs were alleged to have been found parked outside Israeli banks in New York. A search of the car revealed stationery containing Black September letterhead.[24] In the second, April 16, 1973, shots were fired into the home of the New Zealand chargé in Washington. Neatly spray-painted on the building were the words "Black September." Apparently, the attackers were aiming for the Jordanian ambassador who had occupied that building two years previously, probably getting the address from an old telephone book.[25] That summer an Israeli diplomat in Washington who bought military hardware was killed by an unknown assassin as he was coming home from a party late one night, and the Voice of Palestine radio in Cairo claimed responsibility, saying it was revenge for a killing in Paris three days before.[26] But no Palestinian organization had the capacity or the will to operate in the United States, and Black September did not print letterhead. They did, however, launch a letter-bomb campaign from Amsterdam. One of the bombs killed Ami Shachori in the Israeli embassy in London, but all other devices were detected and defused. As a terrorist organization, Black September was well organized and probably not penetrated. It is difficult today to know who was responsible for what. Gunmen did not know one another. During operations they wore masks to remain anonymous, as some security units do. Such amorphous organizations tend to be out of control.

There were a few PLO-connected acts of international terrorism after 1973, and we will examine the significant ones; however, the PLO bailed out of the international terrorism business in 1973, vowing to carry out military operations—what they called the armed struggle—exclusively against Israel. Thus the period of systematic international terrorism by PLO factions stretches about five years, 1968 to 1973. They were headline-capturing, fear-inducing actions designed to prove to the world and fellow Arabs that the Palestinians would not surrender their cause. Militarily, they were of little consequence; they did not help the Palestinians recoup any of their homeland. Many criticized terrorist operations in the October 1972 PNC, and while not wanting to abandon the military fight against Israel, the PLO moved into the arena of politics and diplomacy, a move that was accelerated by the October 1973 war when PLO leaders discovered that even a successful military campaign against Israel could not win them back Palestine.

The undercover war carried out by Israel during the same period had equally negative consequences. In 1972 the Israelis formed teams of assassins to kill influential Palestinians. Israel had other assassination teams to kill Arab nuclear scientists[27] and Palestinians in Israel and the occupied territories that showed leadership abilities. In the early 1960s assassination units and letter bombs were dispatched to kill Egyptian and West German scientists working on Egypt's rocket program.[28] David Kimche, an Israeli leader who would later be involved in the Iran-Contra affair, also conducted letter-bomb campaigns on Israel's behalf, but during the early 1970s covert war fought in Europe and Lebanon, the Mossad aimed at PLO leaders who they claimed were involved in terrorism.

It is commonly understood that Golda Meir established the assassination squads of the 1972-73 period as revenge for the Munich Olympics, targeting those who masterminded the operation. Whenever a Palestinian was killed, Israel leaked information about his involvement with Munich. Several studies have discussed these covert Mossad units, describing the efficiency of the assassinations.[29] One Mossad squad directed by Major General Aharon Yaviv was allegedly named the Wrath of God, indicating a just cause against the guilty.[30] The Palestinians built such a foul reputation that when someone was killed the press were ready to believe that he was a terrorist, killed either by a rival Palestinian faction or by a bomb he was about to plant that exploded prematurely. If we delve further we find that the Mossad worked from bad intelligence and that their assassinations were crude affairs.

These assassinations were part of the covert Israeli-Palestinian war; the Palestinians who died were usually not involved in terrorism. Each assassination took months of preparation: renting safe houses, transporting weapons, tracking the victim, working out assassination and escape plans, arranging false documents and car rentals, bringing in the assassins. It was a multimillion dollar operation which was planned and begun before the Munich Olympics. Among those receiving letter bombs during this period was Dr. Anis Sayegh, a historian and director of the Palestine Research Center in Beirut, who was permanently injured by a mail bomb. Two other Palestinians in Beirut detected letter bombs before they exploded, and a doctor with the Red Crescent discovered a bomb in his car.[31] All were easy, unguarded targets.

However, the first victims were Ghassan Kanafani and his 17-year-old niece, Lamees. Kanafani was a leading leftist poet, writer, sculptor, and spokesperson for the PFLP during the Black September war. Kanafani's poetry kept alive the Palestinian identity, and he was one of the first advocates of coexistence in a democratic Palestine, giving lectures in Europe, being interviewed by Israeli journalists, and having contact with many European Jews active in the antiwar movement in Denmark and Sweden (Kanafani had a Swedish wife). He and his deputy, Bassam Abu Sharif (who would be wounded by a mail bomb two weeks after Kanafani's death), had demanded that Israel release prisoners during the 1970 hijacks. However, their views had mellowed, and both had begun speaking against indiscriminate violence.

One day Kanafani and his niece got into his car outside his Beirut apartment, turned on the ignition, and both were burned alive. It was suspected that Kanafani was killed in retaliation for the Japanese Red Army airport massacre just past, but the assassination may have been planned long before. Abu Sharif takes up the story:

> Ghassan was killed on the morning of July 8th. I was hit on the 25th. On the 17th of July, my bell rang in the early morning, and I went to the door and looked through the glass and saw nobody, but there was an envelope under my door. I opened it. It contained a black-and-white negative which I took to a photographer to enlarge. There was Ghassan's car at the very moment of the explosion. It was clear that the photographer knew and was waiting for the car to be destroyed.
>
> The Lebanese had formed a committee to investigate Ghassan's assassination. I went and gave them the photo as a piece of evidence because it would be easy to check from where the picture was shot and go and check the apartment, find who was there, etc. That could give a clue. They took it. Since that day the file was closed on an unknown criminal. Abu Ahmed Yunis [a member of the PFLP leadership] was on the committee.
>
> Two days later I was back in my apartment, Commodore Apartments on the first floor next to the Commodore Hotel [later used as a base for journalists]. Parking was behind the building. It was hot, and I was in my underwear, my hands folded on the balcony, looking for a breeze. I saw two young men jumping the fence and approaching my Datsun. One got under the car. I said, "Hey, what do you want? What are you doing?" They didn't move at first, but then looked up. I yelled, "What are you doing?" They looked like Arabs. One of them had a bag. They ran and jumped the fence. In my underwear I started running behind them, yelling "Stop them, catch them!" But they disappeared.

A few days later a large letter arrived for Abu Sharif. He would live the rest of his life blaming himself for carelessly opening it. The blast disfigured his body. Later his life was again endangered, as he recounts:

> Another member of the PFLP leadership was executed around 1980 for killing one of the members of the Central Committee, Abd al-Wahab al-Kayeb. Now the guy who killed him confessed that he was ordered to do it by Abu Ahmed Yunis.... He confessed that Abu Ahmed Yunis had enlisted people to kill not only Kayeb, but me. The sniper had actually started to shoot me, then stopped, saying, "I saw his face through my telescope, and I saw how the Israelis had damaged his face, and my finger couldn't pull the trigger."

Israel ordered the bombing of Kanafani, Abu Sharif, and Sayegh. Of that there is no doubt; Israeli spokesmen virtually admitted it. But Abu Sharif claims that Israel collaborated with Arabs in carrying out the executions;

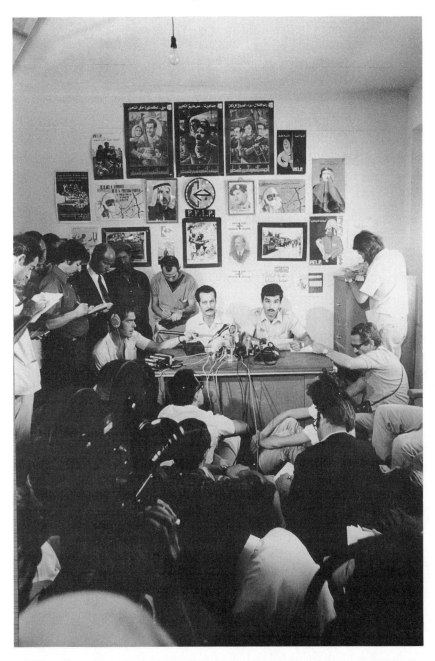

Ghassan Kanafani and Bassam Abu Sharif at a news conference after the September 1970 hijackings demanding the release of Israeli prisoners. Two years later Kanafani was killed by a car bomb and Abu Sharif was wounded by a letter bomb.

Bassam Abu Sharif today.

furthermore, Abu Sharif was implying that a PFLP leader, Abu Ahmed Yunis, had Israeli involvement. This would mean that Israel had infiltrated the leadership of one of the strongest Palestinian organizations. To members of the PFLP Yunis was a stern patriot, one of the most ardent Palestinians, who would not compromise with the Zionists. He tried to radicalize the PFLP during its power struggle when Habash's 1980 stroke left the organization temporarily leaderless. Abu Sharif's accusation is credible. The PFLP executed Yunis in 1981 for embezzlement and for ordering the murder of Kayeb, but they mentioned nothing about collaboration, and his case was not revealed to party members.[32]

Five weeks after Munich an Israeli assassination squad in Rome killed Wail Zwaiter, another noted Palestinian poet who translated *The Thousand and One Nights* into Italian and edited the PLO's Italian newsletter. Zwaiter had lived in Rome nine years, during which he was perpetually broke, working as a clerk here and there while writing and translating. A highly cultured leftist, he expressed the Palestinian position eloquently in Arabic, French, German, Italian, and English. The Israeli version—that Zwaiter's work was all a front and he was actually one of the most dangerous terrorists, responsible for Munich—does not hold up. He was "energetically" opposed to terrorism,[33] consistently wrote against violence, and sought Arab-Jewish friendship. A month before his death he led an Italian peace delegation to Amman.[34] Israeli agents had trailed him for weeks, probably singling him out to be killed before the Munich massacre.

He was coming home late at night, carrying a bag of groceries and a translation of his book under his arm. Two Israeli assassins made themselves obvious by hanging around the entrance of his modest apartment building for most of the evening. Zwaiter went to the downstairs bar to make a telephone call (the telephone company had cut off his service after he was unable to pay his bill). Everyone in the bar noticed a man and woman having a loud argument in what turned out to be the getaway car parked across the street from the bar. When Zwaiter walked into his building, the assassins filled him with silent bullets and ran into the waiting car. The people in the bar watched the car peel rubber and swerve away, almost crashing into a minibus as it approached the first intersection. Only the inefficiency of the local police prevented them from getting caught. An Italian court held an Israeli-controlled squad responsible for the killing of Zwaiter, but no one was captured.[35]

That afternoon Prime Minister Meir told her parliament that Israel would use all methods to defend itself from Arab terrorism abroad.[36] She was speaking about the bomb that had blown up an Arab bookstore in Paris ten days before, in effect saying that the bookstore, which also served as a library and meeting place, was blown up by Israel for self-defense. An organization calling itself the Movement for the Defense of Massada took responsibility for the bomb.[37] Police thought it was a young group ideologically associated with the Jewish Defense League, almost certainly receiving help from the Mossad for the action.[38]

Two months later another assassination squad killed Dr. Mahmoud Hamshari, the PLO representative in Paris, and again, the Israelis leaked the story that he was the brains behind Munich.[39] Hamshari, the most lucid and respected Palestinian representative in Europe, was an intellectual who opposed violence, a philosopher with a strong personality who became friends with journalists and government leaders. He held a Ph.D. in economics, was a political conservative, and understood the Western mentality—he married a sophisticated French woman, and with their young daughter they lived like a typical French family—and he persuasively communicated the Palestinian side of the conflict. Hamshari was also unguarded.

Mossad agents disguised as telephone repairmen planted a small bomb either in the telephone or the stand underneath it. They could have disrupted the telephone service, forcing Hamshari to call for repair, but they broke into his flat and planted the bomb. Another Israeli claiming to be an Italian journalist had previously called Hamshari and requested an interview, which he conducted in a cafe, though there seemed to be no need for this subterfuge. After the repairmen left, the assassins telephoned. He answered, and they pushed the button, sending bomb fragments into his body. He survived until the next morning and was coherent enough to recount the story to police.

There is a report that the French police later arrested two armed Israelis, Yaacov Rak and Michael Marhoub, in Lyon with false passports; one of these

Dr. Mahmood Hamshari, killed in Paris in 1972 by a Mossad hit team.

men was outside Hamshari's apartment at the time of the bombing.[40] The French released them. Another reliable report claims that the Mossad assigned a Palestinian collaborator recruited in Paris to befriend Hamshari. The collaborator had left Palestine to work in Algeria but met many hardships; he could never get himself off the ground. He then traveled to Paris and was picked out by Mossad agents, who have their eyes open for Palestinians with problems. The Mossad gave him money and a comfortable life. In return he was told that they wanted little from him, just to find out about Hamshari's habits. The PLO found out about him, and he supposedly confessed, although he had nothing to do with the killing.

In January 1973 the Mossad killed a Palestinian representative, Hussein Abd al-Chir by planting a massive remote-controlled bomb under his economy hotel room bed in Cyprus. Abd al-Chir had been a language professor before turning to politics and becoming a political advisor to the PLO. In 1970-71 he taught at an Armenian school in Cyprus.[41] He was instrumental in persuading the PLO to stop outside operations and work diplomatically, and he was one of the PLO's experts on the Soviet Union who were constantly advising the PLO to turn away from armed struggle. He was never guarded. News reports claimed that he was a terrorist handling bombs at the time of the explosion.[42]

On the twenty-fifth anniversary of Deir Yassin, Israeli commandos landed in Beirut. We touched on this incident earlier. Lieutenant-Colonel Ehud Barak led the raid, which included Major Jonathan Netanyahu, Benjamin's brother, later killed at Entebbe. Mossad chief Avraham Avnery, whom the Palestinians would kill a dozen years later, helped plan it. They shot dozens of people during the attack, but their aim was the PLO's intellectual leadership, killing three members of the Central and Executive committees.[43]

The Israelis collaborated with paid Lebanese and Palestinian agents, who helped an advance party rent cars and secure a harbor where the commandos could land. Informers gave them locations and habits of PLO leaders. A large force of gunmen took part in the operation, landing at midnight at Khalde,

Kamal Nasser, left, Kamal Adwan, center, and Yousef Najjar, right, PLO leaders killed in Beirut during a 1973 Israeli raid.

south of Beirut. After a short gun battle with Lebanese police, they attacked the DFLP headquarters but found the building empty—their first intelligence failure. Then the Israelis unsuccessfully tried to charge Arafat's well-guarded apartment, suffering casualties and withdrawing.

They then drove to a small street near Rue Verdun, pulling up in front of an apartment building and killing a solitary guard. The commandos stormed the apartment where they thought Abu Iyad was staying and filled his bed with 200 bullets, but he was elsewhere that night. The Israeli team finally succeeded when they broke into Yousef al-Najjar's flat, killing both him and his wife. Najjar, the main target in the building, was a founding member of Fatah and had become the PLO's political advisor, an expert on government relations and negotiations between factions.[44] After he organized the assassination of Wasfi al-Tel, he had little to do with military operations, becoming the PLO's diplomat.

The Israelis then went downstairs and threw a grenade at Kamal Adwan in front of his wife and two small children. Adwan, a bright intellectual who headed the information department and coordinated activities in the occupied territories, had spoken out against terrorist attacks on civilians. Adwan has been called a leader of Black September, but this does not seem to be true; he and Najjar were preaching negotiation and compromise.

Kamal Nasser was the final target, but on their way to his apartment, a neighbor opened her door, and the commandos filled her with lead. Nasser, a poet and spokesman, was nicknamed *Addanir,* "the voice of conscience," because he wrote against violence; in the March 1971 PNC meeting he had denounced hijacking.[45] Palestinian writer Abdullah Frangi tells us that the unmarried Nasser, who held a Ph.D., was at the time working on an elegy for Issa Nakha, a colleague who had died a few days before: "The Israeli bullets tore into Kamal's books and collected poems, as if they hoped to silence his words too."[46] After they shot him, Palestinians claim that the gunmen tore his mouth off with bullets, Mafia style, since he was the PLO spokesman, and laid his body as if hanging on a cross since he was a Christian. He and Najjar and Adwan had been in a meeting that was scheduled to last most of the night—Palestinian meetings usually start when most people go to sleep—but to the luck of the Israelis the three had ended early and gone home.

The Israelis killed 17 Palestinians and Lebanese during the operation and took away documents from the apartments of those killed and from an empty PLO office, carting them away by helicopter. It was later shown that Israel used Lebanese collaborators through the Deuxième Bureau. Lebanese contacts told Abu Iyad that Israel had been contacting Lebanese informers in order to launch an attack, but the Palestinians thought that Beirut was safe. After the raid the Lebanese government made a show of resigning, another step toward Lebanon's chaos.

Terrorist experts claim that the United States helped Israel carry out the raid by supplying information. However, CIA specialist Miles Copeland, commenting on the raid, says:

> One proof that the Israelis were not acting on CIA counterterrorist information—or, for that matter, on their own—is the fact that the Palestinians they killed were not terrorist leaders. It served Israeli purposes to say that they were, but the real purpose of the raid was not to kill terrorists leaders but to force the Lebanese Government to take action.[47]

The Mossad assassination squad struck again in Paris, killing AUB law professor Dr. Basil al-Kubaissi. Although he was Iraqi, he was a conservative leader of the PFLP. He lived modestly. The PFLP says he was on a mission as an unofficial ambassador for them to negotiate with someone in the French government.[48] He had no hand in violence. He usually walked around Paris to avoid paying for taxis. A bevy of Mossad agents shot him in the back one evening, then they ran down the street into waiting cars. He was unprotected.[49]

The Mossad then killed an Algerian named Mohammed Boudia. Boudia was associated with Haddad, so, unlike the others, he may have been part of the dirty war. His friends describe him as a simple man who worked with Fatah. Boudia, who had been active in the Algerian resistance and moved to Paris in 1965, was a cultured intellectual who became a successful theatrical artist. A writer of *Parisienne Orientale*, a theatrical journal, he also helped edit and distribute PLO propaganda.[50] The Israelis planted a car bomb under the driver's seat and blew up his Renault. Newspapers carried the story that a terrorist had been killed by his own bomb.[51]

Military historian Richard Deacon says the government leaked facts about assassinations "to boost morale back in Israel,"[52] but the Mossad would have liked to have kept its most noted assassination secret. It took place in a Norwegian resort town in the summer of 1973. The killers were aiming for Ali Hassan Salameh, who openly declared himself the mastermind of Munich.[53] Carloads of grim Mossad agents converged on the small Norwegian town wearing brown slacks and checkered, 30 percent polyester short-sleeve fitted shirts, different colors. Previous teams of Israeli agents had reported that Salameh was in Lillehammer, working under the guise of a waiter in a health club.

The group was hanging around hotels and cafes, making itself so conspicuous that even the town's handful of police, who normally handle insect bites and double-parking, got suspicious and wrote down the license number of one of the group's rented car. After following their victim for two days, the Israelis decided to attack one night as he and his very pregnant Norwegian wife were walking home from a film. Two men got out of a car and ran up to the man they thought was their target—who was not Salameh, but an Algerian named Kamal Benamane. The assassins pumped him with six bullets each. His wife collapsed in shock. The men ran into a waiting car, which took off at frightening speed to Oslo, probably killing a 16-year-old boy in a hit-and-run accident on the way.

It took the police a while to mobilize. Fewer than half a dozen people a year get shot in Norway, and this was Norway's first encounter with international terrorism. A policeman at a roadblock became suspicious of the nervous foreigners inside one car, noticing that they did not appear to be typical tourists, and also wrote down their names. The two who actually did the killing took the first plane out of Oslo and were never caught. The man they killed hardly even resembled Salameh.

Later, four of the group were arrested in the airport with large sums of money and fake passports. Two others took refuge in an apartment of an Israeli diplomat. Following leads, police barged into that apartment and, ignoring diplomatic immunity which the diplomat demanded, arrested them.

Two women were part of the team: Sylvia Rafael from South Africa, whom terrorist writers regard as one of the Mossad's slickest agents—we will meet her again—and Marianne Gladnikoff, a large woman of joint Swedish-Israeli citizenship, who had no similar experience. When they arrested the group they also found keys to safe houses in Paris and notes that linked the group to the Paris killings. Rafael (alias Patricia Roxburg) was carrying the name of the Mossad man in Oslo, who happened to be the security officer at the Israeli embassy.

Dan Aerbel, one of those arrested, was a Danish businessman. As he was being questioned by the police he not only told them about the team that killed Benamane, but also bragged that he was part of the group that had stolen 200 tons of enriched uranium from a ship in 1968. The uranium had been bound for Genova on the *Sheersburg A* but had been whisked away to

Israel for its nuclear weapons factory at Dimona.[54] There was no reason on earth that Aerbel should have confessed this. The police certainly did not torture him, nor did they know anything about his previous exploits. Marianne and the others told the police about their activities in Norway, at first contradicting each other and themselves, then finally declaring that they were obeying their Israeli bosses.

Israel denied any connection with the incident, even after the trial, during which the five agents told the court how the Mossad organized the operation. Israel never apologized and never paid compensation to Benamane's widow. The five were found guilty, but since none of the arrested agents did the killing, they received light sentences; all were free within two years. Rafael married her lawyer, then divorced him and returned to Israel to a hero's welcome.[55] The group's leader, Michael Harari, was not caught and went on to other clandestine adventures, including organizing security for Columbian drug kings and Panama's General Manuel Antonio Noriega while building for himself a small fortune from his arms business.[56]

The PLO began files on these people, correctly believing that the Mossad would use the same assassins for other operations, but the PLO security department showed its uselessness by not noticing when Rafael went and lived near the PLO a few years later.

The trial also revealed that Israeli diplomats took an active role in the Mossad's activities in Norway and Paris, probably including Avi Primor, intelligence chief in Paris, who became ambassador to Belgium when the Mossad moved its European headquarters to Belgium.[57] Weapons were brought into the country in diplomatic pouches. Furthermore, the revelations at the trial indicated the complexity of international political assassinations. A dozen people were involved in Norway, not counting information gatherers and backup personnel in Israel, demonstrating that it costs a fortune and takes a tremendous amount of work to undertake international terrorist activities. David Tinnin estimates that it cost Israel about $500,000 to kill each person,[58] not one of whom was guarded. Moreover, the people they killed lived economically, not in the style of terrorist leaders, who spend hundreds of dollars a day. *Time* magazine tells us that during the 1972-73 period the Mossad killed 13 terrorist leaders.[59] All were sharp, intelligent people, including poets and writers, who knew the West; most opposed violence.

Historically, political movements like the PLO do not die with the loss of their leaders, but they can be seriously hurt, as when the British deported Palestinian leaders before World War II. By killing intelligent PLO officials who knew and communicated with the West, Israel crippled the organization. The retardation of the PLO's progress toward international recognition was in part a direct result of the Mossad operations beginning in 1972. Those killed had lived in Europe or the United States for a number of years, received European or American education, often married European women, and sent their children to European schools. These people were most fluent, most able to interact with Europeans and present the case of Palestine, and furthermore, they could have positively influenced PLO decisions. Israel had the military might to deal with the combined military force of the Arab world; however, because it never faced the issue of the Palestinian refugees or of Palestinian statelessness, it had to resort to assassination of those who spoke well and propagated Palestinian culture through art, literature, and poetry.

The revelations in Norway also showed the low level of professionalism used by one of the best security services. European police discovered Israel's net of safe houses and its method of operation. In jargon, Mossad operated dirty, and perhaps Lillehammer was not their first mistake; luck and inefficient police kept them from getting caught before. Israeli intelligence kept flopping. A month after Lillehammer two Israeli fighter jets grabbed an Iraqi Airways flight as soon as it took off from Beirut and forced it to Israel. They claimed to have caught a planeload of terrorists, but got instead a group of Japanese tourists.[60]

Generally European governments forgave Israel, and the dirty war turned to using collaborators, penetrating organizations, and giving money and weapons to radical Arab groups in order to intensify the inter–Arab divisions. Months after Lillehammer the Abu Nidal announced its independence, and one of its main activities would be to kill intelligent, lucid Palestinians who opposed violence and understood the West, who spoke well to journalists and government leaders, were effective, and unguarded.

Meanwhile, guerrilla bands kept mounting raids on Israel, and two par-ticularly bloody Palestinian attacks against Israeli civilians in 1974 need to be mentioned. The first took place in April when three members of the Ahmed Jibril group raided Israel from Lebanon and took eighteen hostages—eight of them children—in an apartment block of Qiryat Shmona. The gunmen demanded the release of 100 Palestinian prisoners. Israel refused to negotiate and stormed the building. After a four-hour battle, moving from floor to floor, all the hostages, gunmen, and two commandos were killed. Israel launched reprisal raids against six Lebanese villages, and the Jewish Defense League exploded a bomb at the Lebanese consulate in Los Angeles.[61]

A month later, on the eve of Israel's Independence Day celebrations, three men belonging to Naif Hawathmeh's DFLP crossed the border and, the next morning, broke into an apartment in Ma'alot village, shooting three occupants. They seized 90 children from a nearby school for Israeli cadets in the Gadna community, demanding the release of 26 prisoners, one for each year since statehood, including two Jews convicted of working with the *fedayeen*. The operation was specifically targeted against children, for the DFLP reasoned that Israel could not fail to negotiate for their lives. But they were mistaken. General Mordechai Gur wanted to negotiate, but Dyan and Meir refused (although Meir said on radio that they would give into the demands since "we do not wage war on the backs of our children"). Soldiers stormed the building using bazookas and automatics, killing the three gunmen as well as 20 of the children. Almost all the other children were injured, many seriously.[62]

Edward Said notes that the Ma'alot attack was "preceded by weeks of sustained Israeli napalm bombing of Palestinian refugee camps in Southern Lebanon." Over 200 people were killed during these raids. As punishment for the Ma'alot attack, Patrick Seale observes, "whole settlements were flattened and between 300 and 400 people killed and wounded."[63] These facts should be an integral part of the terrorism discussion.

Chapter 7
The Rise of Abu Nidal

After 1974 almost all Palestinian acts of terrorism were carried out by the Abu Nidal group. Stories about Abu Nidal himself abound and contradict, and several pieces of his life still remain a mystery. Studies declaring that his father had 13 wives and was the richest person in Palestine are nonsense. Abu Nidal was born Sabri al-Banna in Jaffa in 1936. His father, Khalil, was a middle-class landowner from a normal family of merchants and farmers. Khalil owned an orchard in Jaffa (which became a suburb of Tel Aviv), where he grew what became known as Jaffa oranges. Sabri's mother was Khalil's second wife, much younger than Khalil, a woman of the Alawite sect from Syria's north coast, and he married her secretly against the wishes of his family. Some people say she was a dancer, which to the Arabs would have been equal to a whore. His mother became one of the field workers, shunned by Khalil's family, creating unhealthy psychological influences for Sabri. His distrust and hatred for women is a cornerstone of his existence.

It is said that Sabri's father was a close friend of Zionist nationalists, including Dr. Chaim Weizmann, Israel's first president and foremost leader of the Zionist movement, and Avraham Shapira, head of a Zionist militia.[1] This certainly is not true—Weizmann had almost no dealings with Arabs[2]—but some friends believe that the family actively collaborated with the Zionists, which may have influenced Sabri. Other friends doubt Sabri's Palestinian origin, saying that the family came from Egypt. At Khalil's time there were no borders.

Khalil died when Sabri was about eight, and his family fled to Gaza on the eve of the declaration of statehood, when the entire population of Jaffa cleared out overnight. The family then moved to the West Bank town of Nablus, where they had relations.

Sabri's mother had a hard time after the death of Khalil. She went with the family, Sabri and his ten half-brothers and sisters, settling in an uncle's home. The family must have been poor, but better off than those who received Red Cross tents. The brothers had to quit school and begin working; Sabri quit school even before he left Jaffa, indicating that the family had financial

Central Jaffa in 1936, when Abu Nidal was born.

problems and that he was thought of as illegitimate. He received a third-grade education. To this day it is difficult for him to write proper Arabic. This contradicts reports of him being a university graduate.[3]

We have to assume that nothing significant happened to him until after the death of his mother in the late 1950s, when he joined his older half-brother Zakeria in Wreath, Saudi Arabia, traveling via Amman. It is said that he was an activist in Nablus, but from what we will discover of his life, that seems unlikely. He had three brothers working in Saudi Arabia, but Zakeria helped him the most. Sabri began working as a laborer, specializing as an electrician, and became moderately successful. Industrious and hard-working, paying little attention to current world events, in 1960 Sabri established a small shop with the help of his brother. Standing 5'10", he had good health and a big build, wore a mustache like most Arab men, and had thinning hair that would all disappear by his mid-30s; he was neither handsome nor ugly.

At the age of 23 Sabri had a sudden desire to improve himself. His first step was to become literate. He met Abu Daoud (Mohammed Daoud Auda) who was working as a school teacher in Wreath. Abu Daoud, who had left teaching in Jerusalem to work in Saudi Arabia because the pay was better, introduced Sabri to another Palestinian teacher, who from 1960 to 1961 gave him private lessons in reading and writing. Sabri tried hard, but despite his good memory and his cleverness he did not have a brilliant mind and remained of below-average literacy. Nevertheless, he had the skill necessary for reading philosophy and politics, especially relating to the liberation of Palestine. He became active in the small groups of expatriate Palestinians who met in people's houses, holding discussions to the early hours of the morning. The Saudis did not tolerate political organizations (even though King Faisal was firmly anti–Israeli), so these meetings took place informally.

Sabri had three or four encounters with women, but it is unclear if these were sexual. When it came time for him to marry, his family and friends in Nablus helped him find a woman in the traditional Palestinian manner. Sabri's brothers in Saudi Arabia told him that his relatives had several women who they thought would be compatible. Sabri chose, and the woman's family in turn told her, leaving the final decisions to both Sabri and his mate, a good and docile woman named Hiyam from a decent, large family, al-Bittar, from his hometown, Jaffa. In 1962 Sabri came back to Nablus, met her, married in a happy wedding, then took his wife back to Saudi Arabia with him. There was nothing striking about her; she was a typical Muslim woman who enjoyed cooking and entertaining company. He settled down into married life. Years later, however, as Abu Nidal, Sabri would have his wife's brother killed, which effectively ended the marriage although his wife still lives in the same house with him.

At the end of 1964 the Palestinians in Saudi Arabia rallied around a small cause: the teachers from Palestine and Jordan were receiving a lower salary than those from Sudan and Egypt. They united and staged a modest protest in front of the Ministry of Education building. Although everyone was well mannered, the Saudis came down hard on this first political activity. They detained the organizers and asked Abu Daoud to leave the country.

By the mid–1960s Sabri held his own group meetings, with his own unnamed clique that would come together and discuss politics in either his house or the houses of others. In 1966 the al-Bannas had their first child, a little girl, whom they called Bidia. She would eventually marry one of her father's men.

Sabri became the focal point of his group of armchair Palestinian revolutionaries, even though he became increasingly flighty and easily influenced. His friends gave him the nickname *al-Ahmak*, "the crazy one," because he would irrationally switch positions. He also had unusual propensity for exaggeration, so it became difficult to know when he was telling the truth. His friends used to make light jokes about him. If someone said to him that he drank a glass of wine, *al-Ahmak* would tell others that he drank three bottles. They would rib him, and *al-Ahmak* would occasionally laugh at himself.

Al-Ahmak continued speaking politics while working as an electrician, saving and investing his earnings. He was influenced by the Baath ideology and made several friends in the local underground Baath party. But in early 1967, before the Arab-Israeli war, he suddenly changed and wanted to become a member of the new Fatah movement that people were talking about. Really he was not politicized, being more interested in gossip than philosophy. Even in the early days of his career he relentlessly collected personal information about people's weaknesses, fishing for compromising personal information, especially regarding people's sexuality. No doubt his desire for gossip partly stemmed from an unhealthy attitude towards sex, seeing it as something dirty. But he also thought that knowledge of intimate details gave him the power to exploit. This trait he retained: when he was based in Libya he was desperately trying to discover if Colonel Gadaffi had a mistress. He did not, but on various occasions he would provide the Libyan foreign minister with cases of Black Label whiskey, a fact he was no doubt able to use against the Libyan ruler at some propitious time.

During the 1967 war, the Palestinians in Saudi Arabia staged a demonstration against Israel. Prince Fahd, then interior minister, overreacted, rounding up several Palestinians, including Sabri, and detaining them for three or four days. No one is certain if anything significant happened to him during detention, but shortly afterward he either left the country on his own accord or was asked to leave the country, traveling back to Amman. There he met the representatives of Fatah, who were operating underground. Fatah had set up a small front company in Amman, a commercial office, and Sabri joined the others in trying to organize and expand the movement. Because of his proven business skills, the office was partly registered in Sabri's name, and he worked there along with six or seven people. From this office he was able to meet the essential people of the Palestinian movement. He seemed much more sane there—people stopped calling him *al-Ahmak*—but also more serious and dour.

The person in charge of the office was a man called Khadri, a member of the Central Committee, and Sabri became his assistant. Abu Musa, who would later lead a dissident Syrian-controlled militia, also worked in the office while

Sabri was there. Sabri tried to work under Abu Iyad, whose family was also from Jaffa, but the two men at first had little to do with each other.

After Karameh the guerrillas moved their bases away from the Israeli border, making it hard for Israel to hit them, and they operated semi-openly in Jordan—even King Hussein declared that he was a guerrilla. The Palestinians had developed substantial militias in the villages and refugee camps. Because of his problems with writing, Sabri was not an office worker; he was, however, a competent administrator who used to arrange food, clothing, and tents for the fighters. Sabri's responsibilities were similar to a military supply clerk who helped the many Fatah raids into Israel.

As early as 1968 there were signs of disagreement in the Palestinian movement between the conservatives and militants. Sabri belonged to the armed struggle camp, though he was never, could never have been, a fighter, since he was a physical coward who lacked confidence. From those early days, as soon as he proved his organizational ability, he began speaking disparagingly about Arafat, whom he had met a few times, as if his aim was to accelerate a schism. Fatah leaders told Sabri to fight the enemy, not his brothers. But the seeds of his war against Fatah were already planted.

When Alfred Lillenthal, an anti–Zionist Jew, visited Amman to participate in a demonstration, Abu Daoud took him to Sabri's office for coffee. It may have been Sabri's first open contact with a Jew. Sabri took a liking to Lillenthal, indicating that he had no personal hatred for Jews. However, in the 1980s his organization launched attacks on European Jews, and he spoke against Jews with a Nazilike fervor. If his anti–Semitism was genuine, it must have developed later in Sabri's life. To Sabri's delight, in 1969 his wife gave birth to a baby boy, whom they called Nidal, a common Arabic name which means "the struggle." From then on his friends called him Abu Nidal.

Throughout his life Abu Nidal's main interest remained the collecting of personal information; he was more interested in discovering little secrets about people than in discussing the political question of Palestine. Everyone who knew him mentions this. He worked like a petty security officer, unearthing tidbits of gossip that could later be used to threaten or blackmail. This quality raises suspicion about Abu Nidal's real motives from the beginning of his career in the Palestinian movement. While he was in Amman he organized a filing system to keep track of members. In it he kept secret reports and details of people's lives, with special attention on their sexual relations. This he would not show anyone; it was Abu Nidal's idea to create this system, a useful tool for internal security. When Abu Daoud took over the office from Abu Nidal— and Abu Daoud was his closest friend—Abu Nidal would not let him see his own file, and took all the files with him. Abu Nidal also collected information about all Fatah activities, their offices, members, and so on. His job was especially geared to this, but he continued gathering intelligence about Iraq, Syria, and Libya when he moved to those countries.

When Fatah leaders—Arafat, Abu Jihad, Abu Iyad, Hani and Khalid Hassan—began favoring diplomacy, the hawkish members felt that the leaders were trying to impose their will on the rest of the organization, promoting people who agreed with them and giving others unimportant jobs. When Fatah took over the leadership of the PLO in 1969, they gave favors to those who supported their position and sent others away. Abu Nidal was one of those they wanted to get rid of, so they appointed him PLO representative in Sudan, a good decision since it took one of the proponents of armed struggle away from the center of activity and gave the PLO an opportunity to use Abu Nidal's talent for organizing to open an office.

Abu Nidal, with three assistants—including Abd al-Rahman Issa, who was to stay at his side for more than 20 years—took his family and opened the PLO office, working in friendly territory with a government willing to assist the cause. After the physical work of establishing an office, their tasks were light: helping the few Palestinians who were working in the country, distributing information, and meeting government officials. It was an uneventful time for Abu Nidal, and in the middle of 1970, after over a year in Sudan, he came back to Amman, which was buzzing of civil unrest and a coming war.

Abu Nidal was neither charismatic nor articulate, a straight exponent of the Fatah line; few people took notice of him on his return to Amman. He immediately sensed the atmosphere of conflict and became frightened. Some of the people around him saw his fear—he made no effort to cover it up—and tried to make light of the matter. He did not see it as a joke. When he was in the house of commandant Abu al-Montassim, whose family has a marriage tie to Abu Nidal, he made the wild claim that Fatah had brought him back to Amman to have him killed in the coming civil war. Cowardice was all over his face and paranoia shook his body. Perhaps this hysterical cowardice made him a killer; if he knew how to fight, killing would become a reality rather than a fantasy.

He went to his friend Abu Daoud, who had become one of the main leaders of Fatah's military, and pleaded to be sent as Fatah and PLO representative to Iraq, which he chose because there was an opening there and because it would take him out of the dangerous situation in Amman. When pleading his case to Abu Daoud he exaggerated his connection with the Baathists he met in Saudi Arabia. Abu Daoud talked to Abu Iyad, and they agreed to let him have the position. They appointed him to the Fatah Revolutionary Council, a rank just under the Central Committee. Arafat agreed since Abu Iyad had made the recommendation, and Khalid al-Hassan, the PLO's political officer and hence Abu Nidal's boss, signed the paper for him in June 1970 to be appointed as both the head of Fatah and the PLO representative in Iraq.

Upon his arrival in Iraq, Abu Nidal became more nervous, easily provoked; he smoked constantly and drank occasionally. Frank and serious, he rarely smiled, and he began verbally abusing Abu Iyad, Arafat, and Hassan, calling them cowards. Strange though his behavior seemed, however, Abu Nidal would prosper from his new appointment, for this position was to bring him the power and prestige to launch his campaign to destroy the PLO.

Chapter 8
The Rejectionists

The Palestinians remained divided between concentrating on military adventures, what they called armed struggle, or pursuing the path of diplomacy involving territorial compromise. In the 1970s most Palestinians believed in conquering all of Palestine. The argument is, of course, academic since the Palestinians never had the means to gain a square inch, let alone the territory occupied after the 1967 war or the whole country. It was purely a political line. The Palestinians in the occupied territories supported a compromise more than those who had left, since the outsiders had little to gain from a peace settlement; at best they would have to reestablish themselves yet again, while those in the West Bank and Gaza, both the original inhabitants and the 1948 refugees, would gain some form of independence. The diversity of opinion made it difficult for the PLO to take a unified stand.[1]

It took over a year for the PLO to establish a functioning headquarters in Beirut after the Black September war. Terror attacks on Israel were planned from South Lebanon by Dalan Moghrabi and Abu Jihad, who divided Palestine into three regions: the West Bank, Gaza, and Israel proper (what they called inside the 1948 boundaries), with a separate office handling each area. Palestinian militants were able to smuggle the occasional machine gun or a couple of pistols. They instigated more actions than the Israelis reported, but far fewer than the Palestinians boasted. Without the ability to launch guerrilla raids, Arafat and his colleagues were forced to change from revolutionaries to diplomats. They first sought to appeal to the Arab world and the communist bloc to legitimize their leadership. By the early 1970s the Fatah leadership was willing to accept the reality of Israel's presence, although they did not concretely declare their acceptance. Arafat accepted the 1970 Soviet Union proposal for an international conference that would involve the United Nations Security Council as well as all the concerned parties in the Middle East. His avenue of diplomacy angered many Palestinians, especially the PFLP and its splinter groups, and they began congregating in Iraq, the most hardline state, to reject Arafat's line, being bolstered by Syria and Egypt's acceptance of a ceasefire. Saddam Hussein took charge of bringing them together.[2]

The Rejectionists, as they came to be known, led by Habash, came up with their three nos: no negotiation, no acceptance of Israel, no compromise. Many Palestinian groups with similar-sounding names, such as the Arab Liberation Front, the Palestine Liberation Front, and the People's Struggle Front, flocked to Baghdad with active encouragement of the Baath party. Wadi Haddad rejoined Habash in a bid to stem the PLO's peace moves. They did not want the PLO to accept only a part of Palestine—what became known as a mini-state, a quarter of the original Palestine—since they staked claim to all of it.

Meanwhile, Arafat's pragmatism was winning him standing among world leaders, except those of the United States and the Soviet Union, who were always cold to the PLO, lecturing the organization about the need to achieve its goals though diplomacy and abandon armed struggle.

In the important years following the 1973 war the PLO achieved outstanding political success. First, the Arab League recognized it as the sole legitimate representative of the Palestinian people in 1973, and officially reconfirmed that stance during their summit in Rabat in October 1974. Only Jordan opposed the move. The Islamic and African conferences that followed bestowed on the PLO the same status. About 30 Third World nations cut diplomatic relations with Israel. This new prestige also won over many Palestinians since Arafat had tangible proof that his platform was working.

The greatest diplomatic success came one month later, in November 1974, when Arafat was invited to speak before the United Nations, an ambition he had been cultivating for 15 years. He came to New York wearing a uniform and a gun, and he wanted to walk into the General Assembly with his gun as a symbol of armed struggle, but a Palestinian American persuaded him to discard it. He compromised, speaking in front of the General Assembly with an empty holster. The United Nations then voted to give the PLO observer status. Most Palestinians felt elated, thinking that within a short time everyone would see the rightness of their cause and force Israel to give up territory for a Palestinian homeland. The Rejectionists, meanwhile, had nothing but words, and although most never gave up their philosophy, their movement lost steam, and they dispersed—everyone except Abu Nidal and his coterie.

Among the Rejectionists were still those who believed in outside operations. The PLO leadership (including the PFLP, which remained part of the PLO until the 1980s) had abandoned these operations, but Haddad and Ahmed al-Ghafour (Abu Mahmoud) still wanted to carry out raids. Ghafour, who had personal money, was loyal to Fatah, but he had good contacts with the PFLP. In 1972 he began his own terror group called the National Arab Youth. (We touched on their actions in a previous chapter.) Ghafour made an agreement with Abu Nidal, PLO representative in Baghdad, who was also putting together a secret organization. NAY recruits were trained in Iraqi military bases, and the group was later taken over by Abu Nidal. Ghafour also had contacts with Libyan intelligence, who helped him run wild in Europe during NAY's short life.

On the eve of the first anniversary of the Munich massacre a Mossad liaison officer telephoned the Italian police late at night to say that Arabs were planning to launch a surface-to-air missile at an El Al jet that would take off from Leonardo Da Vinci airport the following day. He gave the police the address of the apartment in the town of Ostia near the airport, threatening to strike at the Arabs if the Italians did not. The police raided the apartment past midnight, found one Arab there—Mahmoud Nabil Azmikamy from Tripoli, Lebanon—and, looking in a closet, discovered two surface-to-air missiles and a shoulder-held launcher. The police then rounded up the other four residents of the apartment, who were staying in a hotel in the center of Rome, and charged them with possession of weapons with intent to shoot down the plane.[3] They were part of the NAY.

The judge in charge of the case ordered two of the five released, claiming he had insufficient evidence to charge them. But before the judge's verdict, Foreign Minister Aldo Moro had negotiated with Libya for their release, though it is not clear who approached whom for the negotiation. Moro mentioned this when he himself was being held captive and arguing for his life. Israeli leaders issued loud public warnings to Italy not to release the two suspects. Prime Minister Meir said that Italy needed a warning not to collaborate with Gadaffi. However, on Halloween a group of three Italian secret service (SID) agents ushered the two released Arabs to Tripoli in an old DC3 code-named Argo 16. They could have flown directly there, quietly dropped their passengers, and left, but they inexplicably stopped in Malta for a few hours. The Italian agents, who had become friendly with their charges, took them on a pleasant tour around Valetta and had lunch together. The SID agents then flew the plane to Tripoli, released the Arabs, and returned home that evening. Someone in Malta knew about their mission and photographed the Arabs and the Italians having a good time in a restaurant, then published the photo in the local newspaper.

Italy had a lot of business with Libya, its former colony, including Libyan oil, and the day before the Arabs were arrested Libya had taken a 51 percent share of its oil companies and raised the price of oil by one dollar a barrel.[4] In the 1970s Italy consigned tanks and armor vehicles to nonexistent army units, then secretly sold the weapons to Libya. (So common was this practice among arms dealers in Europe that in negotiations between NATO and the Warsaw Pact the negotiators were counting hardware that did not exist, probably on both sides.) Moro also sold weapons to the PLO, and at least one machine gun found its way back to the Brigate Rosse terrorists, which meant that the Italian government was arming its antigovernment terrorists.

Three weeks later—November 23, 1973—that same Argo 16 fell out of the sky at 3000 feet on the outskirts of Venice shortly after takeoff. All four people aboard were killed, and 30 cars in a factory parking lot were damaged. There was no news about the crash at the time since it involved a secret service plane, and the four aboard were from SID.

The three remaining Arab suspects were scheduled to go on trial just before Christmas. As passengers were crowding the airports and autostradas, five NAY members walked into Rome airport's international terminal, approached the metal detectors, unzipped their suitcases, took out their automatics, and began spraying bullets. They ran outside and went directly to a Pan Am jet that was getting ready to take off to Beirut and Teheran. On the jet, the terrorists hurled eight or ten phosphorus bombs, which immediately ignited fires. The heavily armed gunmen were well briefed and trained. They avoided Swissair and Air France planes next to the Pan Am and climbed the stairs of a Lufthansa, demanding that they be flown to safety—which they were, going to Athens and demanding the release of two of their cohorts who were responsible for the August attack at the airport. The gunmen aboard the plane killed an Italian passenger and threw his body on the tarmac; then, over the radio they playacted killing other passengers, and the authorities believed them, considering what they had done in Rome. The Greeks rushed the jailed Palestinians to the control tower to reassure the hijackers and stop the bloodshed.[5] They eventually gave themselves up and were tried and sentenced by the PLO in Cairo.

This was one of the must brutal acts of international terrorism in the 1970s. Thirty people were killed, mostly on the Pan Am plane, and about 100 were injured. Fourteen of those who died on the Pan Am jet were employees or dependents of Aramco, the Arab-American oil company. There were also four Moroccan officials on their way to a state visit.

The trial of the three remaining surface-to-air missiles suspects ended in their conviction and five-year sentences, considered light.

The connections between these events were buried in secrecy until an Italian judge in Venice, Carlo Mastelloni, reopened the case in 1988 to see if the Argo 16 was sabotaged, which it almost certainly was. The records of the plane and the accident had disappeared from military archives. High-ranking Italian officials from the secret service and the defense department—including General Gianadelio Maletti, who fled to South Africa in 1981 after being implicated in another scandal, and Vito Miceli, the head of security—covered up the affair, possibly on orders from government ministers who wanted to avoid more problems for the already troubled government. Other central players in this drama have taken their secrets to their graves. Speculations abounded that the Israelis planted a bomb on the Argo 16 while it was in a relatively unguarded military base near Venice. An Italian official alleged that Asa Leven, the late Israeli ambassador to Italy who also controlled the Mossad agents, may have had a role in sabotaging the plane. The judge wanted to subpoena General Zvi Zamir, overall head of the Mossad between 1968 and 1974, even though such a demand would be ignored.[6]

Moreover, the evidence surrounding the surface-to-air missiles is incomplete. The missiles, which disappeared before they could be traced, were assumed to be left over from a failed operation earlier that year in which Palestinians were going to shoot down Golda Meir's plane. Officials have speculated that the Mossad set up the incident by selling the missiles to the Arabs, who were students in their twenties from Lebanon, Syria, Iraq, Libya, and Algeria.

When the Mossad telephoned the Italian police demanding that they take action against the Arabs with the missiles, the Israelis were aggravating a frail Italy. Evidence later emerged that Israel wanted to destabilize the Italian government by such incidents. The Italian right wing was throwing bombs at this time, and NAY actions fit into their program. There is a report that the gunmen who raided the airport were housed in Sicily by an American arms dealer named Ronald Stark, and negotiations with the Palestinians were conducted through the Hyperion School of Languages in Paris, a front for left-wing groups but probably run by secret services. Guns, bombs, and dirty deals flowed through Hyperion, which was opened by Corrado Simioni, who suspiciously flipped between supporting left- and right-wing groups.[7] There seems to have been a cover-up of the NAY investigation. According to Arab sources, Ghafour made arms deals with Europeans, and his organization contained people of questionable loyalty. All remains speculation, but it seems highly unlikely that Ghafour's group was clean.

The airport massacre was timed with Arab-Israeli talks in Geneva organized by United States secretary of state Henry Kissinger and presided over by Kurt Waldheim. Israel insisted on excluding even the mention of Palestinians, and Kissinger bowed to the request, making the meeting a nonstarter.[8] He issued a dictum that no United States government could negotiate with the PLO because of terrorism, making it the issue central of the dispute.

The day before Arafat spoke at the United Nations, four members of the National Arab Youth group dressed up as airport mechanics, seized a British VC-10 plane on a flight to Dubai and took it to Tunis. They again demanded the release not only of Abu Daoud from Jordan, but also of the gunmen who took part in the Khartoum operation to free Abu Daoud, plus two of their members imprisoned in Holland and the five gunmen who took part in the Christmas 1973 attack on the Rome airport, all spectacular events. Neither Abu Daoud nor the Khartoum gunmen had any knowledge of these new people and could not understand why someone who did not know them would go to such great lengths to free them. The actions seemed designed to recall Palestinian crimes on the day the Palestinian leader was addressing the United Nations.

The day after the NAY controlled the plane they killed one of the passengers, a West German, to show that they meant business. The Italians and the Dutch gave up their prisoners, but after stressful threatening, the hijackers grew tired and gave themselves up. The Israelis were able to discount Arafat's United Nations speech by saying that hijacking and killing innocent passengers showed that the Palestinians were terrorists. The Israelis also argued that Arafat had no control over his organization and was therefore not the true Palestinian leader.

The day the missiles were discovered (September 5, 1973), five Palestinians approached the Saudi Arabian embassy in Paris requesting visas. When they were inside the gate, they put on masks, took out automatics, and began shooting. Identifying themselves as *al-Iqab* ("punishment"), they held hostage everyone they found. The ambassador was not there at the time. The gunmen demanded the release of Abu Daoud from Amman. It looked like a repeat of the bloody episode in Khartoum six months previous. King Hussein had taken Abu Daoud and his accomplices off death row shortly after the Khartoum disaster. The gunmen negotiated with police and Arab diplomats by shouting up the second-floor window, then freed most hostages and were given a plane to Kuwait, stopping in Egypt to refuel. They disappeared after that, taking another plane out of the country and eventually returning back to Iraq.[9] Syria claimed that the takeover was an Israeli intelligence service plot to disrupt the Algiers conference of nonaligned nations. Abu Nidal had launched his career as a terrorist leader, for this was his first action, and it was designed not to free hostages but to embarrass the PLO.

Chapter 9
Abu Nidal in Iraq

There are several accounts of the problems that led to the conflict between the Fatah leadership and Abu Nidal. Their formal and bitter separation in September 1974 was the culmination of several years of personal and theoretical differences, during which a smoldering philosophical disagreement degenerated into an open battle of words, which further descended to threats and insults and, a few years later, to a fiery and bloody battle. This feud had its genesis in the months after Abu Nidal returned from Sudan in the spring of 1970 and became involved with the self-proclaimed radicals, who talked about armed struggle as the only road to victory. Abu Nidal began calling Fatah leaders capitalists against the struggle, and in Baghdad his position became open as he drew like-minded cadres around him. These cadres compiled a list of complaints against Arafat and his followers and presented them at the third PNC congress in 1971, but the authoritative Arafat did not listen and had his agenda passed without debate.

The radicals also complained that the PLO was corrupt. Leaders put friends in important positions which they were not necessarily qualified to fulfill. They had little financial accountability, with a stream of mini-scandals or gossip about PLO officials spending money liberally, traveling to European capitals, staying at deluxe hotels and eating in fancy restaurants. The truth of these stories is immaterial, for they were perceived as truth, and Abu Nidal used them to accuse Fatah of losing its original revolutionary spirit and becoming a bourgeois organization. During the fourth congress in 1972, Arafat put together an ad hoc committee to counter corruption, and Abu Nidal and his associates at first supported this initiative.

Abu Nidal then asked Fatah for a dialogue to redesign Fatah's political program. Fatah did not want its differences with Abu Nidal to become public, but they also did not want to discuss changing their political line, believing that a dialogue would compromise their leadership, so Fatah initially refused. Abu Nidal claims that he called for a conference because he and his group did not want to splinter the movement, but Arafat was on a diplomatic roll, and he saw no need for discussion.

In Baghdad Abu Nidal became a focal point for the Rejectionists, and he created a vital organization for the hard liners. Having been put in a position of power by the Fatah leadership, and knowing how to exercise charm along with a free hand in gift-giving, he cemented pivotal friendships in the Iraqi government with people who wanted to show themselves as helping Palestinians. Iraqi leaders frequently met with the PLO representative, enabling Abu Nidal to get to know those who would eventually take over the government, including Tariq Aziz, Saddam Hussein, and his brothers Barzan and Sebawi Tikriti. Saddam disliked Abu Nidal and had no direct dealing with him, but Barzan, who became intelligence head (a key post in a repressive government), was close to Abu Nidal until Barzan was dismissed in mid–October 1983.[1] Abu Nidal also worked with intelligence chief Sa'doon Shaker, who later became the interior minister, and he was impressed by Baath political thinker Nizar Hamdoun, who became a key figure in the foreign ministry and ambassador to the United Nations. Abu Nidal often listened to Hamdoun and mouthed Hamdoun's Baathist slogans. He also had contact with Abd al-Qaliq Samarani, leader of the Iraq Liberation Movement, which the government crushed, killing Samarani in the process. Samarani held high ethical principles, in sharp contrast to the opportunist government and Abu Nidal. The Baath eventually gave Abu Nidal's people passports, including diplomatic passports for the leaders, and allowed them to use diplomatic pouches.

The Baath ideology dictated that the Palestinian issue was a problem for the entire Arab world. To them Palestine was Arab land, and in 1969 Baghdad created a paper organization called the Arab Liberation Front headed by Dr. Abd al-Wahab al-Kayali, consisting of Palestinians allegedly working to liberate Palestine. The organization was based in Beirut, and just as Saika and Ahmed Jabril were created and supported by Syria to counter the growth of Fatah, the ALF was Iraq's answer to the Damascus groups. But the rise of Abu Nidal's group made the ALF extraneous; by using Abu Nidal for dirty actions, they could avoid responsibility for failures. Kayali was assassinated in Beirut in December 1981.

Abu Nidal remained a homebody and did not socialize, an unusual trait for a Palestinian male; nevertheless, by virtue of his position, complete with office and staff and contacts within the Iraqi government, he became the face, the image, of the strong line, a political philosophy that drew to Baghdad those who felt that the PLO line did not represent them. Everyone describes Abu Nidal as just one of the men, lacking significant or striking features except for his turbulent mind, which would often make him change his opinions and adopt diverse or opposing positions. He jumped from idea to idea, sometimes talking calmly and persuasively, and at other times acting awkward and introverted. It seemed as if Abu Nidal never matured. He often wore a pistol, but for all his talk about armed struggle, Abu Nidal never used a weapon in all his life. In 1972 he began creating his own secret group.

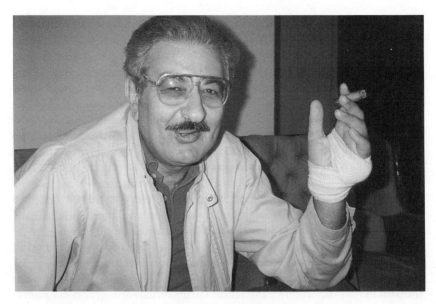

Abu Daoud, key figure for PLO fighters.

That year the PLO selected Abu Daoud and Abu Nidal for one of its del-
egations to China and North Korea. China had been generous to other PLO
leaders, and the two met the PLO representative in Peking, who took them
to visit Palestinian fighters under training in military camps.[2] Abu Daoud and
Abu Nidal took the long train ride to Pyongyang, North Korea, visited training sites there, then flew back for meetings with Chinese officials to discuss
Palestinian military strategy. This was during the Cultural Revolution, and
the Chinese promised them a bigger shipment of weapons—$17 million
worth—which arrived October 1973 at the port of Basra, too late to be of
immediate use in the Yom Kippur War. Like the Chinese shipment that had
arrived too late for the Black September war, they had to be stored in Fatah's
warehouse, located in its training camp an hour's drive from Baghdad. The
Fatah responsible for weapons, a man named Abu Khil, supervised the hundreds of truckloads from Basra to the warehouse. It took about a week to
unload all the supplies. Fatah kept most weapons in Iraq, even though Abu
Nidal was openly rebelling, allowing the weapons to fall under his control as
a way of asserting his independence. He sent weapons to the Palestinians in
Syria and Lebanon, but after he split from Fatah he kept most of the weapons
for himself, only providing a few to Palestinian fighters in Lebanon in 1976
and 1978 at the personal request of Abu Daoud, who tried to create militia
cells in South Lebanon outside the authority of the PLO. The Chinese also
sent to Basra another ship loaded with supplies such as military uniforms and
petrol, but that was distributed straightaway.

Arafat at last agreed to meet with Abu Nidal, and after many assurances and guarantees of safety, Abu Nidal flew to Beirut in the summer of 1974. Abu Nidal was terrified that Fatah would kill him as they killed NAY leader Ghafour. Abu Daoud met him at the airport and took him to meet the Palestinian leadership in a safe house, then drove him back to the airport in the evening with Abu Nidal's empty promises. This was the last time Abu Nidal set foot in Lebanon. While it is true that Abu Nidal was calling for dialogue, he was at the same time creating his own group and openly declaring a fight, publishing bold statements of Fatah's evils, containing not only philosophical differences, but personal hatred for the PLO leadership. In September Abu Nidal's group officially announced that he was the true Fatah who had not abandoned the struggle against the Zionist enemy. They named their organization the Fatah Revolutionary Council, thinking of themselves as true revolutionaries. By calling themselves Fatah Revolutionary Council (FRC) they confused themselves with Arafat's Fatah. Years later newspapers would announce that a gruesome terrorist activity was the work of a Fatah faction, and readers would link it with Arafat. Abu Nidal also called his small news agency WAFA, the same as Fatah, and a program he broadcast on Iraqi radio "The Voice of Palestine," again the same as Fatah, creating serious confusion. In October a squad was dispatched to kill Fatah leader Mahmoud Abbas (Abu Mazin). According to dissidents, Abu Nidal did not order this, and it is unclear who sent them, but it was the final straw, and Fatah began cutting off the Iraqi heretics—which not only gave the FRC validity, but also jeopardized Fatah's relationship with Iraq. Iraq sided with their man; everything that belonged to the PLO, including the Chinese weapons, was now his, and Iraq lavished on him the monthly contribution that they had previously given to Arafat.

Fatah says that in 1975 they held a tribunal *in absentia* for Abu Nidal and condemned him to death, and they attempted later to send a squad to kill him in Baghdad but were stopped by the Iraqis.[3] Before 1978 Abu Nidal had only a driver, no guards. Only after 1978 did he become surrounded by armed guards. The PLO formally asked Iraq to stop Abu Nidal, but they refused, saying that the conflict was an internal Palestinian problem.

Iraq also gave Abu Nidal a large piece of wasteland about 10 km from the town of Heet, less than 250 km from Baghdad, on the Euphrates (al-Farat) River, and he made it his center. The Iraqis were astonished at how he transformed it. He brought in truckloads of earth, water pumps to take out the river water and irrigate, and an electric generator; then he organized the building of houses and the planting of trees and greenery. After four years it was an oasis that became the group's training facility and target practice zone, housing about 100 people (20 to 30 families). The group considers wives and sisters as members. The community had good relations with the local people and helped them improve their land as well. This facility was Abu Nidal's best, one of two he had in Iraq.

When he lost both facilities in 1983—the Iraqis gave the Heet camp to an Iranian dissident group—he relocated in Lebanon in the Syrian-controlled Bakaa Valley near the ancient Roman site of Baalbek. He never had a training facility in Syria. Mustafa Firas eventually took charge of the training of recruits, and it is said that when they left the Heet farm the Iraqis found 30 bodies of former members. It was always easy to be executed in the organization, questioning immediately drew suspicion, but the Iraqi charge was never verified. FRC also used an Iraqi military training camp near the city of al-Ramadi, downriver from Heet, about an hour's drive west of Baghdad. The Iraqis gave a portion of the base to the FRC. Almost all terrorists were trained there until 1983.

The group published a newspaper called *al-Maqawama* with articles written by the literate people who eventually left the group, and it was replaced by Abu Nidal's magazine *Revolutionary Palestine*, again, the title of Fatah's magazine. An excellent physical organizer, Abu Nidal began an importing business. Iraqi Jews had run 75 percent of the country's import trade before their exodus,[4] and two decades later, the country still suffered from a lack of imports.

The Palestinians around Abu Nidal were strong personalities. Some came to Iraq on their own; others were encouraged to come because their views matched those of the radicals that were collecting in Baghdad. Many Palestinian students at Baghdad University joined the group. Mustafa Murad, whom Fatah arrested on the charge of wanting to kill Abu Mazin, joined Abu Nidal as part of Fatah and became his loyal deputy. Another interesting person who joined the band was Dr. Ghassan, who eventually became the political director. He came from a Palestinian family that wanted to think of themselves more as European than Arab. His father, a Western-oriented Palestinian from Jerusalem, collaborated with the British and possibly also with the Israelis. He sent his son to the Feres French Catholic school located just inside Jerusalem's Old City walls, then to England, where he studied chemical engineering.

In the late 1960s Dr. Ghassan became interested in politics and joined Fatah in London. His political views seemed to outweigh his interest in school—he left without finishing his degree and went to Beirut just after the Black September war—and he was later encouraged to join Abu Nidal, so he went to Baghdad in 1973 and initially worked in an unimportant position in the information office. Married to a passive English woman, he brought her and their two children to the Middle East, but she became unhappy with him and the dour atmosphere that hangs over the FRC and left around 1980, returning to London and living a quiet life on a $2000 a month alimony. Dr. Ghassan's strong political philosophy, uncompromising and extreme, as well as his background, made many wonder about his true intentions. Palestinians are widely suspicious of him.

Another group connected with Abu Nidal was led by Naji Alush (Abu Ibrahim), a prolific journalist and writer who inspired Arab nationalism. Alush claims that he was never part of the group, that he thought of Abu Nidal as crazed, and that he hated terrorist operations, those done by Fatah as well as those done by Abu Nidal. Alush was based in Lebanon and was part of a 1978 dispute between Fatah activists and conservatives. He moved to Iraq and cooperated with Abu Nidal, but their bond was tenuous. Abu Nidal dreamed that Alush would expand the FRC into Lebanon.

When the Syrians came into Lebanon in 1976, they began to deflate the Palestinian militias, which had run wild and had become the strongest force in Lebanon. The power of the militias was accomplished by defiance and abuse, and they had far outstayed their welcome. The Syrians used their Palestine Liberation Army against them, forcing Palestinian to fight Palestinian, matching Lebanon's war of insanity, inconsistency, and vanity. On June 1, 1976, the Syrian PLA with their Christian supporters attacked the PLO and its allies at Tal al-Zaitar on the outskirts of Beirut, leveling the camp. The FRC accused Fatah of executing two of its best fighters after the battle, Abu Ahmed and Abu Fouad. Their grandfathers were heroes in the 1936 general strike, and their deaths caused more friction between the two parties, especially when Abu Nidal accused Fatah of first torturing them. Fatah was trying hard to keep all the Palestinian factions under the control of the PLO and to stop armed actions not sanctioned by them. They claim the two were guilty of extortion, but Abu Nidal became even more paranoid.

FRC also claims that Fatah killed their man in Paris in early 1977, Mahmood Salah, who ran the library-bookstore in the Latin Quarter. He was Mauritanian but adopted the Palestinian cause. In the early 1970s he became one of Abu Daoud's fighters in Lebanon, then left to work in the library in Paris, which became a focal point of the radical Arab community. After the killing of Hamshari he became a temporary PLO delegate; then he moved to the no-compromise front and began drawing recruits to his growing network. One day two gunmen emptied their 9mm automatic pistols into Salah's body as he was leaving his bookstore.

The attackers wrote the slogan *Israel vaincra* ("Israel will win") and the letters F.E.J. on the bookstore grate, indicating that the attack was the work of the Jewish Defense League's French branch. There seems to be no question that Salah was killed by a right-wing Israeli death squad who had hounded him before; they had previously planted two bombs at his store and had threatened him many times.[5] The PLO naturally blamed Israel for the killing of Salah, but the FRC accused Arafat, and through the FRC ranks the hatred of Fatah overshadowed that of Israel.

The same day Salah was killed, members of the PLO, headed by Dr. Issam Sartawi, met in Paris with a delegation of Israeli peace activists. After Salah's death Abu Daoud went to Paris with a colleague to bring the body back to Lebanon. They were in and out of the Ministry of Foreign Affairs for four days arranging the details. While the machinery of France's bureaucracy turned, Abu Daoud tried to find out more about the killing. Police were always posted on a bridge overlooking the library entrance, but they did not notice the killing. Abu Daoud concluded that the killers cooperated with the DST police. He accused the authorities, and they arrested him, creating a diplomatic problem. The foreign office had officially welcomed Abu Daoud to France, and they had to step in and order his release. The Mossad gave the story of his arrest to the press, together with a dossier on how Abu Daoud was a terrorist who plotted the Munich massacre and was a double agent of Jordan.[6] Israel made official and public noises about giving terrorists a haven; journalists called France cowardly.[7]

The FRC raided two important hotels in Damascus and Amman in 1976. In both cases the governments reacted with complete force against the attackers and whomever else happened to be in the way. In September 1976, four FRC gunmen seized 90 hostages in the Damascus Semiramis Hotel. Syrian soldiers stormed the building, killing four hostages and one gunman. The other three gunmen were tortured and executed the following day. Two months later FRC attacked the Intercontinental in Amman, where Habash had taken hostages six years previously. All 300 rooms of the hotel were occupied at the time of the attack. Four FRC gunmen walked into the lobby mid-morning with suitcases. They pulled out their weapons, began shooting, and rounded up 150 Western and Arab hostages, taking them to the top floor of the building. At that time the FRC were calling themselves Black June in honor of the Syrian attack on Palestinian positions earlier that year, and they were rebelling against the Riyadh and Cairo Arab League conferences that sanctioned the Syrian intervention in Lebanon.

The gunmen had no time to dictate their demands; orders from the government, probably directly from the king's mouth, came immediately. The army quickly set up a strike force, and just after noon they stormed the hotel, entering from the front and rear doors and landing on the roof from helicopters. The gunmen could have killed many of their hostages, but they chose to fight the attacking army that had turned the luxury hotel into a battlefield. The army fired indiscriminately, killing at least two guests as well as two of the gunmen. They burnt three rooms and riddled others with bullets from their machine guns. The final two gunmen were trapped in a room, and it is said that one of them shot his colleague in the head, then turned the gun on himself. By two o'clock all the fighting was over. Both Abu Nidal and King Hussein had made their points. The government knew that Iraq had given the gunmen weapons and that Abu Nidal had trained them.[8]

Almost a year later, a month before President Sadat went to Jerusalem to speak of peace before the Israeli parliament, the FRC struck another Arab target. A 19-year-old Palestinian, Salah Mohammed Khaled, who had recently

Semiramis Hotel, Damascus, raided by FRC gunmen. Government troops stormed the hotel and killed all gunmen.

joined Abu Nidal, arrived at the modern Abu Dhabi airport and waited for Syrian foreign minister Abdel Halim Khaddam. Khaddam, who had been the foreign minister for four years, studied politics in Moscow and had a Russian wife. Feeling threatened by Egypt's peace with Israel, Syria wanted to come to better terms with its other adversary, Iraq. Syrian president Asad was meeting Iraqi president Ahmed Hassan al-Bakr on the very day the Palestinian was waiting for the Syrian foreign minister.[9] The possibility of an Iraq-Syria alliance posed a serious threat to Israel. Khaled, the Palestinian gunman, was wearing a traditional long robe. When Foreign Minister Khaddam came into the airport at the head of a group of dignitaries, including United Arab Emirates deputy foreign minister Sayf bin Said al-Ghabash, Khaled pulled out a machine gun from under his robe and fired 15 shots, all of which missed the Syrian minister and killed instead Ghabash.[10] It was a strange mistake; the Palestinian was well trained, an excellent shot. He had come from Baghdad specifically for the kill. He was new to the FRC but had been a fighter in Lebanon. There is no doubt that Abu Nidal instructed Khaled to kill the Syrian, and it was unlike him to miss, even more unlikely that the bullets would end up in Ghabash, prompting speculation that someone else gave him different orders. He received his weapon from his contact in Abu Dhabi in the usual FRC manner. No one was convinced it was a mistake. He was arrested, hastily tried, and executed by a firing squad a few days before Sadat landed in Israel. Syria claimed that it was an Iraqi plot.[11]

After the attack FRC representative Abd al-Rahman Issa went to see Fahd al-Fahd, the director of Kuwait's counter-intelligence (he is not part of the ruling family). Thereafter, Kuwait, the United Arab Emirates, and Saudi Arabia made irregular contributions to the FRC to avoid future mistakes.

Abu Daoud tried to reconcile with Abu Nidal two or three more times, shuttling between Abu Iyad and Abu Nidal. The last attempt was in 1977, when Abu Daoud went to Baghdad to convince his friend to return to the PLO. Abu Nidal was interested, but afraid. After talking to Abu Daoud for several hours, Abu Nidal finally agreed to disband his movement, abandon outside operations, and join forces with the PLO. He was promised a position on the Executive Committee in return. Abu Daoud went to bed relieved.

The next morning Abu Nidal changed his mind. His body changed, his face changed, as he flipped in and out of sanity. No way would the "real" Fatah organization join the "mistaken" one in Beirut, he declared. Abu Daoud could do little, though he said later that if he had known that Abu Nidal would turn out to be a criminal and a killer he would have tried harder to change his mind. To all appearances Abu Nidal was a coward who could hardly kill an insect, and Abu Daoud left Baghdad believing that time would eventually settle the conflict. He never understood the underlying cause of Abu Nidal's madness. That was the last time that the two men met. Three years later Abu Daoud was seriously wounded by five bullets in a Warsaw cafe, an attack for which Abu Nidal took responsibility.[12]

Abu Nidal had become an autocratic leader of his Baghdad organization. Others in his group wanted to open up and democratize the group's decision-making, but he would not allow an ounce of power to slip from his grasp. He had complete control over major and minor decisions and the organization's finances. His group collected about 350 followers. Abu Nidal's friends say that as the pressures of his job increased, Abu Nidal began showing signs of schizophrenia. In Saudi Arabia he did manifest signs of mental instability such as irrationally changing his mind, but not schizophrenia, which involves hearing voices and withdrawing from reality. It would be abnormal for a person to begin manifesting signs of schizophrenia at that age, but beginning in 1977 Abu Nidal clearly felt the signs of stress. Perhaps his war with Fatah tortured his already fragile mind; he was obviously run down and pale. He began to employ guards and often changed houses. He owned at least two houses in the upper middle class al-Mansour quarter of Baghdad. He gave a few interviews to reporters but allowed no cameras or tape recorders. Once he brought in three Arab journalists who were driven blindfolded by the Iraqi military to a slum area. At times Abu Nidal was friendly to them; then he threatened the West and Arab moderates.

In 1978, at the age of 41, he suffered a heart attack in his house, collapsing on the floor. His friends took him to a hospital in Baghdad, where he stayed for about two months recovering. Even though many people in his organization were having differences with Abu Nidal, they came regularly to visit him in the hospital and keep him company, steering his problematic mind away from politics and his war against the PLO that kept him under stress.

Abu Nidal needed an operation, so they flew him to Sweden for surgery. He spent about six weeks there recovering after the operation, then returned to Baghdad a changed man. He cut back on smoking—he used to chain-smoke—changing to fancy cigarillos. The doctors told him that it would be good to drink whiskey (or at least he says that the doctors told him that) so he took a glass every day, gradually increasing his daily dosage to a liter and a half of Black Label, an Iraqi specialty. After the operation he began looking after his health, eating fewer rich foods and getting adequate rest. He used to breathe heavily, but after the surgery his breathing calmed. Some things did not change: he remained emotionally cold and quixotic. On his return to Baghdad he dismissed two central leaders, Faraj Isa and Immad Malhas, both honest, hard-working men.

Abu Nidal's doctor also recommended that he stay away from hot weather, so he began spending his summers outside Warsaw, disguised as a merchant under the name Dr. Said, a strange name for a half-literate. Later when he went to Libya he took on the name Dr. Mohammed. He lived more and more isolated, in Baghdad, Poland, and later Syria, so much so that he was ignorant of the news of the world.

During Abu Nidal's time in hospital the differences in his own organization became extreme, especially over Abu Nidal's absolute power. About half the members, led by Naji Alush and Dr. Omar Fahami, left and tried to start another organization, but it dispersed within months. Abu Nidal, still weak from surgery, could not fight the breakaway, and he even offered Alush and his colleagues money and weapons. Alush, taking the ethical high road, did not want the split to involve money or weapons. Alush had seen too many Palestinian organizations fight about such matters, so Alush told Abu Nidal that he wanted nothing. They could have easily finished Abu Nidal, taken over his organization and changed it, but they did not. Alush and the others opposed killing Palestinians and did not approve of military operations outside Palestine. They wanted armed struggle, not indiscriminate violence. Most intelligent men left, leaving those personally dedicated to Abu Nidal, thugs, and infiltrators working for foreign governments. Almost all the political thinkers left. Several military men stayed, thinking they could see action only with Abu Nidal; Mustafa Murad, Abd al-Rahman Issa, and Mustafa Firas stayed. However, with the kind of money Abu Nidal had acquired he could buy new people and create a new organization. Suddenly, previously insignificant members such as Dr. Ghassan and Wasfi Hannoun were promoted to fill the vacuum and became the leader's right hand.

Shortly after, the FRC engineered a mini-war between the PLO and Iraq, culminating in the August 13, 1978, explosion in Beirut near Fatah and

PLF offices, killing 150 people.[13] PLO officials believed that Abu Nidal had no autonomy, that he was a puppet of the Iraqi secret police. Although there were strong ties between FRC and Iraq, Abu Nidal kept autonomy. He had his own money and command structure, and his group was not confined to Iraq. After Saddam had taken absolute control in Iraq, Abu Nidal hardly spent time in his headquarters in Baghdad. Saddam formally expelled the FRC after the Israeli invasion of Lebanon, and Abu Nidal was personally there at that time. He knew the expulsion was coming. The United States was insisting that Iraq get rid of Abu Nidal before they would take Iraq off the list of terrorist countries, which they did in 1983. United States–Iraqi diplomatic relations were restored in 1984 (most Arab countries broke relations with Washington after the 1967 war; Iraq was the last to renew them). In the early 1980s both Washington and Baghdad wanted better relations since they had a common enemy, Iran, and Saddam saw the expulsion of Abu Nidal, whom he disliked, as a small price for Washington's intelligence assistance.

At the beginning of the Iran-Iraq war, the PLO took an unquestioning stand behind Iraq, even though they had good relations with Iran after the fall of the Shah. Arafat was the first leader Ayatollah Khomeini invited to Teheran, and the Iraqis turned Israel's embassy over to him. Thereafter the PLO enjoyed Iraq's oral support for their cause, and the PLO again put much of its military equipment in Iraq. As a favor to Arafat, Iraq also closed the offices of the PFLP and CG, keeping only the PLO and FRC. When Saddam invaded Kuwait in 1990, the PLO again stood firmly by him.

Chapter 10
Intelligence Capability

When the crusaders under King Richard of England defeated the Saracens, the Sultan seeing his troops fly, asked what was the number of Christians who were making all this slaughter? He was told that it was only King Richard and his men, and that they were all on foot. "Then," said the Sultan, "God forbid that such a fellow as King Richard should march on foot," and sent him a noble charger. The messenger took it, and said, "Sire, the Sultan sends you this charger, that you may not be on foot." The king was as cunning as his enemy, and ordered one of his squires to mount the horse in order to try him. The squire obeyed; but the animal proved fiery; and the squire being unable to hold him in, he set off at full speed to the Sultan's pavilion. The Sultan expected he had got King Richard; and was not a little mortified to discover his mistake. — *The Percy Anecdotes*, 1823[1]

Israelis blamed the Mossad and military intelligence for failing to detect Egypt and Syria's surprise attack in October 1973, which began the Yom Kippur War. If it had not been for the massive airlift of military hardware from the United States as well as the bullheaded determination of Sadat not to return armor units to attack a Sharon counter-offensive, Israel might have suffered significant territorial losses. The Mossad invested its energy killing poets and intellectuals and ignored the real danger to its country's survival, perhaps due to an exaggerated sense of invulnerability. For weeks before the war both Egypt and Syria had been fortifying their borders, sending combat-ready brigades and heavy hardware to the front, including flotation bridges to cross the Suez. Both countries had been conducting military drills and exercises involving thousands of troops,[2] but Israeli intelligence knew nothing about them.

Gathering intelligence is a monotonous occupation. We hear about spy novel superagents who speak a dozen languages and penetrate the enemy's secret sectors using ultraviolet and laser gadgetry, but those people fail more often than they succeed. Intelligence means inspecting and cataloging aerial photographs, stationing undercover personnel at a port so they can record the names of ships that travel in and out; drawing maps of waterfronts, train tracks, and roads; debriefing visitors; locating military bases, petrol storage tanks, factories, and government buildings. It means collecting information about a country's finances, personal histories of leaders, imports and exports, ethnic divisions, migration between city and country, standards of military training, relations with other countries, past hostilities, and potentials for social unrest.

Tedious work, involving graphs and statistics, reports about social and political conditions, military invasion and defense plans: that is good intelligence. Many countries, however, dispatch ambassadors and embassy staff who have little knowledge of their host country, hampering information-gathering activities, which are largely centered in an embassy. Intelligence agencies are obsessed with other countries' intelligence agencies to the neglect of the country itself. It could be said that war represents not only a failure of diplomacy but also a failure to understand another country—an intelligence failure.

Although the PLO had an intelligence office, they had no real ability to collect information. The Palestinians who know Israel best are those who grew up inside it, speak Hebrew and understand the country, but the PLO was staffed by 1948 refugees, many of whom had anti–Jewish prejudices. The PLO puts people in office not because of their abilities but because of their connections, which may explain their overall incompetence. Also, either the Mossad or Abu Nidal killed the PLO's best leaders, hurting all aspects of their movement.

The Israeli intelligence, despite its reputation (Kissinger, it is said, preferred Israeli intelligence over America's[3]), also had weak capacity, often relying on mass arrests and interrogation under torture. But while torture may control, humiliate, intimidate, and dehumanize, it is, as theologian Rosemary Ruether concludes, "an inefficient method of intelligence gathering, and such information is likely to be false."[4] Former CIA officer for the Middle East Archie Roosevelt tells us:

> One of the myths widely current in the United States is that of the efficacy of Israeli intelligence; it is simply not very reliable in coverage of its primary target, the Arab world ... Israeli intelligence can rarely count on ideological volunteers inside the Arab target. Furthermore, except for their now-established embassy in Egypt, they have no embassies in the Arab countries from which to conduct operations. So they must try to find recruits without a local base, from afar, a very difficult task... This accounts for Israeli mistakes in pinpointing the perpetrators of terrorists attacks abroad.[5]

Nigel West adds: "Mossad's need to resort to false-flag operations is significant in that it shows how weak the organization is at acquiring highly placed assets inside the Arab establishment."[6]

Besides Lillehammer and the 1973 war, Israel suffered other intelligence failures. During the Lebanon invasion they misjudged their ability to destroy the PLO, the will of the Maronites to join the war, the Shia community in the south. Yet the Maronite government had given Israel copious infrastructure information, and on the streets of Beirut it is said that Israel had 10,000 paid informers in Lebanon (probably a typical Arab exaggeration). Furthermore, Israeli intelligence was unable to predict the Intifada, even though Palestinians in the refugee camps were openly talking about it on the streets; and then they were unable to find its leadership, after many claims to the contrary. They did not predict either of the Gulf wars[7] or Sadat's peace initiative.

These serious, costly intelligence mistakes demonstrate that like the PLO, Israeli intelligence was out of touch with its target. Roosevelt believes that their people could not empathize with the Arabs, "viewing the Arabs as alien, threatening, hateful, and inferior, and as a people with whom they have nothing in common. Hence their own intelligence failures."[8] Defected Mossad agent Ostrovsky believes that Abu Nidal was head of the PFLP-GC and that Ahmed Jabril orchestrated the *Achille Lauro* operation, showing how removed the Mossad is from Palestinians. Also, Israel never viewed Palestinian organizations as an organic force, a revolutionary movement as dynamic as the Zionist movement that created Israel. Even with accurate intelligence, killing Palestinian leaders, arresting teenage boys, and bombing refugee camps can delay but not vaporize such a movement.

Western countries helped Israel with intelligence.[9] Israel signed intelligence cooperation pacts, usually called anti-terrorist agreements, with several European countries. Germany gave Israel a list of Palestinian students in their country as well as information about their political activism. Israeli intelligence personnel had good rapport with many European authorities, and undoubtedly a lot of information was given under the table by Israeli sympathizers who hold sensitive positions in European countries. For example, the sons of former Greek defense minister Ioannis Charalambopoulos have dual Israeli and Greek citizenship and have served in the Israeli army.

Arab countries also exchange information with Israel. Jordanian and Israeli officials have secretly met many times. Miles Copeland claims,

> [Syria] has gone so far as to provoke Palestinian units into making raids into Israel, and then to tip off the Israelis. The Algerian Government donated a number of blank passports to al-Fatah for "Black September," then told the French security authorities how to identify the secret markings they put on them.[10]

Many of Israel's half a million Palestinian and Druze citizens feel more Israeli than Arab. They go to Israeli schools, watch Israeli TV, and speak Hebrew as fluently as Arabic. Druze men control Palestinians in the occupied territories and serve as prison guards and interrogators,[11] and in several instances they helped Israeli commandos by renting cars in Arab cities and working with Mossad assassination teams.

Israel uses a storehouse of Palestinian and Arab collaborators. Some collaborate for money or power, others because they need something specific such as bringing a family member into Palestine or obtaining a license to open a shop. They aim to recruit some of the hundreds of thousands of Palestinians who study abroad, especially those who cannot adjust or who need money. They slowly lure people who are having difficulty, at first offering sexual or financial rewards for insignificant information. The collaborators become more and more hooked, each time feeling it more difficult to escape.

Obtaining recruits is a science that Israel has developed extensively. They immerse a collaborator gradually, step by step, getting him to do something immoral, something that violates his code of behavior. This technique generates the collaborator's hatred toward the person who made him commit the act, but in a weak person it also establishes a bond. The person who pushed the collaborator into an immoral act becomes a controller, the only one the collaborator can confide in. The intricate psychology behind this bond accelerates the road to further collaboration.

From a series of stories about collaborators, a pattern emerges. A PLO military leader told me the story of a young man arrested by Israel in the West Bank when he was about 17. His interrogators must have seen him as a possible recruit right away. They got another boy to sleep with him and secretly took pictures of them together. Later he was having financial problems; the Israelis gave him money, taking pictures of the transaction. They had him then, for they could easily ruin his reputation by exposing him as homosexual and on the pay of the enemy. However, they said they wanted little from him, just a bit of trivial information about the camp in which he lived, information that could cause no one harm.

But collaborating with an enemy is like an addictive drug, and the fellow continued stumbling. The Israelis arranged for him to study abroad, giving him money and taking pictures. They set him up with prostitutes and gave him a comfortable life in Paris. To his friends he looked like a bright and successful young man. He had four brothers who worked for the PLO, and he, too, with the urging of his Mossad controllers, got a job in Tunis. But the Mossad wanted more and more from him. Playing on Arabs' ingrained feeling of duty, they required him to report on meetings and activities. Finally, in early 1990 the Mossad ordered him to poison the people who were gathering at a meeting. That day he broke down and confessed—I am told that one of his brothers almost killed him on the spot—saying that he was spying in conjunction with another person in Tunis who was with Abu Nidal. It was clear to the person telling me the story that the FRC and the Mossad worked together.

Khaled al-Hassan related a similar story, except it was about the FRC:

> Abu Nidal chose someone to kill me by poison. I used to use a certain pill for headaches, and they were going to put a similar-looking pill in my dresser. This man was chosen, and they started training him intensely on weapons until he became an expert on all sorts of weapons. In the mean time they told him a false story about me, that I'm a traitor. When all was ready they told him to kill me. If he fails he will be killed or punished, depending on the nature of the failure. Then he realized he was my relative. He went home and got drunk and told his mother. She said he was stupid. The man came to me saying that I was a traitor. I told him, "Why don't you become my bodyguard for 24 hours; you'll be next to me, and you'll see if I'm a traitor." He started crying and told me everything. He became our man and died bravely in Beirut.

We discussed Abu Sharif's accusation of PFLP leader Abu Ahmed Yunis. In the early 1980s, before the Israeli invasion of Lebanon, Lebanese were operating joint patrols of Beirut with Palestinians in one of the many agreements. One night one of the groups patrolling the Sackyet al-Janzeer section of West Beirut stumbled on two men sitting in a car, purely by chance since that section of Beirut had no street lights, making it difficult to see that there was someone in the car. The patrol opened the door, and one of the fighters identified the man behind the steering wheel as an officer of the Lebanese Deuxième Bureau. They searched the man in the passenger seat and found a pistol on him, and since he had no papers for it, they took him to their office, where their Palestinian boss immediately recognized him as PFLP Politburo member Walid Kadura and stood up. The fighters explained the story to their boss, who turned to Kadura. "Comrade Walid," a wide-eyed Palestinian exclaimed, "What were you doing with that man?"

Kadura was one of the brightest leaders of the PFLP, a sharp exponent of a heavy leftist anti–Israeli philosophy. Respected by some, loathed by others, his extremist political theory created rifts in the Popular Front. Kadura at first made only a partial confession, but eventually, after he became a prominent member of Abu Abbas's PLF and helped mold their political program (which may help explain that group's failure), he came out with hundreds of pages of confession. The PFLP dismissed him for the political inconsistencies, not for collaborating; only later did his full confession, mostly convoluted rambling, appear. As in the case of Yunis, the PFLP remained close-mouthed, but the bits of news that emerged shocked the Palestinian left. Not only was Kadura a clever thinker and analyzer who held tremendous power within the Popular Front, he was a polite, humble cadre whose revolutionary platform was subscribed to by the youth. According to PLO sources, he confessed that in

1963, when he was a student in secondary school in Lebanon, he and other Palestinian boys were arrested during a demonstration. His interrogators discovered that he was clever, the leader of the group of boys, and they recruited him. Since then he was on the pay of the Deuxième Bureau, according to his confession, taking 1500 Lebanese pounds ($500) a month. It is hard to believe that someone of Kadura's stature—intelligent and highly sophisticated—would do what he did only for 1500 Lebanese pounds. He could have earned far more in business—which is what he did when he left Abu Abbas and went to the Arab Emirates.

Here was one who not only gave the Deuxième Bureau information about the PFLP's activities; he was in a position to influence the front's policies, make decisions. Kadura focused on the internal organization, constantly introducing contradictions and polarizing or splitting the group. He never confessed that his role was to discredit the Palestinian movement, but that was the effect of his actions. He was once asked if he could rid himself of his double dealing, but he said that it was impossible: once he agreed to work for them as a student they took control.

This notion of being trapped is repeated time and again by collaborators. Another feature of collaborators is that they seem slightly more loyal, more extreme, than their comrades. They usually work harder, are often friendly and charming. The PLO accused the Mossad of creating Arab-looking organizations that have created terrorism. Collaborators have played a central role in this disguise.[12]

Chapter 11
Death to the Arabs

In 1976 journalist Christopher Hitchens went to Iraq and was given a tour by Marzin al-Zahawi from the Ministry of Information. He wanted to take Hitchens to their man from Palestine, Abu Nidal. Hitchens had never heard of him and was uninterested, but he consented and was driven to a building in a low-rent area of Baghdad where on the ground floor in a humble office he was introduced to the man who immediately claimed to be the real leader of Fatah. His office had a Maoist poster on the wall, and Abu Nidal used extreme rhetoric about the world situation, appearing slightly crazed, moody, and uninspiring. He was disappointed that Hitchens did not want to go to his camp and be trained as guerrilla.

"Did you meet Said Hammami?" Abu Nidal asked his guest, referring to the charming PLO representative in London. Hitchens replied that he had. "If you see him again," Abu Nidal said threateningly, "tell him to be careful. We don't tolerate traitors."[1] Hitchens delivered the threat, but Hammami brushed it off, continuing to meet Jewish leaders, write newspaper articles, and describe the Palestinian cause to members of parliament.

Hitchens, like others who met the terrorist leader, was never debriefed by any official agency, though he later discussed the meeting on the United States television show *60 Minutes*. Had the West been seriously concerned about combating Abu Nidal they would have met with anyone who could have given them information about him.

Although he wanted a political settlement with Israel, Hammami was no pacifist. He was a strong man, a wrestler, who in his youth loved women and sports. He studied English literature at Damascus University and was a political nihilist, not even admitting he was a Palestinian. According to friends, he was one of the last people they thought would become politically involved.

Hammami was born in Jaffa in 1948. His family was put on a truck and taken to Gaza, like Abu Nidal's family; then they went to Lebanon. Hammami changed after the 1967 war, suddenly turning up as a guerrilla in Jordan and the West Bank. Hammami's intelligence enabled him to climb the ranks of Fatah, and in 1973 he was made PLO representative in London. The Arab

League had given the PLO a small office in the basement of their Mayfair building. Said came with his Syrian wife and two children and immediately became friends with many influential people, doing more to improve English-Palestinian relations than any man before or since. He spoke persuasively for an independent state in the West Bank and Gaza, never sparing criticism for the Jordanian and Syrian governments, and although he worked for peace, he never verbally attacked those who preached armed struggle as long as they struggled against Israel.

Arafat assigned him the task of meeting Israelis and telling them privately that the PLO was ready to accept a mini-state and would end their war with Israel and recognize it. Hammami openly made contact with peace activist Uri Avnery and wrote op-ed pieces in London newspapers calling for negotiation and the rights of Palestinians. In 1975 he was interviewed by Moshe Machover for *Matzpen*. In late 1977 British authorities warned Hammami that his life was in danger, but they gave him no protection. They also told the Israeli embassy, who they knew wanted to get rid of him, not to do anything against Hammami.[2] Thus if the Mossad wanted to kill Hammami—and it would be an easy kill since Hammami had no more protection than any other nine-to-five man—they could not get caught doing it. The FRC took on the task, their first Palestinian assassination.

Right after the 1978 New Year an Arab with a Palestinian accent called Hammami and made an appointment to see him that same day. The caller came to his office, took out a gun and shot Hammami three times, killing him instantly. The gunman ran off on foot, unsuccessfully pursued by Palestinian students who happened to be in the office. The killing happened shortly after the introduction of a Middle East peace initiative.[3] Abu Nidal loudly boasted responsibility for the action, claiming that he had helped the Palestinian cause.

The killing of Hammami was FRC's first direct attack against the PLO. FRC had previously confined their terrorism to other Arabs and Europeans; now they hit one of the PLO's best people, the same genre of people that the Mossad killed during their 1972-73 assassination spree. Once again, effective Palestinian leaders, conciliatory, intelligent, and unguarded, became targets.

In June 1976 the PLO helped the United States evacuate 263 Westerners from Beirut, and President Gerald Ford publicly expressed his gratitude, an unusual acknowledgment.[4] About the same time, the PLO warned its CIA contacts about a plan to shoot down Henry Kissinger's plane over the Bakaa Valley, and Kissinger's security people changed their plans. Ali Hassan Salameh, the PLO leader directing this close cooperation with the United States, was the person the Mossad had been targeting in Lillehammer when they killed the wrong man. Salameh was the brains behind Munich. A flamboyant man with an I.Q. of 180, he was educated in the Sorbonne. He came from a distinguished Palestinian family (his father was killed during the

1948 war) and married a Lebanese Christian, Georgina Rizk, who had been chosen Miss Universe the year before Munich.[5] His contacts with both the CIA and Lebanese Christian rulers (including the ruling Gemayel family) were tight. Israel was trying to form an alliance with the Christians against the PLO, and a close relation with the CIA was exclusively Israel's territory. The Mossad failed in their attempt on Salameh's life in 1973, but in the late 1970s there arose a renewed desire to kill him. Did this desire stem from the need to settle the account on Munich, or was it inspired by his successful building of bridges? Probably both.

According to *Time*, Israel used 14 agents, including some of the same people involved in Lillehammer, to kill Salameh. Some came into Beirut with Canadian and British passports.[6] Silvia Rafael, using the name Erika Mary Chambers, took an apartment across from Salameh's, pretending to be an English painter who sketched scenes outside her window. In another PLO security blunder, no one spotted her even though her picture had been all over the newspapers during her highly visible trial in Norway. Furthermore, Salameh did nothing after the Lebanese leadership tipped him off that Israel had a squad ready for him. Salameh, unlike the other leaders the Israelis assassinated, was well guarded.

After Chambers knew Salameh's habits, the agents rented a Volkswagen and parked it on a street around the corner from his house, less than 100 meters from the apartment building that Israeli soldiers had raided six years before, killing three Palestinian leaders.

When Salameh's car passed the Volkswagen, Chambers pressed the remote button on the powerful bomb. Salameh and his four aides who were also in the car died, as did a German nun, an English student, and four other passersby, while at least eighteen more were injured. The Israeli agents escaped the country. Israel had their revenge against the Munich organizer, but they also destroyed an important link between Lebanese, Palestinians, and the United States. As with the assassinations in Beirut in 1973, over 50,000 Lebanese and Palestinians attended the funeral. From the Maronite section of Beirut the Falangists fired a salute in his honor.[7] Hermann Eilts, former United States ambassador to Egypt and Saudi Arabia, told the *Wall Street Journal*, "[Salameh] was extraordinarily helpful—as was Fatah—in assisting in security for American citizens and officials. I regard his assassination as a loss."[8]

Zuhair Mohsin loved a fine cigar, a dark, fat Havana. Imitations would not do. He could smell an imitation before someone offered him one. After dinner he would sink into a plush sofa, ritualistically pull a cigar out of his breast pocket, take it out of its protective tin, and light it up with such delight as to make everyone in the room envious. He loved good clothes with the same relish, and good drink, and the most beautiful women.

When Hafez al-Asad struggled for power during a 1970 Syrian Baath party split, Mohsin vigorously took his side. After Asad's coup succeeded, Mohsin anxiously expected his reward. Asad asked what he wanted; Mohsin said Saika.

Zuhair Mohsin came from a lower-class Palestinian family—he was always conscious of that fact—but in the early 1970s he saw a possibility of fulfilling his dream, enhancing his ego, being a gentleman, living the high life. Since his childhood he had known he was destined to be a leader. In Kuwait in the late 1960s his friends used to call him *malek*, "the king," and he went to Syria and elbowed his way to Asad's side. Despite his arrogance and his physical appetite, Mohsin remained dignified, courteous, and eloquent. Since that time Saika ("thunderbolt"), created in December 1968, had been part of Asad's regime. Before Mohsin took his rightful place, Saika had limited autonomy. All Syrian males serve in the army; the Palestinians, who had separate identity cards, were usually required to serve in what was euphemistically called the Palestine Liberation Army or one of the Palestinian factions. The PLA is controlled directly by Syrian officers or by Palestinians who have shown their complete loyalty to the ruling regime.

In the Palestinian refugee camps only those parties as well as the PFLP and DFLP had offices; Fatah was officially banned. The government treated Palestinians with suspicion, often arresting and torturing activists who did not openly profess the party line and display Asad's photo. Although the PFLP and DFLP kept their headquarters in Damascus, they had strong differences with the government, and many of their people have been jailed. The DFLP and PFLP, as well as the FRC when it was there, received no help from the government but remained in Damascus because their alternatives were less desirable.

The Syrian factions—Saika, Ahmed Jabril, and later Abu Musa—had little support from the Palestinians and did not exist outside Syria. Inside that country, they had use of Syrian military bases, were given guns and money, and enjoyed a political status in the government. When Asad gave Mohsin Saika, he put 7,000 men under Mohsin's command,[9] and in 1976 the group joined Syrian forces in attacking Palestinian positions in Lebanon. Although Mohsin was beholden to Syria, his charisma and organizational talent made Saika a potent force.

Saika attacked Israel in the early 1970s and participated in international terrorism. A few days before the Yom Kippur War, two of Mohsin's men kidnapped three Soviet Jews on a train out of the Soviet Union. They demanded that Austria not be a transit point for groups of Soviet Jews going to Israel. Chancellor Kreisky gave in, saying that he made the decision with a heavy heart. Austria had been a key reception center for Soviet Jews, 60,000 having been processed in the previous two years. Golda Meir went to Austria to plead with Kreisky, but he had already committed himself.[10] The attack helped distract Israel while Syria and Egypt prepared for war.

In the summer of 1979 Mohsin was spending time on the Côte d'Azur, living in a most luxurious apartment in the Gray d'Abion. In order to pay for his high life, he managed finances in a suspect fashion, and his organization was corrupt. Shortly after heading a Palestinian delegation of African unity in Liberia, traveling first class on his Chilean passport, he came home after a late night and rang his bell. A gunman who had been hiding in the stairway came out and shot him three times. When his wife opened the door, Mohsin was lying in his blood on the doormat.[11]

Zuhair Mohsin, head of Siaka, killed in Cannes in 1979.

The killing was no doubt related to the seizure of the Egyptian embassy in Turkey 11 days before. The gunmen, using the name Eagles of the Revolution (a disguise for Saika), had demanded that Turkey break off relations with Egypt for signing the Camp David accords and open a PLO office. Prime Minister Bulent Ecevit conceded to opening the PLO office, quickly denying that he was making concessions to terrorists. The Palestinians had killed two Turkish guards while storming the embassy, and one Egyptian diplomat had leaped out, slipped, or was thrown out of a window to his death.[12] Since Saika was controlled by Syria, which also felt threatened by Camp David, Syria received unofficial blame. The Egyptians blamed Mohsin, who had been maligning Egypt, and promised reprisal. When Sadat landed in Jerusalem, Mohsin had declared him an enemy and exclaimed, "Spill the traitor's blood, spit in his face." Despite his acid statements, however, Mohsin was practical and wanted territorial compromise with Israel. Right before his death he said, "It is nonsense to talk about a secular state when we do not possess a single inch of our territory. The time has come to be practical and realistic."[13]

Syria and the PLO, ever enemies, had been making attempts to cooperate against Camp David, and Mohsin had been an important ingredient in the reconciliation since he had good relations with both parties. After Mohsin's assassination, Saika continued to function, but they became more militant, and like the rest of the Syrian groups, Saika became anti–PLO after the 1982 invasion of Lebanon. Mohsin's brother, Majeed, who was appointed by the PLO to investigate the killing of his brother, came to no conclusion, although the PLO blamed Israel as they always do. Israel had wanted to end Mohsin's life since he was responsible for successful raids against them, but so had the Egyptians. It seems that an Egyptian followed Mohsin from Liberia and tipped off the Mossad on his whereabouts. They sent two assassins, one Arab and the other European, but it remains an unsolved case.[14]

Three months after Sadat returned from Jerusalem, Yusef Sebai, the editor of *Al-Ahram* newspaper and a close friend of Sadat, went to Cyprus for a meeting of the Afro-Asian Solidarity Committee of which he was the general secretary. *Al-Ahram* is an arm of government information, and its editor is always a respected and influential man. Sadat had taken *al-Ahram's* Sebai with him to Jerusalem. Abu Nidal said that was when he decided to kill Sebai.

As Sebai was coming out of the Hilton Hotel in Nicosia, two cars rushed up, and armed men from the FRC, Samir Khadar and Zayeed Hussein Ahmed Ali, ran out and shot him at close range in front of the hotel. Unlike most gunmen who know little about the workings of their organization, Samir Khadar (that is actually his brother's name, his real name being Sameeh Khadar, while his name in the organization was Zuhair Arabá), was a member of FRC's Revolutionary Council, indicating that Abu Nidal placed a lot of importance on the success of this action. This and the June 1982 London attack were the only times the group used such a high-ranking member for an outside operation. Another FRC member, Reyad Samir al-Ahad, played a back-up role. The gunmen, armed with automatic pistols and grenades, then rushed into the hotel and collected about 30 hostages, demanding that Cyprus give them a plane out of the country. The police struck a deal, giving them a plane with a crew in exchange for the release of most hostages. Four PLO officials offered themselves as hostages and were taken aboard the plane.

Khadar, Zayeed, and their captives were put on the Cyprus Airlines plane, but after flying to neighboring Arab countries they discovered no one ready to accept them. Even though Arab leaders had cut off Egypt, they were not enemies of Sebai and did not want to become implicated in terrorism. The plane finally landed in Djibouti, but the gunmen had no where to go from there.[15] Khadar and Zayeed then told the pilot to return to Cyprus, where they hoped to negotiate another accommodation using their dozen hostages. Before killing Sabai the terrorists had had a good time in Cyprus, developing a fondness for the country. For three nights they went out to party in bazouki clubs. On the last day the planner of the operation, Mustafa Firas, gave Khadar instructions, then left for Beirut and later Baghdad. The gunmen suddenly became sad that their happy time would come to an end.

The assassination infuriated Egyptians, not only Sadat and the government but also the people in the streets. When Sadat discovered that the plane had returned to Cyprus, he ordered a planeload of commandos to storm it. The Cypriots discovered Egypt's plan and ordered their National Guard to surround and protect their plane, and the Egyptians found themselves having to fight not the Palestinian killers but Cypriot soldiers. In an intense battle initiated by the Egyptians, the Cypriots overpowered the attackers, killing 15 Egyptian soldiers and wounding over 100.[16] This created a sizable row between Cyprus and Egypt, one of Sadat's most irresponsible actions, and he took it out on the PLO even though the attackers called the PLO a puppet organization. Egyptian newspapers showed Arafat dripping in blood.[17] Anti-Palestinian rioting erupted in the streets of Cairo during Sebai's funeral.[18] Egypt restricted the rights of the 40,000 Palestinians in the country and almost broke relations with the PLO.[19]

Both killers were given life prison sentences, but in 1982 the FRC managed to free them. Ahmed Ali, an Iraqi recruited by the FRC, returned to Iraq and continued working for the organization, while Khadar developed into one of the group's outside operations organizers, helping with the attacks on the Rome and Vienna airports in 1985. Two months later the Egyptian government announced that they had infiltrated and uncovered a FRC cell that was getting ready to kill government leaders and foreigners. They arrested 15 people but produced no tangible proof—Abu Nidal had only sleepers in Egypt. The arrests were no doubt an attempt to justify Egypt's behavior in Cyprus.[20]

The killing of Sebai and the subsequent fight between Cypriots and Egyptians made front page news throughout the Arab world, giving Abu Nidal abundant publicity; his name, for the first time, became recognized.

In the early 1970s the Israelis recruited a Palestinian student in the West Bank named Adnan al-Rashid. The Israelis promised to give him a *towjehi*, or graduation certificate, with a 91 percent average on the condition that he apply to study at Baghdad University, considered a good and strict school that requires a high *towjehi* average for admission. Palestinians were awarded special status to attend Baghdad University, but students usually needed a recommendation. Buying collaborators with a good *towjehi* remained a prime method of recruitment.

They arranged for him to go to Baghdad, and Abu Nidal, then still with Fatah, provided the necessary recommendation. Israel asked almost nothing of Rashid, only that he stay with Abu Nidal's men. The Israelis could at any time blackmail Rashid by threatening to expose him as a traitor who received his *towjehi* from the enemy. There was no need for this. Rashid went to school and was later trained in Abu Nidal's camp, toward which he had no particularly positive feeling, and given trips to Cyprus, where Israeli agents would talk to him. In 1981 he was given an assignment, not by Abu Nidal but by the Mossad. He was going to be sent to Brussels and have a nice time. Nothing would be required of him.

He went to Brussels and took a taxi to a furnished apartment provided by the Mossad. They gave him money and brought him at least one light-skinned prostitute, telling him again to have a good time. On the first of June, in the evening, he was put in a car, given a gun, and told to kill a particular traitor. The Israelis did almost everything for him, dropping him off and picking him up. He simply had to walk up to the traitor while the traitor was on his way to work, pump him with bullets, and run off—which is what he did, throwing off his raincoat and umbrella before being carried away by his get-away car, which had parked well enough away to make sure that if Rashid got caught, the Mossad would not be involved. Although Rashid was the gunman, his role in the killing was secondary, but if anything went wrong, he would be blamed. The Mossad took care of every preparation detail. Rashid quietly slipped out of the country, eventually settling in Libya. Right after the killing, Abu Nidal proudly declared that he had killed Naim Khader, traitor to his own people, and it is widely accepted that Khader was killed by the FRC.

Khader fit the mold. A Palestinian who understood the West—he had lived in Belgium since before the 1967 war and married a Belgium woman—he became friends with journalists and government officials. Khader was a Palestinian Christian from a small town near Jenin on the northern part of the West Bank. He grew up among a family of priests, but he went into politics, taking his Ph.D. from the University of Louvain. As the *Jerusalem Post* declared, "Khader played an important role in winning European support for the Palestinian cause,"[21] and an Italian newspaper adds that with his death the PLO lost one of its most valuable diplomats.[22]

In early 1981 the leftist Khader met Arafat in Beirut to try again to start negotiations with Israel, and he was shot just after he made an appointment with prominent Israelis.[23] Three months before Rashid's encounter Khader had met Israelis from the left-wing Rakah party, including attorney Felicia Langer. A photo of the meeting was published in the Lebanese English weekly *Monday Morning*, not the type of literature that sits on FRC desks. Khader also produced a book coauthored by an Israeli.[24]

As PLO representative, Khadar effectively lobbied the European Community for Palestinian rights. After the killing the Israeli embassy in Brussels said that it was probably another Palestinian faction that killed Khader, while Prime Minister Begin declared that he never heard of Khader, which seems unlikely given Khader's good standing with liberal Israelis and government leaders, including his close personal friendship with Claude Cheysson. For people like Begin, Khader was the personification of evil.

The Mossad struck on its own in Rome several months later, killing the PLO's minister of information, Majeed Abu Sharara, who had come to town to attend a conference of sympathetic journalists. The Mossad planted a powerful bomb under his bed which blew away his body when he came home at

Left: **Naim Khader, noted PLO dove, killed in Brussels June 1981;** *right:* **Majeed Abu Sharara, head of PLO information, killed in Rome October 1981.**

night. FRC was not involved, but callers to Reuters and UPI in Beirut and Rome claimed that it was *al-Assifa,* stating that Sharara represented the "line of surrender."[25] The killing resembles other assassinations. Abu Sharara, a member of the PLO's Central Committee, worked with Naim Khader on drumming up European support for the Palestinians. As an Italian newspaper said on Abu Sharara's death, Menachem Begin had more than once threatened the Palestinian intellectuals in order to stamp out all signs of Palestinian culture.[26]

The day before his death, Abu Sharara met leaders of both major left Italian parties. Abu Sharara was himself a leftist, but he was anxious to see an independent Palestinian state on any amount of territory they could get. In a Palestinian seminar about the West Bank and Gaza held just prior to his death, Abu Sharara eloquently argued that the PLO should establish an office specifically for the occupied territories, stressing their political individuality in order to fight what he called the schemes of Camp David and the Jordanian regime. Other people argued that Palestinians living inside and outside Palestine should be united, not separated.[27] In March 1974 he and Khalid Hassan had a secret meeting in Morocco with United States representative Vernon Walters, who passed on Kissinger's negative wishes.[28] Although Abu Sharara spoke for peace and negotiation, he publicly applauded the killing of

Sadat and never spoke against the violence. He took precautions, traveling under a false name and passport and carrying a .38 revolver.

In the summer of 1978 a lone FRC gunman assassinated the PLO representative in Kuwait, Ali Nasser Yassine. The gunman arrived at Yassine's door, rang the bell, and shot him when he answered the door. Yassine was a Palestinian success story, almost a legend. A slightly shy person, honest and upright, he acted as a conduit between the quarter of a million Palestinians living in Kuwait and the Kuwaiti government. Yassine, who moved to Kuwait in 1965, became an effective and admired leader. He helped negotiate during Abu Nidal's first attack on the Saudi embassy in Paris. At his funeral 70,000 Palestinians and Kuwaitis braved the summer heat and walked more than 25 kilometers to the cemetery. Once there the emotion of the crowd overtook them. The people took his body and passed it around, and it took over half an hour for the family to get it back and put it in the tomb. Instead of their usual accusations against Israel, the PLO openly blamed the Iraqi secret police, calling Abu Nidal their tool and promising that the killing would be avenged.[29]

It was. Next month Palestinian gunmen raided the Iraqi embassy in Paris. The PLO leadership publicly denied that they had any knowledge of this, which is possible, for the tenor of the attack was not in keeping with the PLO's style. Two gunmen were selected for the raid, but one of them apparently lost his nerve and ran out of the building soon after they entered, throwing his gun on the sidewalk outside and taking to his heels. The other Palestinian shot his way into the first floor and took eight hostages; then he surrendered to the police, who came in and convinced him to give up. The French police escorted him out, but anger overtook some of the Iraqis, who wanted him as their prisoner, arguing that the embassy was Iraq's sovereign property.

Iraqi security people ambushed the Palestinian as he was being led away. The police, considering him their prisoner, shot back, killing one Iraqi and wounding another. As well as shooting the Palestinian, the Iraqis also shot a French police inspector.[30] Although 200 police staged another demonstration outside their police headquarters, the Iraqis pleaded diplomatic immunity, and the French government stood powerless.[31] The incident strained relations between Paris and Baghdad, but it also brought the Iraq-PLO war into the open.

Using the FRC, Iraq quickly sought revenge for the raid, first assassinating another valuable Palestinian, Dr. Izz al-Din Qalak, the PLO representative in Paris. Qalak was a genius—a nuclear physicist, short-story writer, painter, actor, and statesman with excellent relations with the press and French officials, one of the most westernized Palestinians. He was one of 13 people in the world at the time who had a degree in his specialized area of physics, an amazing man whom it is difficult to praise enough.

Two gunmen shot their way into the PLO office located in the Arab

League on Boulevard Houssman where both Qalak and Adnan Hamid, a correspondent for the PLO news service WAFA, were working. They shot Qalak and threw a grenade which ripped off Hamid's legs. He died shortly after in the hospital. The gunmen, Hatem Abd al-Kadir and Kaid Hussein, were trapped by police and gave themselves up. They had been recruited in Amman, Jordan, and joined Abu Nidal's FRC a short time before the attack.[32] PLO leaders thought—still think—that the matter was an Iraq-PLO dispute. The gunmen went to prison but were released and rejoined the FRC in Sidon, Lebanon.

Two days later four FRC fighters stormed the PLO office in Islamabad, killing the Pak-istani policeman outside and

Izz al-Din Qalaq, Palestinian nuclear physi-cist, killed in Paris August 1978.

three PLO clerks in the front office, firing 30 to 40 shots. They kept shout-ing the name of the PLO representative, Yousef Abu Hantash, but he was able to hide. The gunmen were distracted by 15 Pakistani students who happened to be inside, and after about five minutes of running around shouting for Abu Hantash, they ran out of the building. Abu Hantash claims that the gunmen spoke with an Iraqi accent.[33]

The PLO Executive Committee then sent an emergency delegation to Iraq to end the conflict. Both sides quickly agreed to stop killing and raiding embassies—an agreement that seemed to stem from FRC's autonomous actions—and Abu Nidal stopped attacking the PLO for a while. Soon after, Saddam Hussein took power. He sat down with the PLO, telling them that he did not believe in their platform, but since he had no alternative to offer, he would not interfere with their activities. Saddam remained frank with the PLO, and although he never helped them, he stopped hurting, until he invaded Kuwait. In the four years before the Israeli invasion of Lebanon, Abu Nidal is credited with killing nine PLO leaders.

Chapter 12
Death to the Jews

Since 1974 two Middle East performers dabbled in international terrorism: Abu Nidal and the Mossad. On May 20, 1978, FRC struck Paris's Orly airport. Three gunmen walked into the terminal, approached the El Al desk, and began firing. El Al security men took out their weapons and returned the fire, stopping the gunmen from throwing their grenades. Three waiting passengers and one policeman were killed, and several others seriously injured, though the policeman may have been killed by an El Al bullet. The flight the gunmen attacked was not for Israelis but for 150 French insurance employees who were awarded a vacation in Israel for their labors. The terrorists missed Israeli ambassador Mordechai Gazit and labor minister Israel Katz, who had gotten off the incoming flight and were in another part of the airport at the time of the shooting.[1]

Paris airport had been the scene of other malicious stupidities in January 1975 when Carlos's group went to a public terrace with an RPG and, supposedly aiming for an El Al flight to New York, hit a Yugoslavian DC9. They came back to the same spot a week later and dropped grenades into a crowded passenger lounge, wounding 30, then took hostages into a toilet and negotiated for a plane, passing notes under the door.[2]

This was followed by an April 1979 FRC airport attack in Brussels demonstrating a similar proportion of malicious incompetence. Four Arab gunmen attacked the El Al counter. They arrived late; the plane had finished loading. Not knowing that, the Arabs threw a couple of grenades and wounded ten Belgians—no Israelis, not even the El Al security people who had stayed behind to shoot back at the Arabs. The terror group named itself Black March, after the month of Camp David, the first and last time Abu Nidal used that name.[3]

Toward the end of 1979 Arabs attacked the Israeli ambassador in Portugal as he was arriving from work. Abu Nidal claims the action was his, but that seems doubtful. There are mixed reports on how it happened: either a lone gunman stood next to the Israeli embassy, or a passing car drove up and started shooting. A Portuguese bodyguard, the only person apparently alert enough to know what was happening, drew his gun but was killed by the attackers. Three other people were wounded in the attack: the policeman guarding the building, the driver, and a woman who was walking on the sidewalk at the time. Although it was a simple operation and he missed his target, the gunman seemed to act professionally and escaped.[4]

The Israeli embassy in Lisbon was new. Portugal only recognized Israel in 1977, and Efraim Eldar was dispatched as ambassador. This was the second attempt on his life; a gunman tried to shoot him just after he arrived, giving rise to speculation that both attempts on his life were planned and executed locally. The second attack would probably not have happened had it not been for a five-day conference in support of the Palestinian people that had taken place in Lisbon the week before, featuring a speech by Arafat, who also hoped to open an office in Lisbon. Shimon Peres, who was in Lisbon a week before the conference to attend a socialist meeting, complained that Portugal had awarded Arafat a "royal reception." After the attack on the ambassador, Peres was able to tell the Portuguese that they "learned the real nature of the PLO" and ask Portugal to ban the PLO.[5] A caller to the Portuguese national radio claimed that the Militant International Workers group was responsible, confirming that FRC was not involved.[6]

The intelligence department of FRC is responsible for assassins and for hiding and transferring arms. Those responsible for the weapons have no idea what they will be used for—most times they are not touched—and they may not know the killers even if they bumped into them on the street. The intelligence department gives a map to the supervisor of an outside operation unit (first passing the map through the administration department). The map points out where the weapons are located. Administration gives the supervisor a detailed plan for the assassination or bombing and a picture of the victim. Weapons are stored in main and secondary sites. The main sites contain major weapons, while the secondary ones have perhaps a few Kalashnikovs, pistols, and fragmentation grenades. They use an array of hiding places, from caves in forests to closets in apartments. After the weapons are taken the storage location is often changed. Although the gunmen fumble, the system established by FRC is tight and deliberate.

Like those who store the arms, gunmen have a specific job and have little idea of the group's other activities. Gunmen think they will die as martyrs, or that the group will protect them from harm. Often they feel they are involved in something they cannot get out of. The supervisor gives the liaison all the instructions, and the liaison collects the weapons and instructs the group leader. The other members of the group, if any, never meet the liaison, who flies out of town before the action. Often the supervisor stays, but the gunmen would have no idea who he is even if the police brought him in front of them.

When the FRC strikes at Arabs, they are usually deadly accurate; when they aim for Jews, it usually becomes a fiasco. A few months after the Lisbon action an Abu Nidal gunman killed a Spanish lawyer in Madrid, the father of nine children, mistaking him for a respected leader of the local Jewish community. The two men did not look alike, but they lived in the same building. It was another in a steady series of blunders during the blundering war.

This unfortunate incident happened early in the morning in March 1980 when the lawyer, Adolfo Cotelo, was driving two of his daughters to school. As he was stopped at a red light, a young Palestinian named Said Salman, equipped with a machine gun and grenade, attacked the car, killing the man and injuring one of his daughters. He then ran down the street with his machine gun until the police leapt on top of him and disarmed him. In his pocket was a fake passport from Oman and a picture of the man he was supposed to kill, Max Mazin, head of the local B'nai B'rith.[7] Nothing could have given the Palestinians worse publicity. The incident occurred as Spain was trying to join the European Community. Spain did not officially recognize Israel, and the European Community wanted Spain to change its pro–Palestinian policy in order to bring its foreign policy in line with the other member nations. Israel blamed the PLO for the incident.

Madrid had become known as a main recruiting center for both the FRC and the Mossad in January 1973 when the PLO lured Mossad recruiter Baruch Cohen to a Madrid cafe and killed him.[8] Both organizations were able to operate quite freely, recruiting Palestinian and North African students who were having difficulties. However, the assassin for this operation was flown in from Baghdad two weeks before, ready to follow instructions from his liaison.

In the middle of the year, there was another attack by an FRC Palestinian on an Orthodox Jewish school. The terrorist, Said Nasser, who traveled to Belgium on a fake Moroccan passport, went to the school and threw two grenades at the children as they were preparing to go on a day tour. He killed a 15-year-old boy and injured 13 others, then took to his heels, running into a police patrol.[9] Nasser claimed he was acting on his own, but he had been given his instructions by Mustafa Murad and had an accomplice named Nihad Declas. Someone called a newspaper and said that it was an action of the PFLP. Some terrorism experts believed that Nasser did act on his own, but individuals cannot obtain grenades in a foreign country, know the location of their targets from abroad, and buy fake passports. His FRC handler gave him his weapon and his instructions.

Besides creating a climate of anti–Semitism, this action seemed timed to stop the European Community's recognition of the PLO. The European Community was scheduled to consider recognition, and it seemed no coincidence that such a repulsive attack against children took place close to where the delegation was about to meet.[10] The message to the delegates was clear: no matter how sincere the PLO's promise about negotiating with Israel, the leadership does not have control over its people and cannot prevent the continued use of terrorism. The European Community failed to recognize the PLO.

In the next couple of years the FRC attacked other Jewish targets in Europe, stirring up anti–Semitism and showing the Palestinians as uncivilized and cruel, the neo–Nazis. On May Day, 1981, the FRC struck in Vienna, killing the head of the Israel-Austria Friendship League, Heinz Nittal. The murder occurred in the morning as he left his house and went to his car. By coincidence the attack was similar to a scene in a movie that had been shown on television the night before, but although the three FRC killers had received their instructions only an hour before the killing, the assassination was planned well in advance. Following the usual procedure, the three arrived separately in Vienna. Each knew only one other person, the contact or liaison, who had woken them up just before the attack and had given them a machine gun and their instructions, then left the city. The actual killer was a Palestinian who was recruited in Iraq. He and his two helpers got away, but he was captured during another attack and confessed to being Nittal's killer.[11] FRC, using the name *al-Assifa*, took responsibility.

Nittal, a leftist and a respected member of the city council, was a Zionist Jew, unlike Chancellor Dr. Bruno Kreisky who was a non–Zionist Jew, but both were sympathetic to Palestinians. Kreisky's Socialist party canceled its May Day celebrations in honor of Nittal, who had been party secretary.[12] Austria had a history of sympathy with the Palestinians, and these attacks had the effect of dampening their support. The FRC operates most frequently in countries that are not strong supporters of Israel—Spain, Italy, Austria, Greece, Cyprus—and works less or not at all among Israel's strong supporters, the United States, Britain, and the Scandinavian countries.

A few months after the killing of Nittal, *al-Assifa* again struck at Jews in Austria. Three Palestinians, one born in Baghdad and the others from Nablus, were separately given Polish machine guns and fragmentation bombs one Saturday morning by their liaison, then told to meet in front of the central Viennese synagogue. The three had not seen each other before, only identifying each other by a red rose that one wore and a green safari cap the other wore. They then produced skull caps and were about to enter the synagogue when two policemen were struck by their suspicious nature and asked them to stop. The police had stationed a car there since an anti–Semite had thrown an unexploded bomb. The terrorists took out their guns and started shooting, killing two pedestrians. They lobbed a fragmentation grenade at the synagogue where worshipers had gathered for a Bar Mitzvah. One of the businessmen attending the service had an armed bodyguard who ran out and wounded one of the Arabs. The other two were both arrested, and the one from Iraq confessed that he had also killed Nittal.[13]

This incident aggravated the bad feeling resulting from a PLO diplomatic blunder of two months before when Gazi Hussein, a member of Saika, was caught at the airport with another Palestinian smuggling guns into Austria. Hussein worked for Syria, who wanted either to scare or to kill Sadat for Camp David. Sadat canceled his visit, but since Hussein was also part of the PLO delegation (Saika was part of the PLO until 1982), the incident implicated the entire PLO mission, and Kreisky asked them not to open another office in Vienna.[14] According to Ostrovsky, Hussein was set up by the Mossad, who sold him weapons and then told the Austrian police.[15] Israel had been turning up the diplomatic heat on Austria for its support of the PLO, and they cited the attack on the synagogue as further proof of Arab terrorism, saying also that the attack violated the ceasefire across the Lebanese border established two months prior. But Kreisky retorted, "The implacable policy of the Israelis toward the Palestinians is to blame for the excess."[16]

The next spate of attacks against European Jews took place after the 1982 Lebanon invasion, when many Europeans, including Jews, were horrified by the carnage meted out by the invading army. It was difficult for even an ardent Israeli supporter to see the invasion upholding the Israeli principle of purity of arms. As Israel's army was surrounding Beirut, the FRC attacked a restaurant in a Jewish neighborhood of Paris near the Bastille. Two Arabs came walking up the street, apparently looking for an ideal store to attack. It was midday on Monday, when most of the shops were closed. Finally, the two terrorists settled on Jo Goldenberg's restaurant, throwing two grenades and then spraying it with bullets. Before a car came up and drove them away, they killed six and wounded twenty-one. The Jewish community instantly rallied, marching down the street chanting, "Death to the Arabs."

The attack received relatively little media attention, the newspapers filling their front pages with stories from the war in Lebanon;[17] however, it helped force a change in France's internal policy. In 1981 France had offered amnesty to 2000 political prisoners, including Jean-Marc Rouillan and Nathalie Menigon, the militant leaders of Action Directe. Following the attack on the restaurant the liberal minister of public security was sacked and replaced by law-and-order advocate Joseph Franceschi, who seized on the restaurant incident to declare groups such as Action Directe illegal.

Five weeks later, as news of the massacres at the Palestinian refugee camps of Sabra and Chitila were beginning to come over the wires, a synagogue in Brussels was attacked by an FRC youth with a machine gun,[18] and three weeks later there was a massive FRC attack against the large synagogue in Rome. Although the invasion dramatically and permanently harmed Israel's image in Europe, these FRC attacks helped soften the blow.

For the Rome operation FRC used the name Martyrs of Palestine—so said a note found in the pocket of one of the five terrorists. Unlike the other attacks, this one was well planned. The attack on the old and impressive synagogue on the banks of the Tiber River came just after the service began to remember the flight of the Jews from Egypt. The attackers dressed in elegant suits; two came in the back door with Polish-made machine guns, and two walked in the side entrance with grenades. The leader of the group, Abd al-Osama al-Zomar, began the shooting. The attackers lobbed their grenades and unloaded their magazines, then fled down the small side streets into two awaiting cars.[19]

Zomar, age 21, had been an engineering student at Bari in the South of Italy. He confessed to a girlfriend that he was going to attack the synagogue before leaving his studies. Abu Nidal always warned his cadres to keep gunmen away from women before the attack, but Zomar had been living in the country where the attack took place, unlike the usual FRC gunmen who are flown into the country just before the kill. After the synagogue attack Zomar's girlfriend told the authorities about him, and the court in Rome handed him a life sentence *in absentia*.

A month later Greek police arrested Zomar crossing the Greek-Turkish border, allegedly with weapons and 60 kilos of explosives. Italy immediately requested extradition, and the Greek Supreme Court upheld the extradition request—to the dismay of Italy, which now had to deal with Zomar. Italy would not have minded if the Greeks had found a way to get rid of Zomar, which they eventually did. After a government reshuffle, the new minister of justice, Vassilis Rotis, overturned the extradition request, saying that Zomar acted legitimately in his "struggle to regain the independence of his homeland." Rotis could not have made such a decision without the approval of the prime minister, Andreas Papandreaou, and Papandreaou may have consulted the Italians beforehand. After that decision the Italians issued a statement of regret.[20] Zomar stayed in Greek prisons for a couple of years, and on his release he returned to the FRC, leaving the organization during the 1989 split.

We should mention here two legendary hijacks planned by Wadi Haddad where commandos were effective in ending the ordeal. Haddad had to turn to the German Baader-Meinhoff group, who had already been involved in the kidnapping and killing of important businessmen. In June 1976 a mixture of Palestinians and Germans hijacked an Air France jet and brought it to Uganda's Entebbe airport, and the Israelis landed two planeloads of commandos who stormed the lounge, killed the gunmen, and rescued the passengers, bringing tremendous respect for the Israeli rescue squad. There has been so much written about the raid that it is difficult to get the facts straight, but it seems that a couple of passengers were killed and at least four Israelis and about 20 Ugandan soldiers also died, and a few Ugandan planes were bombed.[21] On New Year's Eve 1980 a hotel in Nairobi, Kenya, was blown up, killing 16 people. The attack was said to be revenge for Entebbe; the hotel was allegedly owned by an Israeli, and Kenya aided the rescue.[22]

Haddad's final hijacking took place a year later, again using Palestinians and Baader-Meinhoff members, whose leaders had all been arrested. They hijacked a Lufthansa jet and traveled thousands of miles, finally settling in

Mogadishu. A team of German commandos stormed the plane using stunt grenades, a new British product that produces a loud bang and flash but no shrapnel, immobilizing people for a few seconds. The commandos killed the gunmen and harmed no passenger, finishing Haddad's career.

Chapter 13
Lebanon War

We are now suffering the evils of a long peace.
                                        Juvenal, second century

After shuttle diplomacy between Damascus, Jerusalem, and Beirut, United States undersecretary of state Philip Habib concluded a ceasefire across the Lebanon border between Israel and the PLO. Habib could not talk to the PLO directly because of Kissinger's directive, so he used a Saudi member of the royal family as mediator. The agreement was oral—nothing could be written down since Israel and the PLO did not recognize each other and refused to negotiate with each other—but they came up with a truce: the PLO promised not to attack Israel, and Israel would not attack Lebanon. Prime Minister Begin wanted to include in the agreement attacks on Jews anywhere in the world, but Habib rejected that outright, and the ceasefire went into effect on July 24, 1981.[1] It was the closest to negotiations that Israel and the PLO had come to date. Thus the border between Lebanon and Israel suddenly stabilized after over a decade of routine bombing. This agreement was a bargain for both parties following intense Israeli bombing in which tens of thousands of Palestinians and Lebanese fled north to Beirut. On July 17 Israel had bombed PLO offices in a densely populated area, killing 300 and wounding 800.[2] The PLO had opened up their artillery and fired Katyusha rockets into Israel, forcing civilians to abandon northern settlements. Cross-border attacks were no longer restricted to a pair of Palestinian guerrillas trying to cross the two high electric fences and raiding a settlement. After the Palestinians brought all their militias under a unified command in 1980 they had a strong military presence which Israel had been regularly bombing. The PLO had been thrown out of Jordan, was distrusted by Syria, and had been eliminated by Egypt's Camp David treaty; now Lebanon was the PLO's only base, and as such it had become Israel's revenge steam valve. When the United Nations General Assembly gratuitously equated Zionism with racism in 1975, Israel's response was to bomb the camps, killing 107 and wounding 175.[3]

In an earlier chapter we touched on Israel's fueling the Lebanese civil war through a dirty tricks campaign. They provided opposing militias with weapons, and from the tops of buildings agents disguised as militias would fire rockets at opposing areas in order to provoke a response and violate a ceasefire. Between 1968 and 1974 there were 44 major Israeli attacks on Lebanon, resulting in the death of about 880 Lebanese and Palestinian civilians.[4] On March 11, 1978, eight Fatah commandos, led by woman named Dalal Moghrabi who worked with Abu Jihad, landed two rubber dinghies in North Israel and hijacked two busses. The Israeli army stormed the busses, leaving thirty-five passengers and six guerrillas dead[5]; then they occupied South Lebanon in an operation called Stone of Wisdom. CIA chief James Angleton told a friend, "The operation was being used as a cover to build an underground channel that would divert the waters of the Latani River into the parched Jewish State."[6]

Time estimates that Stone of Wisdom killed 2000, mostly Lebanese civilians.[7] Journalist Jonathan Randal adds that half a dozen villages "were all but leveled in a frenzy of violence during which Israeli troops committed atrocities." President Carter told Begin that unless he withdrew all troops within 24 hours, he would cut off United States aid and sponsor a United Nations resolution condemning Israel. Begin complied. After Israel's invasion, several FRC members were arrested by the PLO for attempting to attack UNIFIL forces and thereby undermining the Stone of Wisdom ceasefire.[8] Meanwhile, Israel continued bombing Lebanese civilian targets such as bridges and a main oil refinery at Zahrani to "create maximum havoc for Lebanese civilian traffic and turn the Lebanese against the Palestinians." Randal concludes, "Armed struggle never physically threatened Israel. On the contrary, it gave Israel the pretext for destabilizing Lebanon and eventually smashing the PLO's military infrastructure."[9]

A few months later, Palestinians struck at an El Al crew in London. Abu Nidal claimed responsibility, but it was a professional operation, not in keeping with FRC. The gunmen had an informer at the airport telling them when the El Al flight from New York arrived. Another informer telephoned when the El Al crew boarded the bus that was to take them to their usual accommodation, the Europa Hotel. Three gunmen then went into action. As soon as the bus pulled up in front of the hotel, the gunmen began firing and throwing grenades. A taxi driver was blown out of his car by one of the grenades. Guards aboard the bus immediately fired back (though Israel officially denied it[10]), shooting one of the gunmen, and apparently the grenade he was about to throw blew him up. The second walked away coolly, but the third, Fahad Muhil al-Din, a Jerusalem-born Palestinian, was caught running from the scene and given a life sentence. He claimed that he had been briefed in Beirut by a man named Tariq.[11]

Within a month of the signing of the Camp David accords, Alan Hart notes, "Israel began a five-month blitz on Lebanon. Fifty thousand Palestinians and 175,000 Lebanese fled from the south; thousands were killed."[12] The Habib truce was supposed to bring it to an end. However, the Israeli government found a new need to batter Lebanon. William Polk believes that this need "resulted from Israeli fears that the United States was on the brink of a peace initiative" after the withdrawal from Sinai in April.[13] In response to terrorist attacks abroad, Israel twice tried to declare the truce null and void. First, when FRC gunmen attacked the Vienna Synagogue two months after the agreement, the Israeli deputy prime minister called it a violation of the ceasefire, and the Israelis fired a few shells over the border but received no response. On April 3, 1982, Israel again lightly shelled South Lebanon after Jacqueline Esber, a member of George Abdullah's FARL, killed the Israeli second secretary in charge of political affairs in Paris.[14] Esber ran into a lobby of Yacov Barsimantov's luxury apartments, shot him, and ran down the metro. Israel immediately blamed the PLO, calling it a violation of the United States–initiated ceasefire.[15]

Israeli leaders began planning the Lebanon invasion to destroy the PLO right after Habib's treaty. Shortly after the Paris killing and two weeks before the complete Israeli withdrawal from Sinai (April 25, 1982) United States satellite photos showed Israel massing troops on its northern border. The United States confronted Israel, and Israel backed down,[16] but Israel's ambassador to the United States, Moshe Arens, declared that Israel would shortly invade Lebanon,[17] and Ariel Sharon visited Christian Maronite leaders in Beirut to secure their cooperation. In 1982 both the foreign minister and the director general of the Israeli Foreign Ministry were former senior Mossad officials.[18] Sharon passed the plan to United States secretary of state Alexander Haig for his approval, which he gave on the condition that Israel attack only when it had a clear provocation, stating that an attack from Jordan would not be justified.[19] Former United States president Ronald Reagan adds, "By early June, when I was getting ready to leave for the Versailles economic summit, it was apparent that Israel had already made the decision to attack in Lebanon and was waiting only for an excuse to deliver the blow."[20] This was the difficult part, for the PLO had been rigidly obeying the ceasefire, even following the two Israeli bombings, in order to protect themselves against counter-attacks. Even Jabril's men remained quiet. Israel needed to find a pretext. Then the FRC, who never before or since attacked Israel, had the sudden urge to launch a cross-border raid. They got a few men into South Lebanon, but according to members who left the group, they could not get close enough to the border to give Israel its needed provocation.

Another unforeseen incident occurred: Argentinean troops landed in the Falkland Islands, and Britain and Argentina began warring. Israel often made internationally unpopular moves under the cover of international crisis. The 1956 Sinai invasion was timed during the Hungarian revolt and came at the height of the United States presidential campaign. Israel annexed the Golan Heights during a Polish crisis. They announced the expulsion of Palestinian residents on a Sunday, when most of the world's journalists take the day off. By Monday it becomes old news. The unfolding Falkland drama provided good initial cover for an aggressive operation.

Military strategists tell us that Israel planned their invasion carefully, including the best possible date. Everyone knew an invasion was coming; for months Arafat had been showing journalists maps of Lebanon and indicating the paths the invading army would take. In February the Syrians brutally put down a revolt in the city of Hama by the Muslim Brothers. One Syrian general said that the ruthless force they used was justified since they knew that Israel was about to invade Lebanon and put Syria at risk; Syria, he said, had to avoid internal dissent at such a crucial time.

For both the Israelis living near the Lebanese border and the Lebanese and Palestinians in South Lebanon the 1981-82 truce produced peace and stability, but hawkish Israeli leaders were obsessed with destroying the PLO. They felt that they had permission from the United States and kept their army near the border, waiting for a pretext.

In the weeks before the date set for the invasion, Begin and other Israeli leaders began, as the *London Times* said, "emphasizing that Israel regards the terms of the cease-fire as applying to Jewish targets abroad," retracting the oral agreement Habib specifically refuted.[21] In the early summer of 1982 Begin invited his ambassador in London, Shlomo Argov, to Israel and singled him out, congratulating him for doing a good job.[22] It was a strange gesture; Argov, who had held the job since 1979, not only belonged to the opposition Labor party, he was a liberal, in sharp contrast to the intransigent Begin.

In the late afternoon of June 3, 1982, Argov, back in London, accepted an invitation to attend a reception of ambassadors given that evening at the Dorcester Hotel by the De La Due textile company. He left for the event about the same time as the three London-based members of the FRC went into action. Naif Rosan, the FRC representative in London, a member of the Revolutionary Council and part of its intelligence directorate who had been with Abu Nidal since 1973, was instructed to bring his two boys to the Dorcester. There was a manic urgency in this action—it was not organized like other outside operations where the controllers and the gunmen came from abroad for the killing. Instead they used Rosan and two local students, Marwan al-Banna and Ghassan Said, both of whom, thanks to the FRC bankroll, had been studying in London. An operation was hastily put together. Rosan claims that he made the decision of the action himself and was unable to contact FRC headquarters for their approval because it was late. He was in charge of arms but did not know how they came into the country.

Marwan al-Banna, a second cousin of Abu Nidal, was not smart or well adjusted, but he needed a job, so Abu Nidal gave him money to leave his home in Nablus and train in Iraq. He turned out to be a hopeless recruit and was sent to London in November 1979 with a scholarship and a pocketful of money. Rosan set him up, and his main duty was to live well, an activity he performed proficiently. The FRC sent him on two visits to Baghdad, then gave him the job of keeping weapons in his apartment. He was told to collect information about Jewish organizations in London and possible Saudi and United Arab Emirates targets, a bit of busy work to make him feel that he was contributing to the revolution

Ghassan Said had been a lifelong picture of failure. Like al-Banna, he was never too bright; he failed the exams required to enter college in the West Bank and Jordan. His family collected money and sent him to Madrid to study, but he was no good at school and could not cope with life in the big city. He tried to start again in Barcelona, but failed there as well, remaining constantly broke. An FRC recruit, perhaps in tandem with a Mossad agent, stepped in and gave him a little money, promising to fulfill his dream of studying in England. Said was a cheap recruit. Ben-Gurion once said that it would be worthwhile to pay an Arab a million pounds to start a war, so Said was a real bargain.

He used to meet with student friends who would sit around discussing politics. Several people, possibly agents, were speaking against Arafat, influencing Said, prodding him to make some action to liberate Palestine. The recruiter asked nothing of him, just helped him out of a tight situation, and in September arranged for him to go to London. Said knew al-Banna from Nablus, but both claim that they did not know that they were part of the same organization while they were in London. That is possible. The organization brought him to Baghdad via Amman for three weeks, and he was taken to FRC's Ramlawi camp and given a fighter's training for a week, remaining isolated from the rest of the camp (isolating members with only one contact is an important feature of the organization). He was then sent back to London as a sleeper, enrolling in the same school as al-Banna. Unlike al-Banna, Said never met Abu Nidal, and he knew next to nothing of the organization. He fared slightly better in London, though Rosan gave him only enough money to live.

Rosan, Said, and al-Banna met near the Dorchester. Marwan brought the weapon, a Polish-made submachine gun. Rosan told Said that his duty as a brave Palestinian was to shoot the man that got into a certain car. The man, Rosan explained, was a terrorist spy who killed Palestinians. Said had no idea who the man was; he was too nervous to ask questions, too afraid to appear the coward he was. Rosan gave him a plastic sports bag provided by al-Banna, and Said spent his most nervous half-hour waiting for a man to make for the car, a couple of blocks away from the site of the 1978 attack on the El Al bus. Following FRC policy, Said was given no time to think.

Finally Shlomo Argov walked out of the hotel, followed by the publishing magnate Robert Maxwell.[23] As the ambassador and his guard made for the car, Said quickly took the automatic out of the bag, rushed up, shot him in the face, then ran down the street. Said could not remember his escape plan, but he followed his instincts, running down the busy street and turning the corner. The ambassador's guard, Constable Collin Simpson from Scotland Yard's diplomatic protection squad, ran after him and shot him in the neck.[24] He and his victim both survived, but unfortunately Argov permanently lost part of his faculties.

After hearing the gunfire, al-Banna ran back excitedly to his car. A security guard named Trevor Willis at the Hilton next to the Dorchester saw him running frantically and wrote down the car's license number. Al-Banna and Rosan drove to Said's apartment to clear evidence, indicating that the operation was put together hastily, then drove out of town until they were stopped by police, who discovered a mountain of evidence against them. The group worked dirty, with none of their affairs safe or secure. In al-Banna's flat they found what was obviously a hit list, including a Jewish kindergarten and the PLO representative. Most targets, however, were Saudi and UAE. In Rosan's apartment police found a letter from his controller telling him to seek a UAE target since the UAE had supposedly handed over some commandos to Jordan. Thus the selection of an Israeli target came as a sudden and abrupt change. Rosan also had an inside floor plan for the Israeli embassy as well as a copy of Ambassador Argov's acceptance of the De La Rue invitation.[25] It was obvious that they had inside information, and Rosan confessed that his information came from non–Arabs.

Perhaps it was a coincidence that Abu Nidal gave Israel the pretext they needed for attacking at the right time. Perhaps it was chance that the attack came as Israel had 70,000 troops and 2600 tanks and armored personnel carriers massed on the border with Lebanon and had its air force and navy ready to go. Perhaps Israel, ready to attack, just happened to be lucky in having a pretext when, military experts tell us, Israel planned the attack. Perhaps it was a fluke that the only time FRC attacked an Israeli it obliged Sharon, a guest of Romania's Nicolae Ceauşescu at the time, who rushed back to Israel and began the bombing two days after Argov was shot. Israeli planes flew over the refugee camps in the south and headed for Beirut, bombing the Palestinian and Muslim sections in the city, beginning an ordeal that would last two years. The PLO lost its bases, weapons, buildings, money, and fighters. Fatah leaders began declaring that the shooting of Argov proved that the FRC was at least infiltrated by Israel,[26] but those announcements made little impression. News of the invasion on United States radio called it an Israeli counterattack.

The three FRC members were tried and given harsh sentences. Al-Banna went even more insane and was removed to a psychiatric ward after an inmate tried to knife him. Al-Banna and Said knew little about the organization to which they had dedicated their lives, and they had no idea that their action

coincided with Israel's wishes. Ian Black reported that Rosan was a colonel in
Iraqi intelligence in charge of coordination with Abu Nidal, and that Iraq
wanted Israel to invade Lebanon so it could end its war with Iran.[27] On June
10, 1982, shortly after Israel launched its offensive, Iraq offered Iran a ceasefire;
nevertheless, Black's story has too many holes. If Iraq knew Israel was ready
to invade, why carry out such an operation? Rosan worked for FRC and was
devoted to Abu Nidal, whose relations with Iraq in 1982 were antagonistic.
The story came from Iran, which refused Iraq's offer.

The Lebanon war turned out to be a tragedy for everyone—the PLO, the
Syrians, the Israelis, the Americans,[28] and of course the Lebanese.[29] Both
Palestinians and Israelis had an unusual skill for making enemies. Israel's even-
tual retreat and continued state of war on the border can be directly linked to
its intelligence failure. In a related story, Israel had over 50 paid agents in
Lebanon whose job it was to track down Arafat and other leaders so the air
force could bomb them. These agents reported on small transmitters, which
Israel provided, the exact location of the leaders, and air force jets would come
and bomb.[30] This plan was a lot of trouble for an assassination, requiring 50
people on the payroll with probably twice that many as backup personnel, and
a ready air force. The PLO discovered the group when one woman came and
confessed—they had no meaningful internal security structure—and it is said
that the PLO executed all those caught with the transmitters, without even a
show of a trial.[31]

More than anything the Lebanon invasion showed that the right-wing
Israeli government sought to settle its differences with the Palestinians only
by war. Peace, negotiation, compromise, continuing the ceasefire, living outside a state of conflict was their greatest fear. As one Israeli newspaper said,
the Israeli invasion of Lebanon "flowed from the very fact that the ceasefire
had been observed."[32]

After the invasion Lebanon endured deprivation. The ring of poverty
that surrounds the capital, where once the Red Cross and the United Nations
had erected tent villages for the Palestinian refugees, began to teem with
homeless Shia and Sunni Muslims from the South, and when it rained, the
water mixed with the sewage and ran down dirt streets into large puddles. Such
living conditions are fertile ground for the growth of terrorism.

Abu Nidal was never able to operate in Lebanon until after the Israel invasion. The Israelis closed all PLO offices, and the fighters, the leaders, and the
bureaucrats entrenched themselves in Tunis, leaving the extremists—the Syrian-backed Ahmed Jabril, Saika, and Abu Musa groups, along with the PFLP
and DFLP. With Fatah out of the way, the FRC had no problem opening
offices in several refugee camps. They put up their bold, colorful posters, distributed their magazines, recruited members, and began making Lebanon their
base, although the leaders were in Damascus, Tripoli, or East Europe.

The FRC had money, millions of dollars, and although they preached the philosophy that the desperate people who remained in the camps wanted to believe—winning back all of Palestine by armed struggle—they also offered boys military training and good salaries. They went into the cities buying flats and buildings, creating day care centers and bakeries and social rooms. But for all their effort, most Palestinians stayed away, for although they believed in fighting, they saw Abu Nidal as an outside group, a secret organization interested in defending their part of the camp, killing Palestinians, and shooting out airports. It was rare to meet an intelligent person who liked the FRC. Officials of other groups who had offices right next to the FRC knew little about their neighbor's activities. It is un–Arab not to know your neighbor.

As the Israeli army was surrounding Beirut, the world's press suddenly begun depicting the Israelis as ruthless aggressors, not valiant pioneers. In the aftermath of the Lebanon invasion a few more Palestinian leaders who were effectively presenting their case before the world were killed by the FRC and Mossad. Two PLO leaders were assassinated in Rome by the JDL operating from the information and assistance of the Mossad. First, a student leader, Nazeyk Matar, who was studying medicine, was walking home with his brother from the PLO office after a late night of talking and watching the World Cup football match. Earlier that day they had participated in a 100,000 person demonstration in Rome against Israel with Italians from left, right, and center parties. Matar was active in GUPS, the General Union of Palestinian Students, and worked as a journalist for a Kuwaiti newspaper. As they were approaching home, a dark Fiat approached, and two men jumped out and filled Matar with lead. His brother ran off in fright.[33]

Several members of the PLO office, including the director, Nemer Amad, and his deputy, Kamal Hussein, rushed to the scene of the shooting. As well as comforting the wife and child—Matar had married an Italian woman and had a seven-year-old daughter—Hussein made a statement to the press, automatically holding Israel responsible for the crime. He had been on the podium during the demonstration the day before and had officially thanked Mayor Ugo Votere for his support of the Palestinians. After the death of Matar he returned home sad and angry, but Hussein woke up early the next morning to deal with the situation. In the morning he kissed his German wife and their three-year-old son, got into his car and drove a short distance to a red light. Someone pushed a button, and a powerful bomb exploded, sending fragments of metal into Hussein's body.[34]

A month later another car bomb exploded in Paris, killing the deputy director of the PLO office, Fadil Dani. The killers were the same or used the same technique as the Rome killers. Dani had just said good-bye to his English-French wife and their five-month-old son in a quiet working-class neighborhood. He got into his car and drove for a few seconds; then the car exploded, before his wife's eyes.

The killers struck at these easy targets instead of the PLO directors because the directors were guarded. Dani had previously had 24-hour protection, but he thought it unnecessary and asked the police to discontinue. He was, as *Le Monde* said, peaceful and polite, a good politician, husband, and father, an intellectual and teacher. Either Dani's car was booby-trapped or a bomb was thrown at it. Someone spotted a getaway car which took off like lightning, and its license number was broadcast on French TV. When it was found it had a dent in it, probably from a hit-and-run accident during the nervous getaway.[35] The ruling French Socialist party was just embarking on a Middle East peace mission, and Dani was helping with the arrangements.

After the Lebanon invasion, one of the PLO's most charismatic leaders, Dr. Issam Sartawi, spoke at a press conference with Israeli dove General Matti Peled. Sartawi infuriated Palestinians by calling for negotiations with Israel, whose bombs had just killed thousands of innocent Lebanese and Palestinians; then he infuriated Israelis by saying that Abu Nidal's organization, which had triggered the war, was infiltrated by the Mossad, repeating Arafat's charge of a year earlier.

Sartawi made a habit of angering people. He was a hard-headed man with a hot temper he could not control. No one could tell Sartawi anything different from what he believed. He felt Palestinians should recognize and negotiate with Israel, solve the problem, and move on, always moving, never time for those lagging behind. Hence he was misunderstood or dismissed by most Palestinians, especially those in the refugee camps who lived on the memories of a mythical past glory of a harmonious Palestine. Sartawi lived in the future, his future, a sane Middle East with Arabs and Jews working together. He was one of the first to realize FRC's relationship with Israel. He also had three assassination attempts against him. Abu Nidal had been out to get him for years.

He spoke again in Algiers during the PNC meeting after the Lebanon war, stating his position for recognition and negotiation, but especially after the brutality of Israel's war, Sartawi's position outraged most PNC members, who used a technicality to prevent him from formally addressing the PNC. He wanted the PNC to void its outdated charter and not to reject the Reagan Plan, but to use it instead as a point of negotiation.[36] No one was listening. He had no time for their small minds, so he resigned and in April 1983 flew off to a Socialists International conference in Portugal. Many world leaders were there, heads of socialist parties around the world, including Israeli leader Shimon Peres, who told the delegates that they should not allow terrorists a stage and successfully prevented Sartawi from addressing the conference.

Although Sartawi angered Palestinians, his moderate stand calling for negotiation won him favor in the West and the friendship of European leaders.[37] He knew the West; he had graduated from Ohio State Medical School and become a competent heart surgeon, a founder of the Palestine Red Crescent,

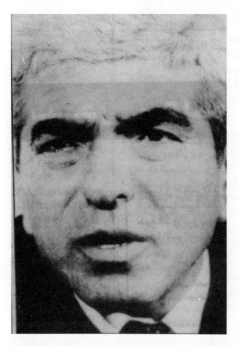

Issam Sartawi, heart surgeon, killed in April 1983.

though politics also drew him. When he was invited to speak, he talked not about bypass surgery but about his homeland and the need to solve the problem. In 1982 he put forward a major peace proposal and encouraged Israelis to meet PLO members.[38] He was a friend of Henri Curiel and was going to meet with him on the day Curiel was gunned down in Paris.[39]

Abu Nidal had known Sartawi personally when, in his radical years, Sartawi was working in Iraq. In those days Sartawi, who was a guerrilla leader in Jordan, started a new organization called the Action for the Liberation of Palestine with about 200 supporters and preached a doctrine of armed struggle and revolution. However, time and war and his friendship with Jews changed Sartawi, and he expected everyone to change with him. He was even ready to met Sharon, but Sharon backed down.[40] Perhaps he knew that the FRC was infiltrated because he had seen inconsistencies during his association with them in Iraq.

Abu Nidal sent one of his best gunmen to Lisbon after him, Yousef al-Awadi, who arrived in Portugal on a fake Moroccan passport and immediately made contact with his liaison, a Revolutionary Council member named Musa. As usual, Musa had been given a map for the location of weapons and detailed instructions for the assassination. It is difficult to believe that the FRC could know that Sartawi was going to attend the Socialist convention in Lisbon and then gather detailed information about the best assassination plan without outside help. The FRC did not have the manpower needed to collect such information; they had people in Spain but no one in Lisbon. Sartawi was unguarded, but he had a secretary.

Awadi went to the hotel where the Socialist conference was taking place to inspect the scene; then he ran back to his liaison and said, "I saw Peres sitting three or four chairs from Sartawi. I could take out Peres just as easy as I can Sartawi."

"No," answered Musa, "kill Sartawi."

Awadi tried to argue, saying that Peres was more important, but he was told to follow his instructions.

The young man thought this was rather strange. Would it not be better to kill the enemy? But Awadi was a well-trained soldier. He went into the lobby of the Montcoro Hotel and found Sartawi and his secretary, Anwan Abu 'Isah, talking to a French delegate. Awadi ran up, shot Sartawi five times, and ran off. Abu 'Isah, slightly wounded in the attack, fell on Sartawi in an outpouring of grief. It was too late; the heart surgeon was shot in the heart.

The police were able to find Awadi and put him on trial, but the court could not pin the murder on him, though most people suspected him. They imposed a much tougher than normal three-year sentence for entering the country on a forged passport.[41] Awadi served his time, then returned to Lebanon, his mind filled with doubt about the organization that made him kill one of his own rather than the enemy. He left the FRC during the 1989 split and began telling his story.

The PLO rarely learned the lesson of security; most of their leaders were vulnerable. Once I had an appointment with a top leader. When I arrived at his hotel room, I noticed the door was open, not just unlocked, with no guards around. At the end of our meeting I questioned him about it, and he answered, "I put myself in God's hand. When my time is up, there's nothing that any man can do." Without arguing the truth of that statement, it shows a passivity, a fatalism innate in Arab culture which made them easy prey for vindictive assassins.

Chapter 14
Deadtime

A lone car drives down the deserted street and turns right one block before the fortified American embassy. The passenger in the back, who has one unarmed guard next to him and two others in the front seat, is in his usual black mood. The driver looks at his watch—5:37 A.M.—and he slows down the slightly aging BMW, pulling it up behind a white 1957 Chevy. The guards look casually up and down the street; then the passenger in the back gets out and walks toward the five-story poured concrete apartment building. He's a big man, and his short walk is ungraceful and nervous as his large feet hit the pavement flat. He has a narrow but slightly flabby face, bald, with thick lips under a dark mustache. His small eyes look from one side to another. The whites of his eyes are slightly yellowish. The downstairs door buzzes open as he approaches, and he enters without losing his heavy stride.

He's the first guest, Abu Nidal, the leader of the organization that has become infamous for mad acts of death and destruction. The flat is owned by one of his few friends, Atif Abu Bakr, the group's political director. It is a large flat in one of the best districts of Damascus near al-Umaeen Square, not far from the main embassy area. Trees line both sides of the narrow street. The buildings are well kept and large, a mixture of flats and houses. The group prefers flats for its members since they provide more security and, more importantly, they're better investments. The front of the building is meticulously clean, like the others on the block. It has a small area of greenery in front, well trimmed and well watered, contrasting with the dry desolation surrounding the city.

Moments later a solitary figure walks down the same street. He's dressed in a dark casual suit imported from France. He looks often at his watch and adjusts his pace. The sun is beginning to give off its light from behind the bare brown mountains east of the city. At 5:42 he walks up the two steps to the front gate; it buzzes as he approaches, and he enters as the door shuts. This man is called Hassan, an unimportant member of the Central Committee, which is meeting today.

Two other Central Committee members arrive, one at 5:44 and the other at 5:49. They walked from opposite directions after small yellow taxis dropped them off at intersections a couple of blocks away; then they walked down the street to the house. The door opens for them as they reach it. The fifth man arrives at 5:52, Abd al-Rahman Issa, officially the group's deputy secretary but in reality one of the main characters in the leadership—or at least he will be until 1989, when he will become aware of the organization's true purpose and risk leaving. He's a coarse man, but he walks with determination through the door that opens before him. Unlike the last three men, Abd al-Rahman is part of the nine-member Politburo, the organization's governing body. In reality the Politburo is the only part of the organization that has any power. This monthly meeting of the Central Committee is only to discuss theoretical issues.

One by one the men come in, two, three, four or five minutes apart. Most are casually dressed; some smoke as they walk. All look straight ahead. At 6:24 Mustafa Murad enters. He's head of outside operations, dedicated and serious. Murad, known to his friends as Abu Nizar, is responsible for most of Abu Nidal's work. In 1988 Abu Nidal will have him killed for knowing too much about the organization.

The sixteenth person to arrive from the 27-member body is Dr. Ghassan Ali, the group's exotic thinker, followed by two other Politburo members: Dr. Kamal, the intelligence officer, and finally Amjed Attar, the second secretary. Like many of his comrades, Attar is married to one of the al-Banna clan. Abu Nidal is a family business. The representative in Baghdad, Abd al-Karim al-Banna, who couldn't attend, is Abu Nidal's nephew. Deputy Issam Maraka, who arrived at 6:08, is married to a relative of Abu Nidal, as is Hussein Ben Ali, head of the investigation department. The group's finances are never trusted to anyone except the family: Abu Nidal; his older daughter, Badia; his son, Nidal; and his nephew.

It's the end of deadtime.

The authorities either don't know or don't care about these meetings. Perhaps they know enough to understand that the meetings are merely window dressing and hardly affect the organization's activities. But this prototypal meeting was held in late April 1985, when the attention of the world, especially the United States, became obsessively focused on this small band of pirates' outside operations: terrorism.

All the Politburo members were well known. Had someone kept watch on this house where several of the meetings were held, he would eventually have discovered the leader. Although this leader almost never attended meetings of the Central Committee or even the Politburo and was living near Warsaw or another East European capital more than in Damascus, he did sometimes come to meetings. Someone could at least have photographed him and distributed prints to border police. He regularly and freely crossed borders with his family, taking vacations in East European countries, flying, sightseeing, eating at restaurants, and staying in hotels like an ordinary Arab businessman. Few people know what he looks like. The Israeli government gives his picture to journalists, but it is of someone totally different. No one seriously tried to neutralize him. He became, supposedly, the most vicious enemy of the West and Israel, and this meeting was held in the house of a former PLO ambassador, a well-known personality who in 1984 publicly left Arafat's Tunis-based organization and joined his old friend Abu Nidal.

The PLO has condemned Abu Nidal to death. No one except Israel has killed as many PLO leaders as this man's organization, but until 1989 the PLO never seriously tried to weaken it. They knew everyone in the organization, as well as the location of their offices and the addresses of their members. They claim that Syria was hostile territory for the PLO. Assad and PLO leaders maintain a personal and bitter enmity, but the PLO has conducted other operations in hostile territory. In Damascus they have two refugee camps full of silent but loyal supporters. The camps were originally built by the United Nations in the early 1950s on the outskirts of the city, but over the decades the city swallowed them and made them part of its decomposed sprawl. Could the PLO do nothing?

Israel has never raised a hand against the FRC.

Abu Bakr first encountered Abu Nidal the year after the Arabs' humiliating defeat in the 1967 war when both were loyal members of Fatah. They became friends and later worked together in Iraq. Abu Bakr believed that the Palestinians shouldn't make any territorial compromise with Israel, mirroring the mainstream of Palestinian thought, especially among the refugees in the neighboring Arab states, where talk of compromise was treason. When Abu Nidal became Fatah's enemy in 1974, Abu Bakr stayed with Arafat, becoming in the 1980s the PLO's ambassador in Bucharest and Prague. Later he left the PLO and joined Abu Musa, which in 1985 agreed to unite with Abu Nidal. Bakr, a short, small-framed man, wears dark-rimmed glasses that make his long, thin face seem gloomy. He's a sensitive man, a poet and intellectual who loves his wife and three children, two girls and one boy named Ahmed.

These meetings were taking place in Damascus at the houses of various FRC members from May 1983 until June 1987. They had offices and businesses and student cells and weapon deposits in many cities, but Damascus remained the base during that period. They always met during deadtime, early in the morning or late at night, when few people notice who walks the streets.

Every intelligence organization should have known where these meetings were being held, and even in that 1985 heyday of terrorism, when millions of tourists were fearfully canceling travel plans, when later that year the United States would gamble on creating an embarrassing diplomatic incident by diverting an Air Egypt civilian plane into a military base in Sicily to capture four terrorists who had surrendered, toppling the Italian government; when terrorism became the most potent word in American politics, surpassing communism; when punishing terrorists became the cornerstone of American Middle East foreign policy; when an AP poll found Mideast terrorism as the editors' lead story[1]—even then the United States left Abu Nidal's deadly group alone. Yet, apart from the actions of this group there were almost no other incidents of Palestinian international terrorism after the early 1970s.[2]

About every three months the FRC's third body, the Revolutionary Council, met with almost twice as many members as the Central Committee, coming together during deadtime to avoid attracting attention. Those bodies never met at one of Abu Nidal's two villas in Zabadany, 30 km from Damascus, but the Politburo did meet in one of Abu Nidal's four flats in the city. The year before Abu Nidal had brought all Politburo members for a special meeting in Romania.

The group will continue to work from Damascus until former United States president Jimmy Carter on a private visit presents Syrian president Assad a confidential report from Pakistani president Zia al-Haq about FRC's murderous 1986 attack on a Pan American Jumbo. Assad, surprised and uncomfortable, will order the group to pack their bags, but Libya will step in and save them.

All guests are greeted at the door by either Abu Bakr's housekeeper or Abu Bakr himself. They walk through the front room and down two marble steps into the sitting room, where comfortable gray sofas with dark brown coffee tables in between line the large room. Most of the men have a folder with some papers. One or two bring briefcases full of papers. As soon as people come in and greet the others in the room, they sit down and put the papers on their laps or in front of them. A 15-year-old girl, Abu Bakr's niece, serves them cups of Turkish coffee. Plates liberally filled with biscuits and candies are on the tables near each guest. Arab hospitality is strictly observed, but not the social requirements of engaging in small talk, asking each other about health and family.

The leader remains in a secondary sitting room, where he is joined by Attar, Abu Bakr, and Mustafa Murad; but when most of the people have arrived, Abu Nidal also joins them, making an unimpressive entrance in the room. Nothing about him is noteworthy, neither his appearance nor his manner. He takes a seat next to Dr. Ghassan, whose real name is Suliman Samreen.

Soon Abu Nidal looks at someone and asks about his wife in a cutting tone, implying that his wife might have been unfaithful while he was stationed at the group's office in Algiers. But the man doesn't give him the satisfaction of a scandal. Then he begins insulting other members one at a time in front of everyone, berating them, haranguing them over petty matters.

Dr. Ghassan says there's talk that a Revolutionary Council member in South Lebanon may have had sex with one of the fighters under him. Abu Nidal gets very excited by the news and asks for more information. Dr. Ghassan says that he heard a rumor that they slept in the same bed while both their wives were in Beirut.

"Who saw them?" he asks. He speaks with a thick Jaffa accent, his voice betraying a lack of refinement. One could mistake him for a hard-hat worker.

Another Central Committee member says that it's true without offering proof. In Arab stories, evidence is unimportant. Abu Nidal's body vibrates with this news. Blood rushes to his dark cheeks. A smile lightens his grim face for the first time, making him look like a kindly uncle.

"How did they act the next day?" he asks.

"They were both happy with each other," Dr. Ghassan retorts as everyone lets out a chuckle. Really Dr. Ghassan heard this rumor third hand and doesn't know what went on, but he knew that Abu Nidal would be interested in the story. Abu Nidal notices every sentence—his memory will enable him to remember accurately every shred of gossip.

Abu Nidal believes the story and tries asking various questions about what happened, prying seriously into the matter. Abd al-Rahman knows that Abu Nidal is going to ask him to see the files of the two men that they're talking about. He's going to pursue this one to find out if there is a possibility of truth to the rumor, and if there is, Abu Nidal will exploit it.

But suddenly Abu Nidal's face becomes a desert. His body is weighed down in the chair as an air of depression hangs all around him. The men take the attention away from him and make light conversation and jokes that might bring their leader out of his somber silence.

"Let's begin," Abu Nidal says at last, businesslike, his mood flipping again, and all the men shuffle their papers and produce the written program for the meeting that had been handed to them either on the day before (along with their appointed time of entry) or when they walked in. But before the program begins, Abu Bakr wants to know about the two outside operations in Athens and Rome against the Jordanian embassy and a Royal Jordanian Airline ticket office. He could have asked Abu Nidal privately, but he wants to bring the matter out into the open in order to challenge the usefulness of outside operations.

"I don't know anything about them," Abu Nidal says, his hand brushing aside the question as if brushing away a fly.

But before he has a chance to begin the meeting Abu Bakr continues pounding: "What do you mean you don't know? They arrested someone who's with us." He doesn't call him one of our people; he's not a real member, he's an expendable.

Abu Nidal waves his hand again. No one else in the room would dare to be as frank with him. "I told you. I don't know who he is. He said he's with Arab *Fedayeen* Cells. It wasn't our action."

People shuffle papers, though no one looks as nervous as the leader, who feels uncomfortably trapped. Even journalists know that Arab *Fedayeen* Cells is one of the names the group uses. A few people in the room have seen the photo of the man who was caught in Rome trying to fire a bazooka at the embassy, and they recognize him as one of the Lebanon recruits. All their new recruits were coming from the refugee camps in Lebanon.

Several eyes glance at Mustafa Murad, who they know helped organize the operation. Like most of their gunmen, the one in Rome wasn't bright. He grew up in the Chitila camp in Beirut and saw many of his family killed by Israeli bombs and Christian machine guns. He had no future until an Abu Nidal recruiter offered him more than elaborate slogans about winning back Palestine through armed struggle; he paid him two and a half times as much money as the other Palestinian groups pay their fighters. He gave him a Kalasnikov. When he was caught in Rome he was ready to tell the Italian police everything, but since he worked for a secret organization, he knew next to nothing, having only one contact. Police and the newspapers could only report that a Palestinian organization attacked a Jordanian embassy.

Abu Bakr makes known his opposition to such outside operations, but Abu Nidal keeps denying involvement. "I didn't plan them," he says. The distinction of true or false is foreign to him; Politburo members know that what their leader says may or may not have a relation to truth, but they don't take part in the conversation. The technical aspects of the operation were left to Murad, head of the intelligence department responsible for outside operations, but the idea for the operation came from either Abu Nidal or Dr. Ghassan. Murad would have picked the gunmen to send to Rome and Athens as well as their handlers or liaisons. The arrangements to pick up the arms were relegated to someone else. In both Rome and Athens the gunmen received their arms from non–Arabs.

Frustrated by Abu Nidal's stiff denials, Abu Bakr drops the subject, but he remains visibly upset most of the morning. His face looks even darker as he sulks silently. Meanwhile, Abu Nidal takes on the character of an efficient leader, taking charge of the meeting. He never drinks during Central Committee meetings.

The group is gearing for a series of outside operations. Abu Nidal takes out a white case of small Dutch cigars and lights one up. The first item on the agenda is the siege of Ein al-Hilway refugee camp in South Lebanon on the outskirts of Sidon by the militia of the Lebanese Shia movement Amal. Abu Nidal calls on the head of the military department, Politburo member Wasfi Hannoun, who is ready to read a report.

This meeting is a copy of a Politburo meeting that took place two days earlier in Murad's home. The Politburo meets about every week; the same points are discussed again in a more abstract vein when the Central Committee meets every four to six weeks, and later when the 56-member Revolutionary Council meets. Members of the Politburo belong to the Central Committee, and members of the Central Committee belong to the Revolutionary

Council. Thus the group has 56 dedicated well-paid cadres. But even though the real power is left to the Politburo, FRC's primary work, outside operations, is the business of Abu Nidal, Mustafa Murad, Abd al-Rahman, Amjed Attar, and Dr. Ghassan.

Hannoun is seated in the opposite corner. He takes out some papers from a black carrying case on his lap, puts on his glasses, and reads the same report he read two days earlier during the Politburo meeting. The report describes Amal's grip on the camp and the inability of FRC fighters to break the siege. It says that the bakery run by the FRC can't get flour. By a common understanding no ill words against Syria, Amal's patron, are spoken. The report says that the morale of the fighters is high. It doesn't say that the Abu Nidal group—the Council, as they call it—is the only Palestinian group in the camp that has not united with the others against their common enemy. All other groups have formed a united front against Amal's blockade. The report doesn't give numbers, but FRC has about 30 fighters there.

FRC is always trying to pass itself off as a regular Palestinian organization, since all such organizations have fighters in Lebanon. Hannoun doesn't say that his fighters serve no function except to protect their own buildings. Even if they wanted to attack Israel, their hated enemy, as Abu Nidal widely boasts, they don't have the equipment or training for that. Despite the group's words, they have no hatred toward Israel, perhaps because it is the source of their life's mission. They won't even use the name Israel, calling it "the Zionist-imperialist entity." Hatred is reserved for the PLO, toward which it flows freely. Abu Nidal has taught his men that women are the enemy and that the evil Arafat is going to contaminate the organization through women; the FRC therefore needs to adhere to a strict moral code of hard work. The group's slogan could well be "Life is bitter," and they look to recruit those with a similar philosophy.

After Hannoun finishes his three-page report there is little discussion. In the Politburo specific questions of practical details can be raised, but in the Central Committee and Revolutionary Council the points become philosophical; certain matters are not discussed. A couple of people add short, pointed comments on the theoretical reasons for the Amal blockade and the Syrian position, and the others nod their heads. Abu Nidal remains silent.

The next item on the agenda is an internal matter: a new way to send communications. Deputy secretary Musa Analawan reads Amjed Attar's report about the current proper way to ask for information. Each member must be sure to follow the exact procedure to preserve the group's secrecy. One FRC branch or department does not know what another branch does. No member is allowed to contact another member directly. Each of the group's eight departments remains closed, and there can be no inter-department cooperation without going through the administrative department. This department knows every aspect of the organization since it receives all communications and then distributes them to others. The strict procedure is to be rigorously followed. Everyone nods in agreement. "Let's do it right or we'll jeopardize everyone," a Politburo member says after the report is read, summing up the room's feelings. Again Abu Nidal makes no comment.

Next the finance officer presents his report, but it is vague, containing no figures or practical news about the group's many investments. It essentially says that the organization needs to be more frugal, that money needs to be transferred to the fighters in Lebanon, and that FRC gave four new scholarships to sons of Revolutionary Council members so they can study in Yugoslavia.

Several more reports are read. Most everyone stays quiet and listens to the stream of rather uninteresting news, which contains not one word about outside operations. The meeting drags on. Abu Nidal, Abu Bakr, Murad, Abd al-Rahman, and Dr. Ghassan do most of the talking. After a short time two girls bring in small glasses of sweet tea and savory snacks, all the finest quality, smuggled by donkey from Beirut and sold by teenage boys on the sidewalks of Damascus. They put the plates on the coffee tables, and each person helps himself as the discussion takes on an air of triviality.

Business is conducted formally. Everything is regimented and organized, even the trivia. Everyone has his job and attends to it with serious industry. The atmosphere is dense, like a room of religious adherents praying to Our Lady while recalling the agony of their sins.

When the formal meeting is over, people are free to leave one at a time, but unlike their entrances, no set exit times are allocated. People just stand up, salute the rest of the company, and go. Some stay talking on the couches. Most people haven't much else to do, this work being their full-time occupation, so they have ample time to talk politics and strategy. The conversation mostly revolves around the coming agreement between Jordan and the PLO, which everyone in the room is dead against, echoing the sentiments of many Palestinians. They want no negotiation, no settlement, and no peace.

Abu Nidal is the last to leave. He stays in Abu Bakr's house until around ten in the evening, the start of nightly deadtime, when the streets will once again be clear. He eats lunch, takes a nap, talks to Politburo members, then watches television at Abu Bakr's house while thinking about his trip back to Warsaw, transiting through Zurich airport, where he can again eat dinner with his wife and children. The same car comes to collect him from the front door and drives him back to Zabadany.

This Abu Nidal group is a Palestinian's nightmare, a hoax against the Palestinian cause. It gave Palestinians the image of demented terrorists, which gave Israel an excuse to avoid negotiating with them. It assassinated the most effective and important Palestinian leaders, the intelligent people who wanted a peaceful resolution to the conflict. Over a third of FRC targets were Palestinian poets, spokesmen, writers, intellectuals, and diplomats. Abu Nidal's gunmen hit embassies and airlines of other Arab countries to create a division between those countries and the PLO. Another third of FRC targets were other Arabs.[3] The targets comprising the final third were mostly European, and they were selected at the proper time to stop Western support for the Palestinians. Abu Nidal's attacks on synagogues and Jewish schools created panic and hatred among the Jewish population.

Abu Nidal has become a household word for assassinations, bombings, and massacres. Nearly two-thirds of his actions have taken place in Western Europe. Two or three actions were performed in East Europe, and the rest have taken place in Turkey, Jordan, Syria, Sudan, Kuwait, Pakistan, and India. America, which the FRC's propaganda identifies with Israel, has been almost entirely free from the FRC's bloody actions. Every operation was well timed, creating a series of coincidences that hurt the Palestinian cause. FRC rarely gives warnings, takes hostages, or makes demands.

Abu Nidal has never attacked Israel.

This circumstantial evidence linking the FRC to Israel is overwhelming. No one has helped Israeli hawks and hurt the Palestinians more than Abu Nidal. Even though Abu Nidal has driven through the streets of Baghdad, Damascus, Warsaw, Tripoli, and other cities, no one has ever tried to eliminate him. He and Abu Bakr have walked the streets of Tripoli, Libya, often without guards. He could have been a simple target.

Instead, he was allowed to pursue his goals to great effect. As a result of his group's activity, at the height of Middle East terrorism, anyone in the United States or Europe who spoke the word "Palestinian" automatically followed it with "terrorist." The Abu Nidal hoax had succeeded.

Chapter 15
The Heyday

In 1985 and 1986 the well-orchestrated Middle East terrorism scare would swell to its greatest crescendo.[1] The political background included an agreement that Jordan's King Hussein had been forming with Arafat following the PNC meeting in Amman in November 1984, culminating in an accord of February 11, 1985, in which the PLO and Jordan declared that they would be ready to negotiate jointly with Israel. Many rank-and-file Palestinians opposed this deal with the king. Israel was ready to negotiate with Jordan but not the PLO, and they produced documents about PLO terrorism to counter the peace initiative.[2] Syria also opposed the Arafat-Hussein accord since it did not want Hussein to make a separate peace with Israel, and since the FRC was based in Damascus during terrorism's heyday, Syria became an accomplice to terrorist activity. Also, United States leaders had a personal hatred for Colonel Gadaffi and repeatedly blamed and provoked him, using the 1985-86 terrorism scare to hit the Libyan leader.

The terrorism scare received impetus from a host of terrorism experts who told us that the way to deal with terror is to offer terror in return; if we give in once, it will lead to the end of the civilized world. Any action against terrorists, including the unfortunate killing of civilians, became justified. For the United States government, propagandists replaced Claire Sterling's bible on the evil Arabs with Benjamin Netanyahu's *Terrorism: How the West Can Win*, which Edward Said rightly calls "an incitement to anti–Arab and anti–Moslem violence."[3] Several caustic terrorism conferences were held in Israel and the United States.[4] Two figures of questionable integrity in the United States and Israel, Oliver North and Amiram Nir, cooperated in 1985 to strike back at terrorism.[5]

This was the only period since the Wadi Haddad hijackings when other Palestinians besides the FRC were involved in international terrorism. Twice Palestinians who were associated with the PLO struck: in Cyprus and aboard an Italian cruise ship. However, 1984-86 was FRC's show, and they took center stage with their usual clumsy tenor.

Many of the terrorist attacks of this period were directed against Jordan.

145

In 1983 Arafat began to make overtures to be part of a delegation led by Jordan, and that is when the heyday began. In October 1983, during the United States invasion of Grenada, the Jordanian ambassador in Delhi, Mohammed Ali Khourma, was wounded by a lone FRC gunman.[6] The next day in Rome the Jordanian ambassador, Taysir Alaedin Toukah, and his Egyptian driver were wounded when an FRC car came alongside theirs and opened fire Chicago gangland style. Police rushed to the scene and stopped and disarmed a car attempting to speed away, but it turned out to be the ambassador's escort in pursuit of the attackers.[7] During that month bombs were beginning to explode in Amman, and on November 7 the FRC tried to storm the Jordanian embassy in Athens, killing a security guard and wounding a diplomat. As usual in Greece, no one was caught. A few days later a Jordanian *chargé* was also attacked in Athens.

FRC concentrated its attacks on Rome and Athens where they had active cells and stores of arms, the one in Rome being administered by a non–Arab. However, on December 29, 1983, gunmen struck in Madrid, again shooting at the Jordanian ambassador's car from another car, killing diplomat Walid Jamal Balkiz and critically wounding another embassy employee, Ibrahim Mamid. The Spanish government called it a provocation against the good relations between Spain and the Arabs.[8] An anonymous caller to AFP in Paris declared that Arab Revolutionary Brigades had struck, a name popular with Abu Nidal during this period.[9]

The FRC temporarily stopped attacking Jordanian embassies until just after the November 1984 PNC meeting, but what followed compensated for the eleven months of quiet. They immediately unleashed one of their students who had been given a scholarship to study in Rumania, Ahmed al-Hersh. They rarely do this, preferring to bring in the assassins, but Hersh was given a gun and told to kill the second-ranking Jordanian diplomat, Azim al-Mufti, which he did as Mufti was taking his child to school. A caller in London where the FRC had financial offices claimed it was a Black September operation.[10]

In a coordinated attack on March 21, 1985, the offices of the Royal Jordanian Airlines (Alia) in Rome, Athens, and Nicosia were rocked by small explosions. All three Alia offices were located a short distance from the El Al office, which, like the nearby offices of United States airlines, the FRC did not touch. In the morning a Palestinian in Rome was given a bomb by someone he had never seen before, who told him to throw it at the Alia ticket office. He entered the office, threw the bomb—wounding the two women inside— and ran. An hour later, three young men speaking Arabic did the same to the Alia office in Athens, injuring three women, and another lone bomber hit the Nicosia office at noon. The simplistic bombs made more noise than damage; explosives experts call them firecrackers. Callers to news agencies again announced the work of Black September, promising more bombs.[11]

A few days later another young FRC hitman named Nawajah Hussein Shedhadeh came to Rome from Lebanon and was given an American-made antitank rocket and a pistol by a Western woman. He met her at a prearranged spot, and she gave him the signal he was told to watch for. He must have been surprised to discover that his controller was a non–Arab and a woman, but he asked no questions, feeling overwhelmed to be outside an Arab country for the first time. She took his fake passport, saying that she would give it back to him when he escaped; like a typical FRC hitman, he was stupid enough to believe her.

The FRC absolutely prohibits contact with women when their fighters are abroad. In the early 1980s some gunmen backed out of an operation after having contact with women. FRC leaders believe that such contact could get the members, who are immature and eager to talk about themselves, to spill information or change their minds about making the ultimate sacrifice. Former members speculate that Abu Nidal's hatred for women is also responsible for this policy.

But Shedhadeh did what he was told, walking to the fashionable Parioli district and stationing himself between two cars that were too far away from his target. He fired his missile, missing the embassy and hitting instead the family who lived on the floor below it. He then fled on foot, an amazing plan for daylight. The police had little problem arresting him after he drew his pistol and waved it threateningly at those around him.[12]

By this time almost all FRC recruits were coming from the refugee camps in Lebanon, ripe areas for bringing in the dissatisfied, the poor, the weary. The next afternoon in Athens another Palestinian from the camps fired a Polish-made RPG at an Alia plane as it was about to take off. It did not explode—hardly anyone noticed it—and he ran off into a waiting car. Again, someone called the press and identified the action as Black September.[13] In July 1985 the first secretary at the Jordanian embassy in Ankara was killed by a gunman, and bombs and shots were fired at the Alia office in Madrid, injuring two people.[14] The gunmen got away in both cities, but the Turks arrested 16 FRC members, destroying FRC's important Turkish network.

By the hot summer of 1985, FRC had attempted about 20 hits against Jordan's embassies and airlines, succeeding in killing diplomats in Madrid, Bucharest, Athens, and Ankara. But suddenly the attacks against Jordan stopped.

FRC terror during the heyday also concentrated on Britons: diplomats, tourists, and British Airways offices. During the attack on Alia in Madrid just mentioned, FRC terrorists simultaneously bombed the British Airways office, killing one Spanish woman and injuring 26.[15] One cadre who left the group claims that Abu Nidal wanted money from the British and hit their targets to put the heat on, but by this time Abu Nidal already had healthy bank accounts, and Thatcher's government would be the last to risk paying blackmail to

It was easy for any group to recruit young men from these Palestinian refugee camps.

Shatila Refugee Camp, Beirut, terrorist recruiting ground.

terrorists. Another reason given for the attacks against Britain is that FRC wanted to release its people in British prisons, including Abu Nidal's second cousin Marwin al-Banna. This too is difficult to support since during none of the operations or subsequent telephone calls claiming responsibility were any such demands made. It seems more likely that the FRC actions aimed at discouraging Britain from supporting the united negotiating front that Hussein and Arafat were presenting. The attacks on the British make sense only as a means to terrorize, and FRC created the maximum effect by choosing cowardly targets.

In 1984 FRC gunmen killed British embassy officials in Beirut, Athens, and Bombay. On 28 March, as Queen Elizabeth II was making an official visit to Jordan, a Palestinian gunman in Athens fired at a car in which two embassy staff people were riding, cultural attaché Ken Whitty and library clerk Artemis Economidou. He killed both, then ran off on foot, yelling in Arabic as he left. The police rounded up several dozen Arabs for questioning, but the killer got away.[16] Later that year two FRC operatives wearing blue track suits ran up to British high commissioner Percy Morris's car in Bombay as it was sitting at a red light and killed him. The attack was a copy of the previous hit in Athens, with the attackers also yelling in Arabic as they fled.[17] Showing a flair for names, Abu Nidal announced that the attack was carried out by the Islamic Revolutionary Socialist Organization. The FRC first used that title in March 1984 when the FRC killed their first British target, Kenneth Judy, the assistant director of the British cultural center in Beirut.

In Athens during the summer of 1985 the FRC bombed two mediocre hotels where working-class Britons were vacationing, first on August 8, then September 3. The hotels are located next door to each other in the suburb of Glyfada, a minute's walk to the polluted beach and a quick ride to the airport. The terrorist checked in for a flight, went and threw his bomb, then returned to the terminal on the back of a waiting motorbike, proceeding to the boarding lounge before the police were able to respond.

Both bombs were crude devices. The first one at the London Hotel was initially thought to have been an exploding gas cylinder. It wounded 13 British guests. The caller taking responsibility—the first time police or reporters had a clue that there had been a bombing instead of an accident—claimed that the British tourists were actually intelligence agents.[18] Next, grenades were thrown into the Glyfada Hotel swimming pool, injuring several deaf-mute Britons who were on a package vacation. A woman caller to the Athens dailies said that it was a Black September action and that they would "fill the city with bombs" unless Greece released Salameh Haten Samir, an FRC member who had been arrested while standing on a street corner with an automatic and a grenade, waiting for the Jordanian ambassador's car. The woman caller failed to explain why they chose a British target to free a member in a Greek prison.[19]

The targeted hotels are truly hideous, typical of the third-rate concrete

Two hotels near Athens bombed by FRC in 1985 while they had British guests.

architecture destroying the Mediterranean. If Abu Nidal wanted to make a statement against the British, why not strike a prestigious hotel such as the Grande Bretagne in the center of Athens in Sintagma Square? Why pick such an obscure place?

Rome took a hefty share of the anti–British bombings during this period. In September 1985, a young man threw a grenade at tourists drinking sodas at a sidewalk café on the fashionable via Venato in Rome. The large device threw metal fragments into the bodies of about two dozen British, German, Brazilian, and Argentinean tourists.[20] The attack received far more publicity than the Israeli expulsion a day earlier of 18 ex-prisoners released in an exchange, contrary to the exchange's terms.[21]

The FRC attacker drove from Vienna and stayed in various hotels before his liaison gave him a disposable RPG, $1000 cash, a fragmentation grenade, and his instructions. The café is located a few meters from the handsome American embassy, which had seen missile attacks by left-wing Italian groups but none by America's purported enemy, Abu Nidal. The man who threw the bomb had no escape plan, so the dozens of *Carabinieri* who guard the embassy and various nearby buildings (including the El Al office down the street) caught him. He produced a fake Moroccan passport under the name Ahmed Ali Hussein Abu Sereva.[22]

Another of the Lebanese recruits who was trained in the use of an AK-47 before he could shave was sent to Rome. Ahmed Ismail Givara was given money and a Moroccan passport under the name Katas Hassan, and he relished

British Airways office in Rome hit by an Abu Nidal bomb. Like other British Airways offices hit in other cities, it is meters away from the El Al office.

the opportunity to leave Chatila, where several members of his family had been massacred by Israelis and Maronites and Amal. He lived in moderate-priced hotels provided for him. Less than a month after his arrival, when he had learned a few words of Italian, he met a man he had never seen before who gave him the magic words, demonstrating that he was his FRC controller. The man looked like an Arab but spoke Arabic with an accent. His instructions were to take the package that his controller was holding and drop it off at British Airways. He was nervous—he had not even celebrated his sixteenth birthday—but he did what he was told, leaving the bomb under the counter in the office where it exploded shortly after, detonated by remote as soon as Givara left the office. Givara began running out of the building, drawing attention to himself and getting himself arrested.[23] A caller then announced the Socialist Muslim Revolutionary Organization was responsible. Givara acknowledged to police that he thought he belonged to that organization. He was put in a juvenile prison and later sentenced to 14 years.[24] One of the British Airways employees he injured, an Italian mother, died a week after the explosion.

The action followed British foreign secretary Geoffrey Howe's announcement that he would meet the joint Jordanian-Palestinian delegation and Prime Minister Thatcher's surprise invitation to host the meeting with Anglican bishop Elia Khoury and Mohammed Milham, both accepted by PLO officials to speak on their behalf in London.[25] The FRC sent a warning via the AP office in Damascus that they would kill any representatives who went to London. Perhaps this growing British support for a political settlement to the Palestinian-Israeli conflict explains the terror directed towards Britain. Also, six days before, Thatcher had signed an agreement in Amman to sell $500 million worth of arms to Jordan. Israel made diplomatic protests against the sale; Abu Nidal threw bombs. When Britain canceled the PLO's visit, FRC's terror against it stopped.

The attacks in Rome seemed designed to hurt the PLO's standing with the Italian government. Both Andreotti and Craxi, the now discredited heads of the two major ruling parties, were personal friends of PLO leaders. Just three days before the bombing of the British Airways office, Andreotti praised both Arafat and the PLO.[26]

In the middle of the terrorism heyday, barely two weeks before the hijack of the *Achille Lauro*, three Palestinian gunmen walked down the pier of the Larnaca, Cyprus, marina to a 38-foot sailboat. The boat, named the *First*, was flying the Israeli flag, as were several neighboring yachts. The *First* often moored in the Larnaca marina, and those aboard were known to be sociable and enthusiastic, making a special effort to meet everyone sailing around Cyprus. A dog on a neighboring yacht heard intruders and began to bark, startling a middle-aged woman on the *First* who turned and saw the three approaching, one holding a Kalasnikov and the other two carrying pistols with silencers. When she began to run, one of the gunmen shot her twice in the back, the retort of the pistol barely audible. She reeled, then toppled on the boat's front rail, her arms hanging loosely in the air. The gunmen held the two men aboard the yacht below deck. They tied their hands and feet and laid them flat on the beds. People in the surrounding yachts who had heard the woman panic and yell called the police, who came swiftly and recognized that it was going to be a hostage situation. They saw the woman draped over the front rail but could do nothing to free her. People had heard her groaning after she was shot. The police cleared the area and began talking to the Palestinians with a bullhorn.

Following long negotiations, the Palestinians demanded the release of 20 members of Force 17 who had been captured by Israel in international waters on their way to Lebanon. There was no need to ask the Israelis for their response to the demand. No one was sure if the woman draped over the rail was still alive. Shortly after noon the Egyptian ambassador who helped negotiate told the gathered press that they were making progress in negotiations, but a few minutes later the Palestinians shot the two men in the back of the head and gave themselves up, walking out brandishing victory signs.[27] One of the gunmen was blond, of Nordic appearance, and the press asked him who he was. He replied in Arabic that he was a Palestinian fighter.[28]

Israel blamed the PLO, saying that terrorists had killed three innocent holiday makers. They asked for extradition and promised revenge. They gave the names of those killed, but contrary to their practice after other attacks on the innocent, they failed to add details of their lives. Even when the victims were buried in Haifa, nothing was said about who they were, what they did, or who their families were.[29] In the fight for public sympathy, the lives of innocent victims are often described in detail to defame the enemy. The lack of details in this case made a couple of journalists suspicious.

The next day a Syrian official declared that the three Israelis were not holiday makers but intelligence agents, but offered no details. Israel discounted the Syrian report but still distributed no background on the victims, only naming them (Esther Pultzur, her husband Reuben Pultzur, and Avraham Avnery[30]). Meanwhile, the PLO denied it had anything to do with the attack, which it condemned. A week later the *Telegraph* declared that the three were top Mossad officials,[31] but Israel had already avenged the attack by bombing the PLO headquarters in Tunis and the area surrounding it, killing about 80 people, including several high-ranking officials.

The Mossad had always operated in Cyprus, in both Larnaca and Limassol ports, often bringing recruits, including FRC members, for discussions and entertainment. The Larnaca attack was apparently sanctioned by Abu Jihad when he got news that Esther Pultzur was in Cyprus. Esther Pultzur was Silvia Rafael, the Mossad agent known by various other names (such as Patricia Roxburgh and Erika Mary Chambers) who was arrested during the 1973 Lillehammer affair and who detonated the 1978 car bomb that killed Ali Hassan Salameh as well as others who happened to be near the blast. After that she worked principally in Israel. There are credible reports that in the late 1960s, when she was young and attractive, she had posed as a journalist in Jordan and become close to a Jordanian cabinet minister.[32]

According to PLO sources, Rafael was the only one that a Palestinian in Larnaca recognized. But they soon discovered that the identity of the two men with her. The first one listed as Reuben Pultzur was actually Zwi Balsio, one of the Mossad's directors of European operations. The other, whose name was indeed Avraham Avnery, led commando raids and was a deputy Mossad director. Abu Jihad gave the go-ahead to eliminate them, and the assassination squad set off to do the job. One of those who volunteered was an Englishman named Ian Davidson who had fought with the PLO in Lebanon and become a Force 17 fighter. The other two, Khaled al-Khatib and Abd al-Khalim al-Khalifa, came from Beirut refugee camps and had joined Force 17 a few years before.

Israel had been planning to bomb the PLO for months, allegedly using information that Israeli spy Jonathan Pollard pilfered from his job as United States Navy analyst to arrange the attack.[33] The bombing in Tunis killed more people than all of FRC's operations during the heyday. The PLO claims it could not declare that the raid in Larnaca was against Mossad agents because that would imply approval by the Palestinian leadership; sanctioning a military action outside Palestine would have violated the PLO's 1974 promise and would have created friction with the Cypriot government, who normally sympathized with the Palestinians since they too suffered displacement. The bombing also seemed a direct attack on the Jordan–PLO peace initiative.[34] Before the Tunis bombing, Abu Jihad celebrated having neutralized Silvia Rafael and two top Mossad agents. After, the PLO spoke with bitterness. Arafat said, "They wanted to kill me instead of negotiating with me."[35] The bombing radicalized the Palestinians.

The hijacking of the *Achille Lauro* cruise ship, the major news item of the period, began three days after the Israeli aerial attack on Tunis. The *Achille Lauro* action received so much publicity around the world, especially in the United States, that it became the battle cry for the war against the Palestinian terrorists. The group responsible, Abu Abbas's PLF, claimed that the attack was hastily put together as retribution for the Tunis bombing. Right after the bombing Abu Abbas went to Gadaffi and said, "Comrade, I need money for an attack against Israel." He got it. Abu Abbas modeled the operation after a failed attempt in January 1973 when four Palestinians disguised as tourists boarded an Italian cruise ship bound for Israel via Greece and Cyprus. The gunmen, organized by Wadi Haddad, were supposed to pick up their arms in Famagusta (this was before the partition of Cyprus). They carried Afghan passports, three listing their occupation as mechanics and one as a teacher, and they stayed in a first-class cabin, rarely venturing out of it; when they did they remained apart. The ship's Italian crew began wondering what Afghan mechanics were doing locked up in a first-class cabin.

Before they got to Cyprus one of the crew tipped off the Arabs, saying that the Cyprus police had already been notified. When the ship landed in Famagusta the police came aboard and graciously gave them the choice of leaving the ship and forgetting the matter, or informing the Israelis. They took a plane to Beirut, and the incident made no news. The Israelis nevertheless found out about it through their contacts with Cyprus security. This followed another major Haddad mistake when his men were stopped at a border because their forged French passports had Swiss visas.

The *Achille Lauro*, a large ship full of American tourists, docked at Alexandria, Egypt. Most of the passengers got off to tour by land,[36] but four dark young Arabs with mustaches never left their cabin. They had gotten on in Genova after coming in from another boat from Tunis and collecting arms from their contact.

The aim of the action remains a mystery. The ship was supposed to land at Ashod in southern Israel, and according to Abu Abbas, the gunmen were going to launch a military attack as soon as the ship docked.[37] The gunmen, today in prison near Genova, believed this to be the case as well. But it makes no sense. Whenever a ship gets near an Israeli port, dozens of soldiers are on hand. Israeli inspectors with walkie talkies usually come onto the ship from a small boat as it is entering the port, and they screen passengers on the ship. An attacking party of four Palestinians would have no chance of getting past the gangplank, let alone being able to launch a full-scale commando attack on the land past the armed soldiers. Abu Abbas knew this. He tried to deny the responsibility of taking over the ship by saying it was meant as transport for an attack on Israel, taking it out of the category of international terrorism and making it a raid on Israel, similar to the Palestinian commando raids from Lebanon, revenge for the bombing of the PLO headquarters.

Discovering that their plan had been exposed, the gunmen seized the ship and her remaining 200 passengers and 400 crew. The captain made a phone call—he did not know exactly whom he should call—and a couple of hours later, after a series of phone calls all around Europe, Italian prime minister Betino Craxi discovered that the ship was sequestered. The Americans quickly provided logistic support. The ship went north outside the waters of Syria, and during that time the gunmen shot an elderly Jewish American, Leon Klinghoffer.[38] The Americans claim that they lost the ship for two days. The hijacking of the ship had made front page news and occupied the meeting times of the highest rungs of the American government. It is unthinkable that the United States did not call for satellite photos or try to track the ship by air. The captain remained in telephone contact with his government, telling them that he thought there was a casualty but had no details. Later, he said that Klinghoffer was probably confronting the hijackers, and they callously shot him, dumping his body overboard to later wash up on the Syrian shore. The Syrians were only too happy to turn the body over to the Americans and embarrass the PLO, who could not deny that Abu Abbas sat on their Executive Committee. One PLO official, speaking seriously, made the wild claim that Klinghoffer's wife killed him for the insurance money.

Former CIA agents contend that the PLF had been infiltrated, so Israel or the United States may have known about the hijack before the gunmen boarded the ship in Genova. In 1990 when the PLF sent boatloads of commandos to raid the beaches of Tel Aviv, the Israelis knew exactly what was happening and casually stopped all the attackers, then used the failed attack to pressure the United States to end its dialogue with the PLO. Gadaffi, who had also financed the 1990 beach operation, was furious at Abu Abbas and gave him and his small band three days to get out of the country.[39]

Although Gadaffi bankrolled and supported the PLF, Abu Abbas was also a PLO loyalist, and when Arafat failed to denounce Abu Abbas, it was difficult for the PLO to avoid the terrorism rap in both the *Achille Lauro* case and the 1990 beach raid. The public relations fallout from *Achille Lauro* nullified all the sympathy that the Palestinians had gained during the Lebanon invasion. All means for stopping terrorism now seemed justified.

The hijackers made a deal with Egypt to release the ship in return for their freedom as long as they did not hurt anyone on board. Everyone agreed, and the four Palestinians arrived in Egypt. The United States government requested that the hijackers be turned over to them, but the Egyptian government issued a statement the next day that they had left the country. The United States, monitoring the Egyptian government's telephones, picked up two messages. The first came from President Hosni Mubarak to his foreign secretary saying that American secretary of state George Shultz was crazy to think Egypt should turn over hijackers to the United States. The second message said that the hijackers plus Abu Abbas were going to be on an Air Egypt flight to Algeria.[40] The message was passed to the White House, who saw the interception of the plane as a tremendous possibility to win cheers at home. Oliver North got the okay from President Reagan, who was speaking in Chicago.[41]

The plane was surrounded over the Mediterranean by four American carrier-based F-14 fighter aircraft and forced to land in Sigonella, a NATO base in Sicily. Egypt immediately felt slighted, since it had concluded an agreement for safe passage. Italy was put on the spot for henceforth being the lackey of the United States and allowing it to overstep its bounds. Other European countries felt that the use of a NATO base for American revenge was uncalled for: NATO bases should be run by NATO for the defense of Europe, not by the Americans for their private war. The affair brought down the Italian government, which had been the longest lasting since World War II.[42]

Viewing the Air Egypt plane as Egypt's sovereign territory, *carabinieri* captain Fisicano, head of Sigonella base, got his men to surround the plane to protect it from the Americans, who sent a general and a planeload of aides from Germany. The Americans surrounded the *carabinieri*, and another group of *carabinieri* surrounded the Americans. There was actual talk by the American officers of opening up on the weak-kneed Italians in order to get to the hijackers. Following heated diplomatic activity between the leaders of the two countries, the American general gave his telephone to his aide and turned to Fisicano, saying, "They're yours," then boarded his jet and returned to Germany.[43]

The Italians freed Abu Abbas, to the outrage of the Americans. The Palestinian boys were given life sentences—one had to be tried in juvenile court[44]—and Abu Abbas was later indicted and sentenced *in absentia*, a common Italian ploy of avoiding responsibility.

It was a masterful, multimillion-dollar operation to capture four gunmen from the Abu Abbas organization, involving the president, state department, and Pentagon. The Americans never attempted any similar action against the real international terror group, the FRC. They could have spent a lot less energy capturing Abu Nidal or his lieutenants, not from a friendly country such as Italy, but from Syria or Poland or Libya, where Abu Nidal lived with a few lightly armed bodyguards. Neither Abu Nidal nor his men were ever under threat of such attacks. The Soviet Union newspaper *Tass* called the United

States action hypocrisy since in a similar incident the United States gave sanctuary to two men who hijacked a Soviet airliner, killing a stewardess in the process.[45]

The main FRC attack during the heyday came at the peak of the Christmas season, when gunmen opened fire on travelers at the Rome and Vienna airports. The raids occurred just after President Assad had invited King Hussein to Syria for talks, indicating a possibility of a shift in the relationship of those two countries. Some journalists speculated that the Rome and Vienna attacks were retaliation for bombing the PLO in Tunis, an incredible idea, since Abu Nidal, who goes around killing PLO leaders, is hardly interested in evening their score.

These operations were planned by Mustafa Murad and Samir Khader, with help from Abd al-Rahman. Khader came to both Rome and Vienna on a Lebanese passport with a Christian name. Originally attacks were planned on three airports, Rome, Vienna, and Frankfurt, but Frankfurt had to be canceled at the last minute for technical reasons. To spice up the terrorist stew, the FRC was trying to persuade other Palestinian extremists to cooperate in the raid on Frankfurt. Finding no takers, they put out feelers to the German Red Army Faction and again received no encouragement. The Mossad informed the Dutch that Europe should be on alert for possible terrorist attacks.[46]

Typically, FRC used their simple-minded fighters, sending their gunmen to the capitals with false Moroccan passports, five to Rome and three to Vienna, and putting them up in third-class hotels where they hardly had contact outside their own group and their liaison. They were told that they were specially chosen for their bravery and their skill to continue to wage the armed struggle for Palestine, but they were not told about the operation until just before the action.

The Rome group leader, Ibrahim Khaled, knew Ahmed Ismail Givara, the one who threw a bomb at the British Army office. Khaled must have thought that their job would be similar, throwing a bomb somewhere and running. But on the morning of the raid, two days after Christmas, their liaisons came with grenades and machine guns, giving the boys the first glimpse of their operation. The liaisons told the Rome attackers that the terminal would be full of Israeli pilots, passing through Rome on their way home from training in the United States, and that it was their duty to kill them all since pilots kill Palestinians in the refugee camps. They told the Vienna attackers that they were going to hijack an El Al plane and explode it over an Israeli refinery. No one in either group had time to think about what he was going to do.

Like robots, the attackers did what they were told. First the terrorists walked into the terminal at Rome, took out their weapons, and began firing at passengers waiting to check in at TWA, El Al, and other airlines. The El Al security personnel took out their guns and fired back. In a few seconds the police guards ran to the scene and also began shooting. Israeli bullets were responsible for killing three of the terrorists and wounding the other two. They managed to pump at least four bullets into each of the gunmen, also killing and wounding some of the passengers in the crossfire. It was a one-minute nightmare that left dead and wounded bodies all over the terminal.[47]

A short time later the three attacked in Austria in the same manner. Compared to Rome, this was a lighter raid, but it left three dead and thirty injured. The gunmen opened fire at embarking El Al passengers, then tried to flee but were caught by Austrian police, who killed one Arab.

Abu Nidal made his mark as the grand terrorist in these dual actions that would always haunt the Palestinians, justifying the phrase *Palestinian terrorists*.[48] Within months of the attacks the French president had unifying discussions with Israel about terrorism,[49] and when ministers of the industrialized countries came together in Tokyo, their main function was formulation of an antiterror declaration.[50] Austria tempered its support of the PLO; Italy and Israel formulated an accord to exchange information on terrorism[51]; and Arafat made the Cairo declaration against terrorism. Israel welcomed each of these moves.

However, by far the most repugnant act of terrorism during the heyday took place in Beirut on March 8, 1985, outside a Shia mosque in the Bir Abed district where the spiritual leader Sheikh Fadlallah usually spoke. A massive car bomb, probably 300 pounds of explosives, went off just as 200 young women were leaving the mosque after Friday prayers. The street was already jammed with shoppers and pedestrians and children. The blast killed more than 80 people—bodies were so charred and thrown in every direction that it was difficult to get an exact count. Another 250 people were hit with bits of metal and concrete fragments; several were permanently injured. The devout young women took the brunt of casualties; the Sheikh was unhurt.

The *Washington Post* broke the story that the United States in collaboration with Saudi Arabia had arranged the bombing, paying $3 million to train and equip a group of mercenaries to kill the Sheikh. Speaking on May 21, Secretary Shultz did not deny the evidence, saying "actions must speak louder than words," alluding to United States involvement against Sheikh Fadlallah.[52] Everyone in the United States government declined to comment. Outside the mosque, the Shia hung a huge sign in English reading, "Made in America." Considering its magnitude and its implication for United States foreign policy, not to mention morality, when compared to the *Achille Lauro* or even Rome and Vienna, the bombing received almost no media attention or analysis.[53]

Chapter 16

The Questionable 1980s

'Tis not in fashion to call things by their right names.
                                                    Dutch Courtesan

In 1985 the Israeli press began a massive publicity campaign against Syria. Israeli leaders were discussing the Assad government's cruelty and link to terrorism while giving estimates of Syria's troop strength and weapons capacity, trying to sell the implausible prediction that Syria was ready to invade Israel and a preemptive strike was necessary. Whenever Syria acquired weapons from the Soviet Union, the Israelis would exaggerate their impact, omitting the fact that the weapons were defensive since Syria feared an Israeli attack. Although Syria had a fairly massive army, soldiers were poorly fed, ill-equipped, and virtually unpaid. The 1982 invasion showed Syrians that their most sophisticated missiles and jets were no match for Israel's. The United States, however, was busy conducting a smear campaign against Libya, perhaps inspired by President Reagan's personal hatred of its eccentric leader. While the Israelis were pointing their finger at Syria as the promoter of international terrorism, the Americans were saying that the source of this evil was Libya.

During the Easter weekend of 1986, an unsophisticated bomb went off outside the office of the German-Arab Friendship Association in Berlin, injuring seven Arabs. Israel immediately gave the Germans intelligence information on how the bombing was a Syrian plot for which a Syrian air force intelligence deputy, Lieutenant-Colonel Haitham Said, was responsible, and West Germany temporarily withdrew its ambassador in Damascus over the incident. The Americans, meanwhile, were eager to show that Libya was the villain. Actually, if either of those countries had been to blame for the bombing, it would have been a more sophisticated bomb. Eventually, Ahmed Mansour Hasi and Farouk Salameh, both Palestinians with Jordanian passports, were indicted, found guilty, and sentenced to 14 years. They claimed at first that their bomb came from Syria, then retracted their statement.[1]

This happened about the time the United States launched missiles in the

Gulf of Sirte, sinking a Libyan ship. Five days later another bomb shook La Belle Disco in Berlin, a watering hole for American soldiers, while it was packed with 500 people, killing three—two Americans and a Turkish woman—and wounding 200.[2] The United States intercepted phone calls on March 25 and April 4 between Tripoli and the Libyan embassy in Germany authorizing a terrorist hit. Defense Secretary Casper Weinberger said that American MPs had been minutes away from saving La Belle since they were going around clearing Berlin bars of American servicemen. Weinberger got caught in a web of United States government lies when he was asked how they knew to clear out bars since the messages gave no specific targets. The Reagan administration declined to offer any details of its intelligence operations, even to its allies.[3] No bars were being cleared, and Gadaffi was not involved in this plot.[4]

Israel implicated Syria. Anti-Syrian rhetoric in the press and by government leaders was worrying Damascus into believing that Israel was going to launch a full-scale invasion, and Syria bought Soviet advanced missiles, including surface-to-surface SS-21s capable of delivering heavy payloads of destruction, possibly chemical. In February 1986 Israel force-landed a Libyan plane carrying Syrian and Lebanese passengers, including a Baath party official, and kept saber-rattling about the Syrian preparation for war.[5] The United States, however, wanted better relations with Syria and did not want Israel's reactionary government starting another war.

Ten days after the La Belle bombing, with a lot of fiery rhetoric in between, United States F-111 bombers based in northern Britain launched their surgical strike on Libya, bombing the French and Swiss embassies, hitting residential areas, firing missiles at a flock of migrating birds, and hitting almost no military targets. At least 63 people were killed and 100 injured, and apparently all were civilians, including an adopted daughter of Gadaffi.[6] The raid justified the hundreds of Israeli bombing raids on Lebanese refugee camps, or as an Israeli reporter said, the raid demonstrated the soundness of the Israeli policy of preemptive strike.[7] One terror expert called it a "step in the right direction,"[8] and it received popular backing in the United States. In reality the raid was a sham, a grudge killing resulting from an irrational hatred that generated more Arab-Western friction, later avenged by the destruction of Pan Am flight 103 over Lockerbie, Scotland.[9] Reagan's press secretary Marvin Kalb resigned over what he euphemistically called a government policy of misinformation about Libya.

The United States bombed and almost killed Gadaffi, spending several million dollars on missiles alone in order to destroy the terrorist scourge, risking friction among European allies who did not believe President Reagan's accusations. The United States never tried to hit Abu Nidal, the master terrorist, a much easier target than Gadaffi. If the United States knew Gadaffi's whereabouts, they could have also known Abu Nidal's (he was in Damascus at the time of the bombing). Since the beginning of President Reagan's first term there had been at least 16 attacks against Americans in Europe by Middle Eastern and left-wing groups,[10] but the United States chose to ignore the other attacks and concentrate on Gadaffi.

As an aside, a CBS crew interviewed FRC spokesperson Abu Bakr in Beirut just after the raid and reported that he threatened Oliver North and other American leaders. Abu Bakr claims that he was not threatening but giving examples of what he called American-sponsored terrorism against Cuba and Angola. North sent a letter to Congress about the Abu Nidal threat, which he cited as justification for using thousands of dollars from weapon sales to Iran to install a home security system.[11]

Two days after the bombing, a pregnant Irish working woman, Ann Marie Murphy, unwittingly tried to sneak a bomb aboard an El Al flight from Heathrow to Tel Aviv. The airport security people inspected her bag and passed her, but she was stopped for a second check by El Al personnel. She was not acting suspiciously since she did not know she had a bomb, but they found it. It turned out that her Palestinian-Jordanian boyfriend, Nizar Hindawi, had planted the bomb and had taken refuge in the Syrian embassy, whose staff tried to get him out of the country as a crew member of Syrian Arab Airlines. The ties to Syria were irrefutable, as Paul Wilkson observes:

> The evidence of Syrian involvement which engaged the Hindawi trial was unusually detailed and damning…. Hindawi gave a detailed account of Syrian complicity in the crime. He claimed he was briefed by Syrian intelligence on how to set the bomb on the plane, that he was paid US $12,000 by Syria to undertake the attack at Heathrow, and that he was in touch with the Syrian Embassy in London.

It was neat—too neat. Hindawi (the brother of Hasi, the one caught in the first German bombing), did not just leave his fingerprints everywhere; he enshrined them into everything he touched. In an interview later that year French prime minister Jacques Chirac said that Germany's chancellor, Helmut Kohl, and foreign secretary, Hans-Dietrich Genscher, had concluded that the Heathrow attack "was a provocation probably organized by Israel's Mossad secret service and renegade Syrians in an attempt to bring down the government of Syrian President Hafez Assad." Chirac added, "I am always suspicious of this sort of affair [terrorism and Hindawi], especially when it fits into a certain policy. First it was Libya, and now it's Syria."[12]

It would be difficult to find logical motivation for Syria, one of the most cautious and ponderous governments on earth, to attempt to blow up an El Al plane. At that time Assad was making moves toward the West, and the last thing on his mind was a confrontation with Israel, which was sure to again destroy his army and air force within hours. Such a defeat would undoubtedly topple his unpopular regime, which was kept in place by fear and the pervasive secret police. It is not possible to see how the bombing or attempted bombing of an El Al jet would help Syria.

The Hindawi family knew little of Palestine. Their father came from Palestine and the mother from Jordan, both respected families. Hindawi's father, who worked as a cook in the Jordanian embassy in London, seems to have been an Israeli spy who escaped a death sentence in Jordan by remaining in Britain.[13] Sources describe Hindawi as an opportunist who worked for anyone who would pay. His cover was a job in London for an Arab newspaper, but he remained a braggart and liar, common traits for agents. This was almost certainly not his first undercover operation. Hindawi and Hasi were working under Colonel Said and his deputy, Colonel Mufid Akhour, who was later suspected of being an Israeli agent, though the Syrians kept this a secret. FRC deserters say that their group provided Said, FRC's liaison with Syria, the explosives Hindawi gave to Murphy. It took years for Syria to repair the damage caused by the Hindawi brothers.

Although terrorism continued, the terrorism scare stopped shortly after the Libya raid and the Hindawi affair. It appeared to be an insane period involving indiscriminate acts of death and destruction, but analysis shows that most acts were orderly and directed. Over 2 million Americans canceled overseas trips in 1985. In the two weeks after the Rome and Vienna airport attacks, TWA lost 4000 bookings.[14] During the heyday summer, tourism in Israel was down 40 percent to what it had been the previous year, according to the Ministry of Tourism. This decline had a harsh effect on the infusion of badly needed hard currency in the country's then-troubled economy.[15]

After the Lebanon invasion, militant Palestinians under the Syrian-controlled Abu Musa faction, whose rejectionist line was popular in Lebanon, began an armed revolt against the PLO. Abu Bakr left the PLO and joined Abu Musa, as did a handful of PLO military officers. In 1983 Abu Musa's chief political thinker, Abu Khalid al-Amleh, began negotiating secretly in the Bakaa Valley with Abu Nidal leaders Dr. Ghassan and Mustafa Murad, planning the anti–Arafat takeover. Amleh was the driving power of the group, a PLO colonel who had left the Jordanian army during the 1970 war and was a commander in the battle at Tel al-Zaitar. Abu Nidal followed these talks from Warsaw and Damascus. The Abu Nidal and Abu Musa groups decided to begin formal talks to unite their organizations in January 1985. Representing Abu Nidal were Murad, Dr. Ghassan, Abd al-Rahman, and Mansur. On the Abu Musa side were Abu Bakr, Amleh, Abu Ahmed, and Elias Sufanni, a Palestinian-Israeli who studied in the United States and became a mediocre scholar at the Palestine Research Center, then worked with Fatah in Sidon. He became an extremist, suspected by many to be a Mossad agent.

They sat around the table until the end of February and reached agreement on a political program under one united leadership. The draft of this merger would effectively take over the Palestine movement in the Middle East with backing from Syria, since the PLO was far away in Tunis and had burned its bridges in Egypt, Jordan, Lebanon, and Syria. They asked the Syrians for a formal invitation to sign the agreement in Damascus, but Syria refused. The government had no formal relations with Abu Nidal and did not want to begin them, so Abu Musa and FRC went directly to Gadaffi. The Libyan leader was anxious to sponsor the new movement, officially welcoming them in Tripoli on March 6, when they formed what Libya called a "pan–Arab command of revolutionary Arab forces."[16] Abu Nidal himself was not part of these negotiations and was not received in Libya until early September, when he met Gadaffi's deputy, Major Abd al-Salam Jallud.

The new movement lasted only two months, since FRC was not interested in unity and only wanted to take over and disrupt the Palestine movement. During the meetings Murad and Abd al-Rahman encouraged Abu Bakr to join them, and he did, while Dr. Ghassan and Sufanni worked closely together, coming up with several aspects of the agreement separately. The latter two had a lot in common: two Western-educated extremists (Sufanni grew up in Israel), both leaders of questionable organizations, making an agreement with a crazed Arab leader and almost taking over and radicalizing the entire Palestinian movement, at the same time that Israel was linking Syria with terrorism. It is difficult to believe that Western-educated, intelligent people like Dr. Ghassan and Sufanni could mouth simplistic slogans about American-Israeli imperialism. Simple people who have never left their villages adopt this extremism—simple people, or *agents provocateurs*.

The 1983–85 split harmed the Palestinians more than the Lebanon invasion, and in 1986 the Soviet bloc countries tried to heal the rift by arranging meetings of the different factions in various East European capitals. Finally, in early 1987 the PLO looked as if it would again be united. The Syrian groups, including the PFLP and DFLP, wanted Arafat to repudiate the Amman accord with Hussein prohibiting the Palestinians from negotiating for themselves. Since the accord ran out of momentum, partly from the heyday of terrorism, Arafat obliged, and almost all factions were set on reuniting at the 1987 PNC.

But Algeria, the host country, threw a wrench into the works when they brought Abu Nidal and his deputies Abu Bakr and Murad in an attempt to reconcile the FRC with the PLO. Abu Nidal had given two rare newspaper interviews in which he struck a conciliatory tone and began talking moderation.[17] News spread that he had been forgiven by Arafat and was going to be back in the mainstream. [18] These reports linked Fatah to FRC's terrorism and discredited the PLO's newly formed unity. As editor Maxim Ghilan put it, Abu Nidal's presence would "deliver to the Israeli peace camp, already in crisis, its worst and most disastrous blow."[19] What Israeli could talk to the PLO when it included the terrorist who had recently killed Jewish worshipers in Turkey and previously targeted Jews in other European cities?

Abu Bakr shuffled back and forth between Abu Nidal and the Fatah leadership, trying to rectify the split between the two. Finally, he arranged a dialogue between Abu Iyad and Abu Nidal, and they are said to have talked for 20 hours (perhaps an Arab exaggeration). What must it be like to have a long chat with someone who planted a bomb in your car seven years before,[20] who speaks nothing but insults about your organization and killed your closest friends? During that meeting Abu Nidal confessed to Abu Iyad that he had Israeli agents in his organization.

There is a revealing picture of the PLO leadership taken in a hotel lobby during the conference. All the main characters of the Executive Committee and a few other leaders are standing close together and smiling, with Arafat in the middle surrounded by Abu Jihad and Abu Iyad, Habash and so forth. At the left end of the group stands Abu Abbas, who had gained infamy from his *Achille Lauro* episode. He is a big man, standing with the pack and smiling. A few feet away is Abu Bakr, a third the size of Abu Abbas, his arms folded on his chest, a disgusted look on his face because he hates Abu Abbas so much he does not want to stand next to him.

The PLO claims it could not have killed or arrested Abu Nidal because he was protected by Algeria, a strong PLO supporter; such an action would go against acceptable Arab tradition. But they could have done something— trailed him, arranged an auto accident, subdued him. By that time his FRC had killed the best PLO leaders and was more effective at maligning the Palestinians than Israel's public relations campaign. The PLO did nothing. Abu Nidal tried to meet his old friends Abu Daoud and Naji Alush, but no one was interested, and he returned to Libya after taking away the victory achieved by the PLO in its reunification.

Ismail Sowan did not want to become an Israeli collaborator; not really. He wanted money, the chance to live high. He wanted to study abroad and have a good time, meet women. His family had been collaborators and done well for themselves. They came from the town of Silwan just outside Jerusalem and thought the Arabs were a backward lot. His older brother Ibrahim was notorious in the West Bank, collecting information from the local Palestinian community and openly receiving money and protection from the authorities. (Ibrahim would be killed in March 1990 when the Palestinians of the *Intifada* went on a collaborator-killing spree.) Another brother also passed information, sometimes making up stories for extra pay.

Ismail joined the Mossad at 18 while he was living in the West Bank. He was a less obvious candidate than Ibrahim, but the Mossad wanted to develop him, so they sent him to Beirut in the late 1970s to collect trivial information in return for money, the promise of studying abroad, and a bit of sex. They gave him an apartment in Beirut and put money in his pocket so he could spend it in front of other people. He offered his services to the PLO and did small jobs for them,[21] meeting Abd al-Rahim Mustafa, a not-too-bright member of Force 17, the security branch of the PLO headed by Abu Tayib, a semi-literate who worked from Amman until he was dismissed in 1991. Force 17 personnel sit in offices pretending to be central to the struggle to liberate Palestine.

The Mossad sent Sowan to other cities, including Paris in 1982. In 1985 Sowan appeared in London, where he began talking to people in the PLO office, claiming to hold a degree in civil engineering from Beirut and to belong to Fatah, trying to strike up relationships. But someone in the office who served in the same prison as Sowan's brother became suspicious when Sowan asked his rank in Fatah. "No one asks a question like that except a collaborator," he told Sowan, directing him to leave the office. PLO representative Fiasal Aweida claims he also knew Sowan was a spy the first time he met him.

FRC had problems operating from Britain since it is more difficult to bring arms into Britain and border formalities are tighter than in all other European countries. On January 27–29, 1985, Scotland Yard arrested and deported without evidence four FRC members traveling on Syrian diplomatic passports. The police asked the Syrian embassy about them, but the Syrians had no idea who they were.[22] They were staying at the Cumberland Hotel, hardly venturing out, waiting for their liaison to give them instructions for an FRC action. Police thought they were going to kill PLO representative Aweida, but they were actually being cultivated for a Jordanian target.

After the four were expelled the Mossad brought in a collaborator named Khalid al-Usta, a Palestinian from Nablus. Like Sowan, he was recruited in Tel Aviv as a student and promised money and education abroad in exchange for bits of information. He came to London and tried to become active with other Palestinians, helping the PLO office whenever he could. The Mossad told him to tell PLO officials that he hated Israel so much he would be ready to kill anyone for the cause. According to PLO sources, his Mossad handlers suggested the idea as a way of inspiring confidence, having told him not to worry: "We'll kill for you; we'll plant bombs wherever they want. We'll do the whole thing for you. It will give you standing in the PLO." But the PLO had been out of the assassination business for a decade. After leaving the Arab League's building and moving to South Kensington, the London PLO operated almost like an embassy, and Aweida had good contacts with many government leaders.

Usta began drawing suspicion from the PLO people in London, so the Mossad sent him to Tunis in late 1985 to spy on Abu Jihad. He went there and told the PLO security office under Abu Hol that he was a spy and wanted to amend his ways, saying he had a lot of information to offer. But the PLO had already been burned by that trick, and after a couple of cold showers Usta admitted that the Mossad had given him the line about wanting to confess, with bits of unimportant information to spill, in order to win the confidence of the PLO. Later, however, the Mossad would use that tactic effectively to sneak an agent right next to Abu Hol and the top leadership of the PLO.

When Usta was no longer any use in London, the Mossad sent Sowan, and he was delighted. Upon finding himself unwelcome in the PLO office, Sowan began hanging around a Palestinian medical charity, trying to make himself helpful and reporting back to the Mossad. James Rusbridger claims that the Mossad wanted Sowan to set off bombs in London to make it look like the work of Arabs.[23] Fortunately for the Mossad, Force 17 sent Mustafa, Sowan's friend from Beirut, to the London office as a security officer, and Sowan began working him over in an effort to win his trust. Mustafa had had a hard time in Lebanon after Sowan left. He was captured by Shia gunmen during the siege of the camps and released on payment of a ransom. His wife, a Lebanese Shia, was tragically killed during the camps war, and he was given the post in London as compensation.

Sowan told another Palestinian, "Last night I slept with an Israeli." Then he mentioned that he was going to marry her—Carmel Greensmith—adding that she was a "good Jew." There have been other cases where agents, whether Mossad or Abu Nidal, were told to marry. In the summer of 1986 they had a large wedding, and he invited every Palestinian he could to the reception; six or seven showed up, one being Mustafa. Sowan was still a student, but the Mossad was giving him £600–800 a month plus expenses, as well as paying the rent on his flat. His controller was a man in the Israeli embassy posing as an attaché named Arie Regev. The fact that Mustafa, a security specialist, was one of the only people who did not know Sowan was a spy makes an indicative statement about Force 17 and PLO security. Mossad agents in London worked out of the Israeli embassy and under the cover of a private business.[24] London was not a recruiting station for either the Mossad or FRC; agents were sent in. Besides Sowan, they employed another Arab, a Druze from the Golan named Bashara Samara, who the PLO claims was in Tunis spying on the PLO before he came to London. Although an Arab, he, like most Druze living in Israel, was a faithful Israeli citizen.

Mustafa drifted out of the PLO office and bought a petrol station in Essex, working long hours and forgetting about politics. But Aweida found out that Mustafa was probably trading in weapons and informed the police, telling them that Mustafa was no longer part of the office. The last thing Aweida wanted was some thug jeopardizing what he thought was a good relationship with the British. The police said that they would keep Mustafa under surveillance. In 1986 he left London and went to North Africa, turning over the running of his filling station to a friend.

The FRC launched two of its most bloody attacks in September 1986. The first operation, in Karachi, Pakistan, was planned by Samir Khader in conjunction with Abu Nidal and Mustafa Murad. It seemed unusual since it was an attack on an American airliner, Pan American; the FRC generally avoided attacking the United States or its airlines. But the decision to attack Pan Am was made by the group leader. The planners originally wanted to attack a Saudi jet in Karachi. (According to two different sources, the Saudis were not paying the FRC and needed gentle reminders.) However, the confident leader, a man known by the code name Abbas, knew the timetables and saw that a Pan Am jumbo was going to be taking off at about the same time as the Saudi jet. He decided, contrary to the orders of his superiors, to go for the Pan Am.

Abbas was the nephew of Mohammed Sufarini, an important FRC Central Committee member who left Jordan in 1985 (his name in the organization was Omar Hamde). Breaking FRC's rules of conduct, Abbas was able to meet his uncle on his way to Karachi, and they spoke at length. The uncle convinced Abbas that he was a tool of Israel, but Abbas, rather than abandon the operation, changed targets. Since he was the only contact with the liaison, the other members of the group know nothing about this. Samir Khader helped plan this action, but he had no contact with Abbas. The liaison carried the instructions from Khader to Abbas.

The four gunmen arrived at the airport after receiving their weapons and altered instructions. They got onto the tarmac and stormed the 747 after it had finished loading passengers (about 400), climbing up the ramp and shooting. Abbas, calling himself Mustafa, told the passengers to keep their hands over their heads, roughing up anyone who did not comply. According to the newspapers, the hijackers demanded to be flown to Cyprus, but their motives were never completely clear.[25]

Reports conflict as to why the plane was stormed by Pakistani commandos. One official said that Abbas or Mustafa began to rape a stewardess. The plane's power unit was allowed to go out so the plane would be dark for the storming.[26] The commandos climbed up the ramps and emergency exits, firing, acting very much like the terrorists they were aiming to get. There was pandemonium, with gunfire everywhere. Hardly a passenger left the plane unhurt—many were killed or wounded by the commandos—and it would have been worse had the hijackers used the belts of explosives they wore. Telephone callers in Cyprus and Beirut rushed to claim credit for the operation, using previously unheard of names. The London *Times* remarked, "Lebanese police suspect that various intelligence organizations in the Middle East are often behind the claims." Using the name Fedayeen Revolutionary Cells, Abu Nidal claimed the action. The gunmen would be convicted to death in July 1988 but later taken off death row by Benazir Bhuto.

Hours after the bloody resolution of the attempted Pan Am hijacking, two FRC gunmen walked into the Neve Shalom synagogue in Istanbul with submachine guns and hand grenades. They let fly their grenades and began shooting, creating a nightmare for a congregation who had nowhere to run, leaving 21 of the faithful dead and several injured. Apparently the gunmen either killed themselves, possibly with their own grenades, or they were shot by someone who was never identified. It was the bloodiest attack against Jews since the Nazi atrocities of World War II, and it understandably rekindled fear in Jewish communities around the world. (A Jewish community has been living in Turkey since its ancestors were expelled from Spain in the 1490s.[27]) Investigators had little to go on, but there was no doubt that the attack was staged by the FRC, as the FRC boldly acknowledged.[28] The next day Abu Iyad had to hold a press conference condemning the act and adding that it only supported the enemy.[29]

The following June the Italian police arrested two Arabs on a train between Turin and Milan. According to Reuters, they confessed to being part of the group that attacked the synagogue, saying that the group's controller chose by lot who would be the suicide attackers.[30] A female caller in Beirut claimed that the synagogue attack was in revenge for the destruction of a vessel carrying weapons to the PLO, but it seems hard to imagine that Abu Nidal would be interested in avenging the PLO. One thing is certain: these two attacks blackened the name of Palestinians.

In July 1987 a Palestinian writer and cartoonist submitted to the widely read Kuwaiti newspaper *al-Qabas* a sketch making fun of a girlfriend of Arafat named Rashida. It became instantly and hilariously famous throughout the Arab world, reprinted in many newspapers. This was not the first time that the cartoonist, Ali Adhami, known by his pen name Naji al-Ali, had lampooned the PLO. He often depicted them as money-hungry and corrupt, out of touch with the Palestinians in the camps, a bourgeois revolutionary movement. Right after the cartoon appeared the Mossad flew Sowan to Israel to discuss the matter.

Some who have written about this affair have concluded that Naji was a traitor, but he was a strong patriot and nationalist who grew up in South Lebanon. PLO leaders were angered at him for that last cartoon, but he knew the leadership personally, and they knew that he made fun of all Arab leaders, considering all regimes backward and oppressive. He was kicked out of one Arab country after another. By 1985 he had to move out of the Arab world altogether and work from London. Several PLO officials in Tunis say that they had wind of something and phoned Naji several times to tell him that his life was in danger. But Naji had been threatened before.

By chance Abd al-Rahim Mustafa, the former PLO security specialist who had become acquainted with Mossad undercover agent Ismail Sowan, came back to London at the end of 1986 to settle his affairs. When the cartoon came out, Sowan and Bushara Samara approached Mustafa and got him thinking that he would please Arafat if he killed Naji. Mustafa gave Sowan 6 suitcases of arms, including 4 assault rifles, grenades, and 145 kg of Semtex, to store. Probably the Mossad set up Mustafa through another agent. Sowan called his Mossad contact, Dave, who seemed to know all about it and told the nervous Sowan not to worry; they would handle everything. One evening as Naji was going to his office near Sloan Square, an Arab gunman came up and emptied his pistol into Naji, then walked calmly down Draycott Avenue.[31] Naji stayed in a coma for over a month, then died.

The finger of blame automatically pointed at the PLO for wanting to silence their critic after the infamous cartoon, but Aweida kept telling skeptical police investigators that the Mossad was responsible. Scotland Yard's antiterrorism chief Allan Talbot was especially interested in Mustafa, who left the country about the time Naji was killed. Samara also left the country. The Mossad sent Samara back to London from Italy with forged papers, and he was stopped as he was crossing the English Channel. The police detained and questioned him. They found in his diary the address of Sowan, who had moved to Hull by the Sea and enrolled in college. When the police arrived at Sowan's apartment on Westbourne Avenue, they discovered the six suitcases, and during Sowan's second court appearance for possession of weapons he began spilling the Mossad's beans. The police deported Samara, and the man who pulled the trigger on Naji was not caught. Mustafa almost certainly had a hand in the killing, and possibly Samara, but they were not the gunmen. Sowan went to trial and got 11 years for illegal possession of arms. He knew nothing of the killing of Naji and is now bitter. His wife never visited him, but the Israeli counsel did once.

The British were unhappy with Israel. Thatcher ordered five Mossad agents to leave the country, giving them a warning that if they continued playing dirty in Britain they would suffer more serious consequences. Israeli deputy ambassador Jacob Barad, who had also been directly involved in the affair, having "coordinated the work of the Mossad at the embassy with Mr. Regev," was declared *persona non grata.*[32] In a move to be evenhanded, the British also expelled one of the PLO diplomats, Zaki Abu al-Hawa, forgetting that he was not in the country at the time and knew nothing of Sowan. It turned out to be a diplomatic slap in the face of the Israeli embassy, since it put that office on equal standing with the PLO.[33]

The assassination of Naji came hard on the heels of a scandal involving the Mossad's use of forged British passports. It is said that the Mossad was running an operation in West Germany to kidnap or kill German scientists who were going to work for Pakistan. One of the Mossad agents left a stack of the passports in a German telephone booth. Israel initially refused to apologize, even though the Mossad was caught red-handed. It took a lot of diplomatic threats to persuade Israel to offer even a half-hearted apology, which was not accomplished by any promise not to do it again. The Mossad likes forged British passports.[34]

A few years before this activity the Israelis were using their diplomatic immunity to kidnap a former Nigerian transport minister, Umaru Dikko. British police, ignoring immunity, opened a crate and discovered Dikko and a Mossad anesthetist and arrested two other Mossad agents who were abducting Dikko.[35] After the killing of Naji, several members of Parliament openly voiced their displeasure about the incident. However, months after Naji's death, Israel and Britain resumed their exchange of intelligence.[36]

It is difficult to underestimate the effects of the Palestinian uprising that they named the Intifada; not only did it change the politics of the Middle East, but it helped change the world. The images of the young people defying the mighty Israeli army with stones, standing a short distance from heavily armed, quick-to-shoot soldiers, inspired the revolutions of East Europe that began within a year of the Intifada. There has not been a study on this, but for the oppressed people of East Europe, seeing the youth of Palestine taking their fate into their hands must have provided an impetus to rebel against their own oppression.

Throughout the Arab world the boys and girls of the Intifada became glamorized heroes to whom every leader paid homage. Several Arab countries tried to link their own governments to the Intifada by intercutting television images from the Intifada with pictures of their leaders in front of various crowds. The Intifada also attracted public sympathy outside the Arab world as hundreds of thousands of demonstrators took to the streets of European cities to support it. Even the White House voiced "concern" about Israel's use of force.

The PLO had a bright but unoriginal public relations idea for a story that would dramatize the plight of Palestinians. They would launch an unarmed ship of distinguished Palestinians who had been thrown out of their country, sailing it back to Haifa, in imitation of the Zionist ships that had brought Jews to Palestine a half-century earlier. The political office in Tunis put out press feelers and got a positive response for the story. They found 131 volunteers and even more members of the international press ready to accompany them.

Israel feared the PR potential of a shipload of unarmed Palestinians. A shipload of fighters they could handle, but a group seeking peace and wanting to return to their country posed a major threat. The Palestinians rented a ship from Greece, one that already made regular trips to Haifa via Cyprus. It was the dead of winter, and the company had hardly any passengers, the Intifada having driven away more tourists. But the Israelis threatened to sink the ship, forcing the shipping company to renege on the agreement.

The PLO then bought a ship of its own, the *Sol Phryne*, a Greek ferry. They docked it in Limassol, Cyprus and christened it *al-Awda* ("the return"), the new Exodus. They flew the Palestinians and the press from Athens, and amid a hubbub of publicity they were ready to embark. Israel said that the ship would never be allowed near Haifa.

Actually, the Mossad had a plan based on the poor security that characterized any project the PLO undertook. Cyprus was one of the Mossad's centers, and they went after one of the main organizers, a high-ranking PLO leader named Mohammed al-Tamimi, who had been in Athens and had flown to Cyprus when the ship was secured. The Mossad planted a remote-control bomb in a Volkswagen owned by Marwan al-Kayyali, another important official who was also working out the details with Cyprus authorities for the event. Riding in the car as well as was Mohammed Ibheis, a third PLO official. The Mossad got three officials in one shot.[37]

The triple killing put a damper on the project. Tamimi had been a courteous, bright, and popular young man. He and the others had had no security protection, and the PLO had not thought it necessary to add any even though they knew this project was driving the Israeli government mad.

To make sure *al-Awda* did not sail, Israeli frogmen planted a mine on the side of the ship which blew a hole in the hull and made it unseaworthy. The project lost steam, and everyone went home. Terrorism succeeded.

Cyprus complained that Israel, who denied involvement, was using their country for terrorism, but most of the press paid little attention. In terrorism studies the incident is hardly mentioned. The PLO's incompetence in the ways of the world allowed Israel to defeat the project, ending another PLO propaganda opportunity. When the three murdered PLO officials were buried in Amman, tens of thousands turned out to pay their last respects,[38] but the ship was forgotten.

In March 1988 the FRC struck another Asian airport. This time a lone gunman went to the Bombay airport and attacked a bus carrying an Italian flight crew, wounding a pilot. He had forced his way onto the bus and begun shooting; two shots hit Captain Santeleillo, then the gun jammed. He threw a grenade, but it did not work; then he threw another, which also failed to explode, and two off-duty plainclothesmen rushed to the scene and wrestled him to the ground. According to an FRC official, the attacker was supposed to hit a Pan American crew bus, but he could not tell the difference between a Pan Am and an Italian crew, demonstrating the mental abilities of FRC personnel. It seemed obviously an action designed to fail.[39]

That was just before the Mossad killed Abu Jihad in a complicated operation that involved an assassination team of up to 40 army commandos, dozens of secondary personnel, and a Boeing 707 full of senior military commanders. The killing has been well documented. Abu Jihad was well guarded, but his villa was vulnerable to a sea attack, and that evening he gave most of his guards the night off. The assassins drove up in a mini-bus and filled his body with several dozen bullets, also killing three guards.[40] It was a right-wing government's attempt to tame the Intifada.

Two months later the FRC devastated the British Club and Acropole Hotel in Khartoum, Sudan. They used five gunmen who stormed the hotel with machine guns and grenades, killing at least seven, including two children and four British nationals. Three of the FRC members, using the name Arab

Three PLO officials killed by car bomb in Limassol, Cyprus, February 1988. *Left to right:* **Mohammed al-Tamimi, Mohammed Ibheis, and Marwan al-Kayyali.**

Fedayeen Cells, were Lebanese recruits. There were stories from the terrorism experts that the attack was revenge for the assassination of Abu Jihad,[41] but again, Abu Nidal does not even the score for Fatah. The senseless killing of innocents seemed a direct affront to the passive resistance of the Intifada, which was probably also the reason for an attack that occurred about the same time on a Greek ferry called the *City of Poros*, which was carrying a load of European tourists. Nine died in that attack.

In a new type of terrorism, the Italian press reported in April 1988 that Israeli grapefruit had been injected with a blue poison. The health ministry, taking the claim seriously, fed the suspect grapefruit to mice, which died. When the results of the tests hit the newspapers, several people were also reported to have died from eating Israeli grapefruit. Israeli produce was banned until scientists convinced the health ministry that any citrus would kill a mouse. An Italian radical group had created the scare by injecting a few grapefruit with a blue dye and leaking the story of poison.

One day around the same time, a four-wheel-drive Mitsubishi with a man and woman inside was trying to park outside the Israeli embassy in Nicosia, Cyprus. The Cypriot guards shooed the driver away twice. The police spotted a suspicious-looking Arab standing nearby with a device in his hand. As soon as he noticed that he was being watched, he ran down an empty area and dropped the box he was holding. When it hit the ground, the car exploded while it was on a bridge, killing an elderly pedestrian as well as one of the occupants. The person in the passenger seat survived.[42]

The action is often reported as an FRC attack—FRC claims it—but outside of the stupidity of the action, it does not resemble previous FRC attacks. FRC does not attack Israeli embassies or use women. The attempt may have been the work of Hizballah. But an anonymous caller to NBC-TV in New York—the FRC never had anyone there—claimed that the attack was carried out by Abu Nidal. This was reported in the press and by the United States State Department, even though when the FRC attacks, they never use the name of Abu Nidal. Actions like attacking Jewish worshipers are characteristic of the FRC, while trying to attack Israel or its embassy is not. It is not possible to park near the embassy, and whoever planned the attack either did not know this or planned it with that fact in mind, the amount of explosives being small and without the ability to harm the embassy.

Chapter 17
The Business of the FRC

The Terrorist and the policeman both come from the same basket.

Joseph Conrad, *Lord Jim* (1900)

I began examining the FRC in 1987 after having dinner with some Israelis and hearing one person, who had worked for Israeli security abroad, mention that Israel ran the Abu Nidal group. It was an open secret among the Israeli security establishment, he said. I wondered about the veracity of the claim. I had met many militant Palestinians, and although their militancy was usually armchair rhetoric, Abu Nidal did represent a strand of Palestinian thought. There are Palestinians who hate Jews, hate America, hate Britain. The refugee camps are teeming with the volatile desperation of a stateless, hopeless people ready to throw their empty existence in front of Nasser or Saddam Hussein or any other crazy who can rock the boat, even if everyone drowns in the process.

Over the years I interviewed about 200 people, often during late-night gatherings in safe houses or cafes, talking to people who either knew or pretended to know about terrorist actions. Palestinian leader Abu Iyad had taken special interest in my research, and his name opened many doors to information, rumor, and gossip. Norman Antokol and Mayer Nudell observe, "The typical terrorist is young, highly educated, and intelligent."[1] That has not been my experience. The world of gunmen is not a happy or healthy one, nor is it intellectually or emotionally developed. Many people I met were dishonest and immature. Good sources do not exist.

I studied terrorist incidents and traveled through Europe, looking at the sites where actions had taken place, interviewing police and journalists. According to the United States State Department, which compiles accurate information on FRC actions, the group killed or wounded nine hundred people on three continents, not counting the hundreds of their own fighters.[2] I talked to people who knew Abu Nidal as a young man, and to those who left

174

his group after the 1978 split and the 1989 split. I went to Lebanon and talked to members of the organization. It was terribly easy to discover their buildings, how many people worked there, their activities. FRC worked like a religious cult, in which immature members think they are special and believe that everyone will eventually realize the rightness of their cause. At first I wanted to meet Abu Nidal, but later it seemed that such an interview would not be worth the effort.

FRC's killings, their major activity, can be divided five ways: (1) Internal killings: the group massacred 200–500 of their own members, mostly their best fighters. (2) Killing of Palestinians: we have seen how they targeted intellectuals, moderates, and effective leaders. (3) Killing of other Arabs: attacks on diplomats and embassies, Jordanian and Syrian for political reasons, Saudi and Emirates for extortion. (4) Attacks against the West: tourists and airlines. (5) Attacks against Jews in Europe and Istanbul.

Patrick Seale also researched the Abu Nidal group, and I have tried to avoid duplicating the items presented in his study. In European capitals terrorism experts talked to me about the Italian Brigate Rosse (BR), the French Action Directe (AC), the Greek November 17, the German Red Army Faction (RAF), as well as Abu Nidal. These groups seemed to do nothing but discredit their cause. They had no popular support, and those who were wise to terrorism were telling me that in reality they did not exist. Abu Nidal had no popular support and not one prisoner in an Israeli jail.

"There isn't much difference between all these groups," one Western expert told me in Athens. "They're fabricated." He went on:

> There's no such thing as November 17 or the Red Army Faction, or Abu Nidal. The IRA has an ideology, popular support, a movement. So do the Basque ETA and ASALA.[3] They made logical actions against their enemies. The other groups have money only, and how could a small group get money like that? Do you know how much it costs to keep safe houses, run training camps, make false identities, pay gunmen, secretaries, accountants, arms smugglers? Look at Rome and Vienna airports or a professional operation like the kidnap of Aldo Moro. They cost a fortune, and these are supposed to be struggling leftists. Only countries with armies and secret services and embassies can run operations on that scale.

At first groups such as the BR picked appropriate targets such as fascists or Mafia bosses—their enemies. Then they began to turn against the progressives.[4] When a group begins to target friends instead of enemies, we have to suspect that it has been infiltrated by those who showed themselves as more extreme, more patriotic, and climbed the group's hierarchy. Infiltrators chant slogans of defiance and preach a line of no compromise, becoming the epitome of revolutionaries, usually splintering the movement by creating internal dissent and by getting people to hate them simply because they are so hateful.

They often get rid of the original leadership by informing on the old leaders so they can be arrested; then the infiltrators become the new leaders. I saw this happen in anti–Vietnam War demonstrations when a few people pretending to be more gung-ho would pick fights with police and turn a strong civil movement into an antisociety farce.[5] In Greece since 1974 not one November 17 member has been caught though the organization has assassinated at least 15 diplomats and Greek officials. The BR began in 1968 as a group of idealistic intellectuals, but by 1977 their actions had degenerated into a senseless killing and destroying spree, targeting communists and union organizers.[6] It was shown that BR leaders did not have the organizational or military skills for their broad activities. Such an armed movement without a proper ideology is easy to control.[7]

In Europe no communist party came to power, though communist coalitions in Athens, Rome, and Paris were realistic possibilities; left parties commanded over 20 percent in France and 35 percent in Italy. When Moro wanted to include the communists in the majority, he was kidnapped and killed. Secret services infiltrated these radical groups and made them militant.

When a group is infiltrated, it suddenly has millions of dollars to finance a mini-war. The Abu Abbas attack against the beaches in Tel Aviv cost over $3 million and took two years to plan. Abu Abbas has 100 men; probably 10 percent are plants.[8] The secret of these groups is money. If they can show boys safe houses and weapons, yell fancy slogans, they can attract simple recruits. Only a few are necessary. Many of Abu Nidal's recruits were under 16. Baader-Meinhof had 20 core people, and with that number they successfully discredited other leftists.

Guerrilla movements start with a handful of loyal supporters, but they have an ideology. A thousand men and no ideology produces chaos, but ten men and an ideology can ignite a revolution.[9] The other Palestinian groups had followings, people who supported Habash or Arafat or Jabril. Those were real organizations who performed logical though often repugnant actions. But Abu Nidal aimed to kill Palestinians and Jordanians and deaf-mute English tourists, to spray the Rome synagogue and toss bombs at British Airways.

"Look at the outcome," people kept telling me, "and you'll determine the cause. See who benefits." Abu Nidal appears to be a true nationalist, and his speech appeals to the young men who live without hope in Chatila, but he has not carried out one operation against Israel or the United States. Other marginal groups such as Jabril, Abu Abbas, and Saika attacked Israel. I told an Arab journalist about a road in the West Bank that runs through an Arab town to a Jewish settlement. One day a boy threw a molotov at one of the yellow license plate cars and killed a child. The Israelis arrested a hundred boys, slapped on curfews, blew up houses, and dug up an orchard of olive trees, but for over a year the settlers stopped using that road.

"Exactly what I'm illustrating," he retorted. "An action against an enemy

Stark FRC office in Mar Elias Refugee Camp with photos of "martyrs," none of whom were actually FRC members.

is understandable and effective. It may be immoral and disgusting and a dozen other adjectives, but it makes sense that someone would do that. It wouldn't make sense for that boy to collect a hundred thousand dollars and come to Athens to throw his molotov at French tourists or to go around killing other Palestinians in Paris."

Abu Nidal spends his energy eliminating Palestinians, the most effective people, the brains of the movement, the same type the Mossad killed. They seem to be literate intellectuals, Westernized, moderate, effective. I am not sure why, but almost all those killed by FRC or Mossad were leftists. Other governments benefit from the work of Abu Nidal, since he helped avoid the creation of a Palestinian state. Any time there is a massacre or an assassination, people instinctively turn away from what is frightening and insecure and toward what is safe: the status quo. An unchanged Middle East map represents stability for those in power. Repressive Arab governments gain when Abu Nidal shoots Christmas tourists.

People who knew Abu Nidal are divided over whether he was an agent or was manipulated by others. Everyone believes one or the other; I have never met anyone apart from members who believes FRC is clean,[10] and no one disputes that his power comes from his money. Abu Nidal is thought to have tens of millions of dollars, perhaps up to $200 million. Where did he get this money? Ostensible sources would include sponsorship, first from Iraq, then Syria, then Libya. Just as widely accepted are reports of blackmail and arms sales. However, it is impossible that he should have amassed such a fortune from those means.

His first sponsorship dollars came from Iraq, which had originally pledged its support to the PLO. After the Arab League recognized the PLO in 1974, Arab governments committed themselves to annual donations. Iraq pledged between 40,000 and 60,000 Iraqi dinars a month ($150,000–200,000) to the PLO. When Abu Nidal announced that he was the true Fatah and split from Arafat, the Iraqis began giving Abu Nidal the money they had been donating to Arafat. Abu Nidal told members who left that he received more than a million dollars a month from Iraq, but 50,000 dinars is probably accurate, and he may have not gotten it every month; the PLO generally had to chase down Arab heads of state in an often unsuccessful attempt to translate their pledges into cash, and FRC likely met with the same sort of difficulty.

Abu Nidal also took for himself the PLO's real estate in Baghdad, of no translatable value, and the weapons and supplies that China had donated to the PLO. By the time of the split, less than half of the $17 million shipment was in Iraq, and he had to give a quantity to the Iraqis; one source told me that Iraq took all the Chinese weapons. In 1978 Abu Nidal passed on more weapons to a group led by Abu Daoud, who was trying to raise a militia in South Lebanon outside the authority of the PLO. Nevertheless, FRC clearly retained a large arsenal.

A monthly 50,000 dinars was barely enough to meet Abu Nidal's expenses, even though the FRC had been a streamlined organization from the beginning, and his expenses were low (unlike the PFLP or Fatah, which have thousands of men on their payroll and need to maintain hundreds of buildings and vehicles). If Abu Nidal's men were paid 40 dinars each a week, including food and shelter expenses—a bare minimum since many of his men had families—and payroll accounted for 40 percent of his expenses (in most corporations payroll is usually less than a third of total expenses), with the other 60 percent going toward newspaper publishing, fighter training, travel, office expenses, vehicles, and so on, he would be able to support only slightly more than 100 men on the Iraqi contribution. These figures do not even take into consideration the cost of building his desert training camp or the enormous amount of money needed for outside operations. Yet within a couple of years of the split he had over 200 men on his payroll. By the time of his sickness in 1978 he had perhaps 300 men. This would mean that he had to come up with two or three times the amount of money he got from Iraq just to keep in the black.

Abu Nidal claims that in the 1970s he made a few huge arms deals with African countries and Yemen netting him $50–60 million profit. There is no proof of those deals anywhere; nor is there proof that he had the contacts or the transport necessary to make such deals, unless he dealt in conjunction with people in the Iraqi government or, more likely, with the Israeli government.

Perhaps he sold the Chinese weapons, but he would have needed Iraqi government help to ship them out of the country.

There is no doubt that Abu Nidal sold small arms through his complex financial network. He built an import-export business in several cities, dealing with everything from cans of green beans to crates of hand grenades. Abu Nidal began establishing this international network in the 1970s, concentrating on outlets in Warsaw and East Berlin. Later, he had branches in London and Athens. In the beginning, Abu Nidal's company, known by several names but principally Zibado, would buy cheap products in the East Bloc and ship them to the central office in Baghdad, where they would be sold to wholesalers at a profit.

Abu Nidal never mixed finance with terrorism. Though he did use his import-export connections to deal in weapons, each office of Zibado was run only as a business, and the office directors knew nothing of the squads of researchers and killers that the FRC intelligence department sent. Each branch, including London, dealt in weapons, but the actual weapons did not pass through Zibado offices, any more than did crates of canned tomatoes.

Zibado was a good business. It would have made Abu Nidal personally wealthy, but it would not have provided the funds to run the FRC on the side. Abu Nidal was a good organizer and businessman, but he was not a wheeler-dealer who traveled far and wide rustling up business. He had sharp businessmen working in each Zibado branch, finding food products and arranging export to Baghdad. It is too hard to know exactly how much money he made on those export deals.

The director of the East Berlin office of Zibado was a man named Derar Abu al-Fatah al-Silwani. He had an office in the Foreign Trade Building and a few accounts in his name, but most of the money remained in the name of Abu Nidal's family. In 1986 Silwani escaped to West Berlin and gave the authorities information about Abu Nidal's financial network in exchange for asylum. According to the United States State Department, the United States mounted a diplomatic campaign on Poland and other East European countries in 1987, seriously inhibiting Abu Nidal's financial network.[11] Poland had viewed Abu Nidal's company as beneficial since he exported products, bringing in hard currency, and some Polish officials may have not known that Zibado was a front for Abu Nidal. Silwani vanished in Europe, possibly in the United States, joining another former Central Committee member, Adnan Zayed al-Kalani, who left a year earlier.

The United States State Department also pressured the Greek government to close down Abu Nidal's Athens branch of the company on Solonos Street, which operated under the name al-Noor.[12] The Athens office was opened right after the Israeli invasion of Lebanon, and it acted solely as an import-export office, sitting next to hundreds of similar offices in Athens. The branch was run by a man named Musa Mohammed Mufeed, a Palestinian who was recruited in Iraq. When the branch closed in 1987, Mufeed returned to Sidon.

The Warsaw office was the most important, apart from Baghdad. It was run by Samir Najmeddin, an Abu Nidal loyalist, who was treated well and rewarded handsomely. As head of the Polish branch called SAS (the Arabs pronounce it "Sash"), which operated in the Intraco building on Stawski Street in Warsaw and had a branch in London, he traveled throughout Europe on business, largely dealing in weapons.[13] Acting on information from Silwani, the Swiss apprehended Najmeddin when he was in their country, but he was freed and went to Libya, where Abu Nidal demoted him to a secondary position.[14] Abu Nidal had three front companies in London, including an insurance business, laundering and moving money with the knowledge of the CIA.[15]

In addition to his alleged deals with Yemen and countries in Africa, Abu Nidal boasts that he earned $90 million from arms sales during the Iran-Iraq war, selling weapons to both sides—an interesting claim, since Israel cornered the market in supplying arms to Iran. Knowledgeable sources estimate that Israel indirectly provided half of Iran's weapons during the war. After in-depth scrutiny by journalists covering the Iran-Contra affair, we know many of the channels of weapons sales, the principal arms dealers, the shipping routes where arms were directed. Nothing points back to Abu Nidal. There is no reason to believe that Abu Nidal sold any great quantity of weapons during that war.

As for blackmail, Abu Nidal claims that he received protection money from Kuwait, Saudi Arabia, and the United Arab Emirates. There seems to be no doubt about that. He targeted those countries for terrorist attacks in order to extort them. However, it is doubtful that they made continuous payments to his organization; Abu Nidal had to make many operations against them to convince them to keep paying. Defectors say that Saudi Arabia made only one payment of $5 million. Whatever the payments, Abu Nidal had money for outside operations before he began blackmailing the Gulf.

Some sources that finance other Palestinian groups are not available to Abu Nidal. For example, in addition to government contributions and investments, the PLO collects a tax from Palestinian workers in Arab countries. Because Abu Nidal has no popular support, he receives no such donations. Several militias made money during the early stage of the Lebanon war by raiding downtown banks and blowing up their vaults, but Abu Nidal could not operate in Lebanon until after the Israeli invasion. Ahmed Jabril receives money from Syria, but the Syrians are intelligent enough not to give the group more than it needs to cover expenses. They would not want Jabril to act independently. By the same reasoning, Iraq would have been stupid to give more money than needed to Abu Nidal.

After Saddam Hussein seized power in Iraq, Abu Nidal stopped receiving money from the Iraqi government. When he went to Syria in 1983, he received no money from that government either. Instead, he was expected to provide income for Syria; one of the attractions of bringing in Abu Nidal was his ability not only to embarrass the PLO but also to bring in hard currency, buy houses, and provide jobs.

By the time the group went to Libya in 1987, any money they might have received from the Libyans was unimportant. The group had been rich since the 1970s.

While Abu Nidal was in Libya his organization was spending between $1.25 and $1.5 million a month on normal expenses, almost $20 million a year, which is high for a small organization, reflecting the staggering cost of outside operations. When the group went into Syria and Lebanon in 1983, they went in buying apartments and houses. They owned 150 flats in Damascus; 100 in South Lebanon, mostly in Sidon; and another 200 in greater Beirut as well as a few apartments in Tripoli, Lebanon. These flats are either rented for income or used by the organization. Because of the strict rent control laws in Lebanon coupled with an extreme deflation of the Lebanese pound, the apartments in Lebanon proved to be sour investments.

By looking at FRC offices in different cities, it is difficult to see that the organization has money. Their buildings are stark—as are almost all Palestinian offices—and not well kept. Apart from Politburo and Central Committee members, none of the members seem rich. Abu Nidal himself has simple tastes. The FRC puts out a slick magazine and full-color posters, but printing is cheap in Lebanon. However, Najmeddin had an FRC account in the London branch of the fraudulent BCCI containing $60 million, with the knowledge of British authorities.[16]

Abu Nidal had other investments in Europe and the Middle East. I kept stumbling on small businesses here and there, a bakery in Beirut run by a family, an oriental restaurant in Cyprus run by two brothers. He used numbered accounts in Swiss banks and had an extensive network of investments in the cities where he ran his business. (If any state is a supporter of terrorism, it is Switzerland, which protects terrorists, dictators, and drug lords through its secret banking policy.)

Terrorists have several avenues for bankrolling their activities: dealing in weapons, robbing banks, kidnapping, dealing in drugs, blackmailing countries, or receiving contributions. The FRC never dealt in drugs, robbed banks, kidnapped for ransom, or received donations. The amount of arms dealing seems questionable, and they did not receive blackmail money until, at the earliest, 1980. A more in-depth analysis of his finances is difficult because hardly anyone knows about them, even high-ranking defectors. Abd al-Rahman Issa knew a limited amount, but when Abu Nidal's older daughter, nephew, and son became of age, he introduced them to his finances, putting bank accounts in their names. His accounting seems the most impenetrable part of his organization.

To sum up, Abu Nidal is undoubtedly rich, and he controls his organization by holding all its financial keys and maintaining a diverse investment portfolio. His combined assets are certainly over $50 million. An unstable man like Abu Nidal is easily manipulated and could be easily overthrown by others in the organization if he did not have absolute control over the group's finances. Unlike most businesses, FRC employees are in a non–financially productive role (i.e., assassins are a financial liability, not an asset, since they do not produce income).

The financial leverage Abu Nidal wields is kept in place by the FRC's highly structured organization, excessively ordered for a small group. Used to maintain secrecy, it also assures the smooth working of the group. Everyone has his function, and if a member tries to discover the function of others, he has to be reported. Thus most members know little about the FRC. They may have only one or two real contacts known only by false names. As we look at the organization it will become obvious that it must have been engineered and run by an efficient and well-ordered group or individual. No madman or drunk could have devised and kept together such a tight, orderly framework.

The group had four ranks. The highest order, the Politburo, with 9 or 10 members including Abu Nidal, controlled the organization, made daily decisions, and implemented all internal and external functions, holding the organization's secrets. The 25 to 27 members of the Central Committee, the Politburo members among them, discussed situations in general and had no power to implement policy or deal with specific situations such as money and terrorist actions. The third rank, the Revolutionary Council, with about 50 members, including all those of the Central Committee and Politburo, looked and functioned as a parliament and took on constitutional and theoretical issues. Finally came the rank and file, the recruits, gunmen, fighters, and students who had no say in the organization. The FRC worked through departments, of which there were eight, each one controlled by a Politburo member. All departments were strictly closed; departments could not mix functions or obtain information about one another's activities. Abu Nidal was organized almost exactly like the Mossad.[17]

The *Political Department* had three subdivisions. The first was responsible for political ties with Arabs and Europeans, coordinating the secret relations and deals FRC cut with countries and political organizations. The second branch was responsible for printing and public relations, issuing the internal newsletter *The Path*, written by the leadership, and its external magazine, *Filistin al-Thoura*, ("*Revolutionary Palestine*"), which came out more or less weekly, full of hyperbole and bold slogans repeated time and again about the Zionist-imperialists. (It is amazing that a group of only 200 to 300 members could put out such a slick product. It takes a tremendous amount of work, personnel, and money, to produce a weekly magazine. The other Palestinian organizations also produced weekly magazines, but they had thousands of members.) The political department's third branch was the office of the spokesperson, which is the only contact outsiders can have with the organization.

The *Intelligence Department* (in Arabic it was called "information"), which is of most interest to us, became divided between Sidon, responsible for intelligence matters in Lebanon, and Libya (between 1987 and 1990), responsible for work outside Lebanon. The Libyan branch, called "resistance," controlled outside operations and was headed by Murad until his murder. This department had a rigorous agenda, being tightly regulated through its bylaws. It was highly compartmentalized, so that those knowledgeable of some actions were ignorant of others. It was also responsible for taking over (from the political department) secret relations with other countries and groups if those relations reached a stage of cooperation.

The *Military Department*, located in Lebanon, was responsible for FRC fighters. Created in 1985, the military department operated in the refugee camps and had no connection with outside operations, though a few people responsible for outside operations were trained in the military camp in Lebanon's Bakaa Valley, and also some fighters were transferred to the intelligence department and thus performed outside operations. A person could be chosen by the intelligence department, at which point he would be isolated from the military department and then transferred. In this sense the intelligence department was higher than the military one.

The *Economic Department* had two distinct branches. The first dealt with daily expenses: payroll, bills, mortgages, and the like. The second branch, FRC's backbone, handled investments and was under the direct control of Abu Nidal and his son.

The *Organizational Department* was responsible for members studying or working outside Lebanon, the nonfighters in Arab and European countries. It maintained contact with them and kept track of their needs. It was not, however, responsible for recruiting new members. The FRC divided the world into six regions, each headed by a Central Committee member: the Arab countries; Asia; Africa; East Europe; Western Europe; and the countries of Turkey, Greece and Yugoslavia, where they had offices and weapon dumps.

The *Scientific Committee* was responsible for explosives. This department developed weapons and bombs needed by the intelligence and military departments. Its field was technical: car bombs and special weapons necessary for operations. It sounds ominous, but actually the Abu Nidal group used standard weapons, rarely employing plastic explosive or sophisticated arms.

The *Secretariat* was a most powerful department since it handled all communication. All information from the Politburo, Central Committee, and Revolutionary Council passed through this department, making it a store of information that served as an internal security net.

The *Membership Committee*, a small group of three or four people, was responsible for each member's file in which his real name and all his personal information, including information that could be used against him, was contained. This committee, too, acted as a sort of internal intelligence, for it knew the strengths and weaknesses of every member.

With the organization divided so strictly, it would be possible to work next to someone for 10 years and not know anything about him. The FRC membership roll varied from period to period. When the group was in Iraq, from 1974 to the 1978 split, it had between 300 and 400 members. When the group was in Syria, from 1983 to 1987 it had fewer than 200. After the group moved to Libya it had 350 to 400 members; many of those were fighters in Lebanon. Any of Abu Nidal's people who discovered something are now dead, killed by Abu Nidal.

On November 25, 1987, Jabril's GC organized an ultralight plane raid into an Israeli military camp. The pilot, Khaled Aker, threw grenades and opened fire, killing six soldiers and wounding seven before he was later killed.[18] Less than two weeks later the Intifada began after eight Palestinians were killed by a truck, but many people believe that Aker, who became known as a Palestinian Rambo, sparked the revolt. That type of terrorism had a vastly different effect on both Israelis and Palestinians than the FRC operations, which were cowardly and had no connection with the conflict. Like his organization, Abu Nidal's activities were closed and secret, and their effects were subtle and distorted.

Chapter 18
Holy Wars and Hollywood: The Manufacture of Modern Terrorism

Terror and Force are the only way to triumph over reason.
Adolph Hitler, *Mein Kampf*

In the 1980s the first thing visitors entering American embassies saw was a large "Wanted" sign for terrorists, a frightening illustration of someone pointing a gun at all who entered with a notice that the United States is ready to pay up to $2,000,000 for information on terrorists. It was an unpleasant way to greet visitors.

When the *Achille Lauro* was commandeered by Palestinians, Italian cabinet minister Guilio Amato said that the Reagan administration kept pressuring the Italian government to attack the ship even though, in Reagan's words, it "would be a high-risk operation."[1] The Italian government opposed such adventurism.[2] Arafat called Prime Minister Craxi and said he would help negotiate. They struck a deal with the hijackers, who agreed to release the ship in return for safe passage to Egypt. Had the Italians attacked the cruise liner it might have resulted in dozens of people being killed. The hijackers, who were equipped with automatics and grenades, had most of the passengers and crew in one of the large dining rooms, a confined area. Had they been raided — and there was at least one person on the bridge to notice — the hijackers could have killed many before the raiding party came close to them.

The desire to raid in a hostage situation indicates the United States government's obsession with terrorism. The terrorism scare was at its height, the central agenda for the United States government and the press, giving rise to

185

an anti–Arab media extravaganza. Cartoons, articles, and documentaries featured bloodthirsty, dagger-waving fanatics ready to pounce on civilized values. From Hollywood, dark-skinned, masked Arabs mounted an onscreen campaign of destruction against the Western world but were stopped by methodical and dedicated American and Israeli agents who ridded the world of their menace. One columnist wanted not just revenge, but a policy of geometric escalation: "For every American passenger you kill thereafter, we will kill 10 of your brothers."[3] The Reagan administration created a terrorism office whose director held ambassadorial rank and "enjoyed direct access to Shultz."[4] Surely, during this frenzy it was difficult to think straight. Even the Crusades may have been less fanatic. Terrorism experts were talking about trends, citing the *Achille Lauro* (as if one action makes a trend), and formulating an international conspiracy logic.

"Terrorists, terrorists, terrorists," lamented Robert Fisk during the Lebanon War:

> The word was ubiquitous, obsessive, cancerous in its own special way. Terrorists were animals. Animals had to be put down. The PLO was a terrorist organization. Terrorists, terrorists, terrorists. Israel radio used the word in every broadcast, almost every sentence.[5]

Professor Edward Said sums it up:

> Today's discourse on terrorism is an altogether more streamlined thing. Its scholarship is yesterday's newspapers or today's CNN bulletin. Its gurus— Claire Sterling, Michael Ledden, Arnaud de Borchgrave—are journalists with obscure, even ambiguous, background. Most writing about terrorism is brief, pithy, totally devoid of scholarly armature of evidence, proof, argument… The worst aspect of the terrorism scam, intellectually speaking, is that there seems to be so little resistance to its massively inflated claims, undocumented allegations and ridiculous tautologies.[6]

Alex Schmid observes that governments usually have a stake in how terrorism is reported: "The facts made available to the public media are not infrequently instruments in the contest for the allegiance of the public."[7] Richard Rubenstein adds that "governments frequently misrepresent the political strength of terrorist groups."[8]

Coverage of terrorism is often selective. The *Achille Lauro* hijack received front story coverage for days. The *New York Times* devoted 1043 column inches to Leon Klinghoffer, the elderly Jewish American killed during the hijacking. A movie and even an opera (*The Death of Klinghoffer*) were made about his life. The hijacking was one of the most covered events in the 1980s. Meanwhile, as the ship was under the control of the gunmen, the JDL planted a bomb at the Los Angeles office of the Arab-American Anti-Discrimination

Committee, killing a 41-year-old Arab American, Alex Odeh. The *New York Times* devoted 14 column inches to the incident,[9] and much of that space was used to quote the head of the JDL, who said that Odeh got what he deserved. In his memoirs, George Shultz dedicates an entire chapter to the *Achille Lauro* hijacking, while the Pollard affair, a major United States intelligence disaster, merits a sentence; Odeh is not mentioned.[10] No one remembers Odeh, a kind, outgoing man who had three daughters and, like many assassinated Palestinian leaders, published a book of poetry (*Whispers in Exile*). It would seem that Odeh would have been more of a romantic hero for a movie than Klinghoffer, who had cancer and knew he had only months to live.

But terrorism is not a matter of guns and killing; editorial decisions of newspapers and TV networks and movie producers manufacture the modern terrorist, and politicians who use tricks and clichés instead of issues to win campaigns reinforce our perception of him. Odeh's killer, Robert Manning, was living in the West Bank, carrying an Uzi and moving freely.[11] Why did the Reagan government not storm his settlement and capture him as they did the *Achille Lauro* hijackers? The FBI called the JDL the second most active terror group in the United States,[12] but the government left it alone and bombed Gadaffi.

Terrorism has also become a business for companies who manufacture metal detectors, train bomb-sniffing dogs, and provide dozens of "security experts" for frightened individuals and institutions. In 1988 the Israeli antiterrorism business brought in $100 million of foreign capital to the two main Israeli companies, ATLAS and ISPS, who sell their services to United States and European airlines and international corporations.[13] According to an Israeli newspaper, 800 Israeli arms and security companies operate around the world.[14] Terrorism pays well.

Six weeks after the *Achille Lauro* affair, an Egypt Airlines flight with 97 people on board was hijacked and forced to Valletta, Malta, despite Malta's objections. This was one of Abu Nidal's services to Libya, for at that time a few Libyan pilots were escaping to Egypt, where they were given safe haven. The United States encouraged Egypt to attack the hijacked plane, asked the Maltese to delay the plane's takeoff—the hijackers asked only for fuel—and gave logistic support to the Egyptians. That the United States should have become involved in this episode at all indicates the fanaticism which had taken hold of American foreign policy and public opinion. This should have remained the worry of Egypt and Malta. The raid ended in disaster, with 59 or 60 people killed and almost everyone else wounded. Because the soldiers encircled the plane and came at it from all sides, they also killed each other as they attacked. Storming the plane showed a callous disregard for the lives of everyone involved.[15]

We have already discussed the 1986 takeover of the Pan American flight in Karachi, Pakistan. There were about 400 people aboard when gunmen rushed onto the plane and claimed it was theirs. This attack, as well as another bloody action the following day at the Istanbul synagogue, was Abu Nidal's. The Pakistanis claim that they only began the rescue after hearing the hijackers begin shooting passengers, but that is probably not true. It was another disaster, resulting in the deaths of at least 21 passengers, while another 120 were wounded.

Not negotiating with terrorists seems on the surface a sound tactic, justified by the idea that giving into terrorist demands only encourages more terrorism. But such a policy usually stems from a fear of confronting the outstanding issues that the terrorists raise. Is not a refusal to negotiate with terrorists a front for the government's refusal to negotiate at all? When terrorists think of themselves as revolutionaries, they are not crazy, (perhaps if they were, there would be all the more reason to negotiate.) Instead, they have a cause, and their actions are rational. Furthermore, the "no negotiation" policy is not consistent. Negotiation does not mean weakness. When North Korea seized the USS *Pueblo* off its coast on January 23, 1968, the United States negotiated for months until it obtained the release of its sailors. Why not negotiate with gunmen holding a plane?

The policy of not negotiating with terrorists is essentially a desire to maintain the status quo of conflict, a policy that constrains rather than frees a country's foreign policy.[16] It does not deter terrorism; it inflames it, propels it to a higher and more vicious level, while keeping it secret and underground. Terrorists are after political or social change. They think of themselves as revolutionaries. Their use of terrorism demonstrates the fervor of their conviction, for terrorism is a group's last resort. Revolutionaries who have conviction in their cause do not abandon their struggle when they face stronger odds; they seek to strengthen themselves in order to win. Negotiation does not encourage terrorism. It encourages more negotiation.

Aldo Moro negotiated to free Palestinians caught red-handed.[17] But when Moro was kidnapped, his Christian-Democrat party refused to negotiate. The United States government sent Steve Pieczenik, who encouraged the Italians not to negotiate,[18] claiming that Italy must stand firm against terrorists. "Exchanges of prisoners have frequently and widely been undertaken in the past in order to save hostages, to spare innocent victims," Moro said. He argued that it is worse for the state in the long run to not negotiate since it intensifies the battle, triggering "a sequence of disasters such as you cannot countenance."[19] In Italy, the no-negotiation policy proved a disaster when Aldo Moro was killed by his captors.

The terror threat created an ugly world of fear and suspicion, in which security equipment and guards and complicated airport procedures are the rule. Such measures may be necessary and even effective in protecting ourselves from individual and organized crime, but the most efficient way to combat political terrorism is to resolve the political issues from which the terrorism sprang. Having studied five terrorist groups, Christopher Hewitt observes that expanding the security forces and enacting emergency legislation does not lower terrorist activity.[20]

The PLO says that Israel's bombing of Lebanese refugee camps or shooting of unarmed youths in the West Bank is terrorism. While it may be true that Arabs are mostly the victims of terrorism rather than its manufacturers, they have little idea that headline-catching, sensation-grabbing, individual operations focus negative attention on the perpetrators much more than an army bombing civilians, even though such bombing inflames violence. As Stalin put it, 100,000 deaths is a statistic, while one death is a tragedy.

Those who use terrorism usually justify it by the military actions against them. Let us examine three examples of Shia (Shiite) terrorism.

The Shia attacked several Kuwaiti targets beginning in 1985, including the bloody hijacking of a Kuwait Airlines jumbo in 1988, demanding the release of 17 comrades in Kuwaiti prison who had been convicted on December 12, 1983, of other terrorist attacks against the state. Those who hijacked the jumbo felt that the trials were unfair, and they took it upon themselves to free their comrades. Let us speculate that the trials were indeed unfair (and many do doubt that justice was really served). What recourse do the Shia have? They have no other avenue for their grievance, no court or human rights body to which they can plead their case. Their choice is either to abide by Kuwait's decision or take direct action to force their case. This is the birth of terrorism. Finally, after one of the longest hijackings, the Algerian government patiently negotiated between the Shia and Kuwait, and an undisclosed deal was struck.[21] As we would expect, the United States government encouraged Kuwait not to negotiate and denounced the deal.[22]

After Israel invaded and occupied Lebanon, it threw thousands of Shia in makeshift prisons in Lebanon and transported others to prisons in Israel. Anyone familiar with the way an army arrests knows that they often go out and pick up young men at random. Such arrests are not an act of justice but a method of control. International pressure forced Israel to promise that they would release 340 Shia prisoners, but on the scheduled day (June 10, 1985), Israel changed its mind. The Shia have no army to fight Israel. They cannot turn to any court or overpowering authority. Either they can accept whatever Israel does to them or they can resort to what is called terrorism. Four days later they hijacked a TWA jet to Beirut in order to get the United States to force Israel to release their comrades.[23]

When the United States Marines arrived in Lebanon for the second time in 1983 they were welcomed as a peacekeeping force by all parties, including the Shia. However, in September the United States opened fire on Druze and Syrian-backed positions near Souk al-Gharb using the large guns of the USS *New Jersey*. The shells from these guns are as heavy as a small car, and because they are fired from such a distance, they have little accuracy. This decision was

Above: Cemetery in Beirut, where, as in other Arab cities, Jews lived in large numbers; *below:* Beirut's Green Line separating east and west.

one of the most myopic and foolish the United States ever made, indicating a low level of Middle East understanding. The Marines ended their role as a peacekeeping force and became a party to the Lebanese conflict.[24]

For years after, Lebanese mothers would get their children to eat everything on their plate by threatening, "The *New Jersey* will get you if you don't." An American seaman killed during the TWA hijacking just mentioned, Robert Dean Stethem, had identification on him that said he was assigned to the *New Jersey.* Secretary of State George Shultz claimed that the *New Jersey* was protecting United States citizens. Defense Secretary Casper Weinberger linked the Christians' defense of Souk al-Gharb to the defense of the United States. But two American professors living in Beirut responded in the *New York Times*: "When the first shell from the U.S. gun was fired ... we had to fear reprisals... The recent American casualties in Beirut were as good as inflicted by the *New Jersey's* guns... Terrorism does not spring from a vacuum, nor does it exist without a logic."[25] Does this shelling help explain why a month later the Shia staged a suicide bombing on the Battalion Headquarters Building, killing 240 Marines in one of the largest explosions since World War II?

The Shia felt that the United States was waging war against them. By contrast, the Italian peacekeeping contingent remained neutral. They met Shia leader Sheikh Fadlallah as well as Christian and Sunni leaders and donated blood to any side that needed, developing a bond of friendship with the Lebanese. Who was more effective?

As an aside, former Mossad agent Ostrovsky claims that Israel knew about the Marine bombing beforehand.[26] *Israel and Palestine Report* speculates that Israel helped to plan or execute it because the truck had to pass several checkpoints, a complicated operation.[27] Robin Wright quotes a Lebanese army liaison officer with the Marines who said, "To prepare an action like this required a lot of information. You need to know how the building was built, where it was structurally weak, and what the behavior of the guards was."[28] Israeli troops had been repeatedly harassing and firing at the Marines, even after the United States officially protested to Israel and gained a promise to stop.[29] *I&P Report* and other sources claim that the Mossad helped in the April, 1983, truck bombing of the American embassy, killing 63 people, including the entire CIA staff, who were having a meeting at the time of the attack under the leadership of Robert Ames, a senior Middle East intelligence analyst who was investigating terrorism.[30]

Terrorism is a poor man's war. In the invasion of Lebanon, Israel killed over 18,000 people, 70 to 80 percent civilians. Many books have been written about this war. Some contain horrific pictures of boys and girls hit by phosphorus bombs, running while brown smoke pours out of their mouths, and families mutilated by cluster bombs that spray heavy jagged pieces of metal. We all know that grim face of war. However, when the Shia attacked Israeli military units in Lebanon, they were often called terrorists. What other type of warfare can the Shia make? They have neither tanks nor jets nor missiles, and in this case they were responding to Israeli aggression and attacking an occupying force on their own land.

The oppression of a people results in their resort to terrorism. After touring the Middle East, John Cardinal O'Connor of New York said that the condition of the Palestinians "has to spawn terrorism." [31] Unless we can address the causes of terrorism we will never be able to solve conflict—which, indeed, seems to be the intention of certain governments who are unable to yield. If we would have the courage to examine the underlying conditions that breed terrorism, we might also find the wisdom to address these problems in legitimate ways. To yield need not be to retreat; sometimes it simply offers the flexibility needed for forward motion.

Chapter 19

Greece

Athens has seen dozens of assassinations, hit and run accidents that killed prominent leaders, murders whose perpetrators happened to slip through police hands. Ever since World War II when Greece was plunged in a brutal civil war that ravaged the nation, when trucks roamed the streets of Athens picking starved bodies off the sidewalks, the country has been marred by political violence, unsolved murders, and riots. After the Nazis and the Fascists and the British and the Communists raped the country, Greeks scrambled to leave their homeland, crowding boats for America and Australia. Mediterranean islands with a 1945 population of 50,000 were condensed to 5,000 by 1950.

In the 1960s and 1970s tanks rolled down city streets and riot police clashed with demonstrators who lobbed the odd Molotov. Greeks have also heard bombs exploding in the dead of night, placed in front of banks and government offices—always unsolved crimes—or tossed at dictators and ambassadors. They have also heard an occasional car bomb, usually directed at foreigners. No one, however, had ever heard anything like the explosion of a car bomb at the onset of the 1988 tourist season on a street adjacent to the sea. The car was vaporized, and the explosion drilled a meter-deep crater in the pavement, melting metal and plastic into the asphalt.

No one is sure how many people were inside, probably two, possibly three; probably men, but possibly a woman. Residents from a mile away came out of their homes and formed a circle around the thing wondering what it was. The police began poking through what was left, finding a few pieces of flesh. One policeman recovered two charred hands which they could not sex. There was an unrecognizable head and a disfigured foot. They also found a piece of a magazine and told the reporters (who arrived as quickly as the police) that it was in Arabic, but they discovered a few days later that the language was Farsi (Persian). Western embassies sent their terrorism experts to the scene, but none of them stayed with the reporters more than a few minutes. The police found a piece of a picture, which they later said was of Samir Khader, killer of Egyptian editor Yusef Sebai and planner of terrorist operations in Europe such as the Rome and Vienna airport attacks and the Karachi hijack of Pan Am.

A short time after the bombing a ship of vacationing tourists suddenly turned into a nightmare when men with guns and grenades ran around the decks killing passengers and each other. The *City of Poros*, a medium-sized ferry, was filled with European tourists on package tours. A French travel agency had booked on it 163 vacationers who were touring Santorini and other Greek islands. Four other French people had booked individually: Laurent Vigneron and his 21-year-old fiancée Annie Audegean, both students at the Lille school in northeast France, and two other women, Isabelle Bismuth and Rossanne Tortorelli. There was also at least one Arab gunman aboard, Sojod Adnan Mohammed, a 21-year-old Jordanian, probably a Palestinian, who was identified by a half-dozen names including "Zojab." At the time, the ship was happily sailing a couple of miles off the island of Aegina, about 90 minutes from its home port at the Trocadero Marina near Piraeus, the spot where the ship was about to land and where the car blew up.

The captain radioed his distress but sailed the crippled ship to port on its own. He was greeted by ambulances and the port police, who declared themselves in charge of the investigation. Regrettably, these officers did not have the competence to investigate so much as children writing graffiti on bathroom walls. Their most sophisticated function had been handling fishing disputes from their impressive office at the head of the port, where a few well-meaning, pot-bellied, middle-aged men pass their days reading newspapers, drinking coffee, and occasionally filling in forms—a low-anxiety job, even by Greek standards—but they welcomed this new opportunity to demonstrate their ability. By rights they had jurisdiction, and so they beat away the national police who were telling them about the advantages of their connections with Interpol and their experience in interviewing.

An investigation could hardly have been conducted worse. People aboard gave conflicting accounts of what happened. Everyone was understandably in a state of shock. Nine were killed and about 100 injured, and several highly potent bombs or grenades had destroyed the sun deck, sending pieces of metal and flesh everywhere. It was a revolting scene of carnage.

The port police agreed among themselves that they needed to interview everyone they could and type out their testimonies. They had no set questions. Some passengers said that there was a speedboat that ferried people away. Several tourists had seen Laurent Vigneron and Zojab shooting, but most could not tell who was doing what. They found a picture of Zojab's girlfriend sitting with Vigneron. The testimonies made no sense. The police confused Vigneron with Zojab, because their photos seem to look alike, and they gave out photos of two Arabs they described as killers, naming each of them, until reporters compared the photos and saw that they were the same person. Finally, the exasperated national police stepped on toes and took over.

They discovered that Rossanne Tortorelli, who had talked to Zojab and found him "nice, friendly and inoffensive," had not signed her statement. They looked for her all over Greece, eventually discovering that she was on a three-day tour to Olympia in the Peloponnese. It seemed unusual for someone who had just seen her friend Isabelle Bismuth blown to bits, with blood and guts lying over the ship, to take off on a pleasant vacation. Even the port police concluded that Vigneron was one of the killers, and undoubtedly they were correct, but on July 17 the Greek and French foreign ministers met behind closed doors and came out promising to "cooperate" on the *Poros* case, which reporters interpreted to mean "alter information." Thus, although the Greek Ministry of Public Order had a good idea of what had taken place, they clammed up, retracting blame of any French national and issuing statements that contradicted their previous ones. The deeper one delves into the episode, the more confusing and irrational it becomes.

No doubt the massacre on the ship was connected to the car explosion. The scrap of Farsi indicates Shia involvement, but that could have been a plant, as could the picture of Khader. The usual account is that the FRC wanted to hijack the ship, then bring it to port, where the car with Khader was waiting. (He was initially identified as Hejab Jaballa, 38, who had rented the car and a hotel room near the scene of the bombing.) But the car blew up, and instead of hijacking the ship, the gunmen sprayed the passengers with bullets and threw a couple of powerful grenades.

The FRC was involved in this, but Greek sources say that at least two other organizations were also involved. For at least a week before the incident various secret services were running around each other in Athens, changing hotels and playing cat-and-mouse. Oral sources claim the Mossad was definitely involved and that they were using Abu Nidal's people,[1] and it seems likely that a speedboat pulled off agents. The fingerprints of the hands that were found at the car were compared with Khader's—the Cypriots sent the Greek police his fingerprints—but they did not match. However, after the talks between the Greek and French foreign ministers, they issued a statement saying that they did match and said that Jaballa was Khader. Abu Nidal told Abu Bakr that he had Khader and a girlfriend killed in the car, but he also started a rumor that Khader was alive.

A search of Jaballa's hotel near the marina found traces of plastic explosives in his suitcases. These chemical tests for explosives are unreliable, but the investigation led the Swedish police to a cell of five Palestinians run by Khader in Sweden. The Swedish prosecutor, Torsten Jonsson, had issued a warrant for Khader's arrest a year before the *Poros* attack. In August Swedish police found in a forest near Stockholm's Arlanda airport a small FRC arsenal of communist-manufactured small arms and five kilos of Semtex. The following February, after interrogating several Palestinians and Khader's wife, Arja Saloranta, they declared that Khader had had a cell operating there for some years, even though the only terror action in either Norway or Sweden had been the 1973 Lillehammer affair.[2]

On instruction from his superiors Khader married three times without getting a divorce. His first wife was Palestinian, his second Finnish, and his third Swedish, through the third marriage he had Swedish citizenship. It seems that someone phoned his Finnish wife and told her that Khader was alive. She had not known him very well but had once gone on an errand to Israel for the group. His third marriage had been arranged by the FRC intelligence department to exploit the Swedish woman as a cover for the group. FRC regularly sent her money in the name of Khader. It was common practice for the group to send money to families of members they killed, telling the family that the member was on a secret mission, and if the family asked an FRC member, he would not know. Terror experts tell us that FRC wanted to control the ship by bringing the booby-trapped car on board, and because of the heat or an accidental electronic signal the car exploded. But gunmen could control the ship without a booby-trapped car, and if Khader had planted the explosives, of which he was knowledgeable, would he have sat in the car waiting while someone else held the detonator? It seems unlikely that the people in the car planted the mountain of explosives; crime reporters doubt that Khader was in the car, and some Western diplomats privately speculated that it was an Israeli action.

The FRC had two prisoners in Greek jails, and it was thought that Abu Nidal was trying to pressure Greece to release them, but Abu Nidal never thought about FRC prisoners. The best explanation is that one group of gunmen opened fire on another, killing tourists who came between them. The tremendous explosion on the sun deck was caused either by an extremely high level grenade or possibly by explosives that had been planted; there is strong evidence for the latter. Inside the FRC Abu Nidal boasted that the action was his and that five of his people were involved. The United States claimed that the whole thing was the work of FRC. Abu Nidal explained to his Politburo that bad intelligence had informed him that the *City of Poros* was an Israeli ship going to Haifa. It seems unlikely that someone could have made such a huge error about the island-hopping ship.

A funny sidelight comes from one of the ubiquitous anti–Arab terrorism experts, who claims that Abu Nidal himself landed in Greece dressed as a Greek Orthodox priest, ready to negotiate with or to threaten the Greek government.[3] One can only wonder how Abu Nidal, with his third-grade education, was supposed to converse in Greek, especially enough to pass himself off as a priest. His downfall would have come when the first customs officer greeted him with "Kalamara" (hello).

Guns and gossip flew through Athens. The weapons came from Yugoslavia across the loosely regulated border in Macedonia, supplied by either Austria or the East Bloc countries. Once in Athens, comfortably in the European Community, they could be shipped to militias in Lebanon and to other Arab countries. Gossip, either real intelligence or controlled leaks, landed in the city and was picked up by dozens of waiting ears, then passed to various agencies. Athens was one of FRC's principal bases and weapons deposits during the heyday of terrorist operations. In 1987 police discovered one of FRC's deposits of arms buried on a hill in Athens, including a 9mm Browning similar to the one used to kill British diplomat Ken Whitty.

The *City of Poros* attack was the culmination of years of Mossad and FRC terrorist activity in Greece. Two days after Sereya threw a grenade at Rome's Café de Paris in 1985, the FRC used one of its members to assassinate the outspoken Arab writer and publisher Michel al-Nimri, a respected man from a well-known Jordanian family who had become a Syrian citizen in the days when he supported the Syrian regime. Nimri's career was speckled with politically flip-flopping, supporting and then denouncing different Arab governments, until he became unwanted in most of the Arab world. In 1980 he ended up in Cyprus, where he published the magazine *al-Nushra*. He moved to Athens in late 1983 and later wrote about a purported failed coup against Hafez al-Assad staged by the Syrian military, resulting in the execution of 21 Syrian air force officers and the arrest of 300 Palestinians. A few days before his death he had returned from visiting Arafat in Tunis and had applied to visit Iraq.

One PLO leader claimed that Abu Nidal killed Nimri as a favor to Syria. A few days before the killing Syrian defense chief Mustafa Tlass, who has a major publishing business on the side, visited Athens, and it is thought that he gave his approval for Nimri's demise. Most experts on terrorism believe that the Mossad or Syria ordered this killing, but it is doubtful that Syria would risk its good relations with the Greek government over Nimri. A lone FRC gunman, Jihad al-Amari, a member of the Revolutionary Council, shot Nimri and ran away. Like every other assassin in Athens, he got away, but soon after he was killed on orders from Abu Nidal, who alleged that he was an Israeli or Jordanian agent. The killing of Nimri probably hastened Amari's untimely retirement. The PLO issued their usual statement blaming Israel for the killing, though no one took their statement seriously. Most speculated that Syria had hired Abu Nidal. Syria gained a bad reputation as the killer of Nimri, with all the sideways condemnations that come with such blame. Greece asked that its soil not be used for the exploits of others.

After the bombing of Libya the Mossad launched a couple of its own attacks against Palestinian military leaders rather than activate the cumbersome and unreliable FRC. In June 1986 they got word from informers in the Greek government that a PLO chief of military operations in the occupied territories was in town. Khalid Nazzal, a Central Committee member of Naif Hawathmeh's DFLP, had come from Tunis for a brief vacation without checking in with the PLO office or the DFLP responsible in the city. In reality his job, launching military operations against Israel in the occupied territories, had a big title but involved little activity. After 1970 there were few PLO military operations, but he did coordinate a few attacks, possibly the Bus 300 hijack.

Israeli embassy in Athens, a main intelligence facility.

As Nazzal was coming home a lone Mossad assassin was waiting at his hotel, his gun fitted with a silencer. It was a simple matter to shoot Nazzal as he was walking into the hotel lobby. The killer had a backup, a suspicious second person hanging around who ran off after the operation, but the primary assassin needed no help. He shot, ran out to the street, and was whisked away by a motorcycle. Despite this easy kill, the Athenian police managed to arrest him. He claimed to be Argentinean, but police discovered that he was Israeli. Because of either police incompetence or a desire to avoid a complicated diplomatic incident, the man disappeared. Local crime reporters say that he was taken to the airport and shipped away by Mossad agents working with Greek security, the ones who originally found out from immigration that he had come into the country.[4]

In October of the same year the Mossad was able to silence a PLO military commander who had managed to stay alive since the stand at Karameh, Mondher Abu Ghazalah, officially in charge of naval operations and also a member of the DFLP, who came from a military family. Abu Ghazalah was in Athens to buy a large speedboat in order to launch an operation against Israel. He first called on an old friend, a gregarious and talkative man who understood little about security. His friend promised to help him, and although Abu Ghazalah tried to disguise himself as an Arab shipping tycoon and traveled on a fake passport, his friend went around bragging that Abu Ghazalah was Abu Jihad's assistant. The two went around the Athens port of Piraeus, looking and talking. His friend told people on the one hand that he wanted a boat for his pleasure; then out of the side of his mouth, with a twinkle in his eye, he would hint about the real nature of the project. He also stayed at a fancy hotel, attracting more attention.

Talk traveled, and the Israeli embassy found out about the boat. The new PLO representative, Fouad al-Bittar, who knew Abu Nidal because of a family connection with Abu Nidal's wife, met his old friend Abu Ghazalah and tried to get him and his friend to tone down their talk. A couple of local Palestinians saw the simplicity of this bubbly duo, and knowing the situation in Athens, they suggested point-blank that Abu Ghazalah go back to Tunis. Amazed that a person appointed to such a high position could be so naive, one person with Mossad connections told Abu Ghazalah that the Israelis were following him. But Abu Ghazalah also had personal reasons for staying in Greece. He wanted to visit friends, including a girlfriend, though he apparently saw her only in the presence of others and remained a faithful husband.

Abu Ghazalah had the mentality of a farmer, trusting and polite, lacking the required discretion for military ventures. He could work in an office or with a militia, but his assignment showed that the PLO did not have the required maturity to select people by their skills instead of their connections.

Despite security incompetence, Abu Ghazalah was in a position that could hurt Israel's inviolate borders, and so the Mossad blew up his car. There are two versions of the story: either they planted a bomb in his car during his three-hour stay at the home of a lady friend in Neo Smerney, or on the way back to the Intercontinental he picked up two girls who asked him for a ride, and one planted a bomb under the driver's seat. On a residential street the bomb exploded. People heard him crying for help, but minutes later a second explosion, probably the gas tank, destroyed him beyond recognition, blowing the car's top onto a Mercedes parked on the other side of the street. It cut a hole half a meter deep in the pavement. The style was similar to the Mossad killing of Majed Abu Sharara in 1981, but the motive was similar to the August 1983 killing of Mamoun Mreich.

Mreich, working for Abu Jihad, was also in Athens, posing as a Moroccan shipowner after returning from Tunis. At the time of his killing he had only been in town a short time, but he had worked out of Athens and lived there undercover for 18 months. He was killed in his car by a man on the back of a motorcycle who, together with two backup cars, pulled up and shot Mreich through the open window while he was stopped at a red light, also wounding his four-year-old son and his driver. Mreich, a PLO lieutenant colonel, held a central position during the siege of Beirut. Like Abu Ghazalah, he came to Athens to buy a fast ship in order to launch an operation against Israel. He managed to shell out 450,000 PLO dollars for the *Santa Andrea*, but although Mreich was security conscious, changing his habits and using a driver, word filtered to the Israelis about his new ship. It was not the first ship he bought that was subsequently used for a raid on Israel.

The Mossad had FRC agents in the city, and according to Abu Bakr and the United States State Department, Mreich was killed by Abu Nidal. But there seems to be no doubt that he was being followed by the Mossad, probably trailed from Tunis, and this killing seems to have involved direct coordination between FRC and Mossad.

Chapter 20

The Departure of Abu Bakr and the Death of Abu Iyad

The real slavery in Egypt was that the Israelites learned to endure it.

Simcha Bunim

Abu Bakr is an Arab rebel, a most unlikely man to belong to a terrorist organization. From his home in Tunis he tells his story:

At first I didn't suspect Abu Nidal. I knew he had criminals in the group and made errors of judgment. I joined during a period of major contradictions inside the PLO, and I wanted to change Abu Nidal's line of killing. I led negotiations with several countries. I was the only one who had relations with Eastern European countries. I opened the door for him to some Arab countries. From 1985 I was the only one who lived with him a long time, especially after we moved to Libya in 1987 and were in daily meetings. Before I considered his faults as mistakes, but in Libya my thoughts changed. I first felt that his relationship with Libya was an unequal intelligence relationship, an exploitation. They were using him as a tool against Libyan opponents. For me it was taboo, their problem, not ours.

I talked with him openly that outside operations serve our enemy, and I tried to stop the bloodshed while pushing two points: to defend the camps and put forward our concerns to the Palestinians. Abu Nidal never considered these matters. If you sat with him for one month you wouldn't listen to a single word about the Intifada or about Palestinians inside the occupied territories. I asked him how we can justify our existence as an organization if we have no relationship with our people. He would say that

Atif Abu Bakr, FRC deserter.

outside operations is one way, or he would say that we failed to create an organization inside the occupied territories. At least you can discern if he is speaking about obstacles or running from the subject.

Day by day my doubts mounted as I began seeing things in another way. At first I thought that the operation against Argov was by chance on 3 June and by chance the invasion began two days later. I thought Abu Nidal didn't know they were preparing for an invasion. Later I began to suspect—everyone knew they were preparing for an invasion. I began explaining things to myself in another way. I saw that all the results were going to Israel's pocket. In 1988 I took the decision to leave them and to destroy them. I didn't have the idea of destroying them from the beginning, but I became convinced that they are one of the main obstacles and dangers to the Palestinians. Especially after the Intifada I noticed contradictions and was fully convinced that they were serving the Mossad. I began to fear what the group can do.

Now we are fighting them. Some are hesitating or escaping. We know that we can lose our lives. In Abu Nidal's mind there's no such thing as debate, only physical fighting, but this phenomena is enough. Fifteen years is enough.

Abu Bakr deserted Abu Nidal in November 1989. He tried to get other of his comrades in the organization to leave with him. Abd al-Rahman Issa and the widow of Mustafa Murad, Sobhia—Abu Nidal had killed his deputy Murad the year before, as Murad was harboring the same thoughts as Abu

Bakr—issued a statement saying that they were beginning a corrective movement of the FRC because of Abu Nidal's role in crimes and terrorism, because he made all the decisions by himself, and because he kept money in Swiss banks under his name and the names of his family.[1]

Abu Bakr comes from a large, prosperous, well-educated family. He went to Amman to visit his sister, a bank manager, who told Abu Bakr that the family held a meeting among themselves when they discovered Abu Bakr's break and decided to crush Abu Nidal's family if necessary. (Such complex clan codes help account for Arafat's failure to destroy Abu Nidal.)

Abu Bakr's rebellion came hard on the heels of a bloody internal fight. In September Abu Nidal is said to have killed 90 of his followers in Lebanon, including members of the Central Committee. They were killed by leaders who observers believe have links with the Mossad. The killers claimed the executed were agents of Israel, Egypt, Iraq, Britain, the United States, or Germany.[2] Deserters report that hundreds were killed, their best fighters, including almost everyone involved in outside operations. It appeared as if the group had outlived its usefulness and imploded. Gadaffi voiced his displeasure with Abu Nidal and made noises against the group during one of his mood swings, perhaps trying to ease the strain of his relations with the West.

Within weeks many members in Lebanon joined the Issa and Abu Bakr split-off group. Within months, almost half of FRC had left, creating a schism similar to the split that occurred in 1978, except this one had been accompanied by slaughter. Abu Bakr went to the PLO and tried to get support for their goal of destroying Abu Nidal. On June 16, 1990, Fatah raided FRC positions in two Lebanese refugee camps, Rashidia and Ein al-Hilweh, killing several FRC fighters, including FRC commander Omar Hamid. The PLO never explained why they had not done that before and why they did not attack all FRC positions. The FRC was not popular; no Lebanese or Palestinian group would have come to their aid had the PLO extinguished them. The next day, after a 9-hour battle, 40 FRC men surrendered to Fatah. On September 10 Fatah claimed victory after a 3-day battle with FRC that left 78 dead.

FRC still had 150 loyal members with their base near the Ghassan Hamoud hospital in Sidon and the Beirut refugee camp of Mar Elias, just behind a Christian cemetery. There then began tit-for-tat assassinations between Fatah and FRC in Lebanon, but FRC's effective power was greatly weakened.

Abu Bakr and Issa fled Libya on diplomatic passports to Tunis and Algeria with wild stories of human butchery in Libya as well. They claimed that Abu Nidal had 30 of his men, including his most senior advisors, killed and cemented in his bedroom. They said that men loyal to Abu Nidal jumped on Central Committee members in the group's Asswani military camp, located southwest of Tripoli, and killed military commandant Hussam Yussef and political department head Abu Musa. Abu Nidal, however, continued to

Abu Iyad, PLO's number-two man, killed on the eve of the 1991 Gulf War.

control the finances and could buy new fighters and recruit new gunmen. Abu Nidal had been trying to form new groups in Asia and South America, but with the splintering of the group these faded away.[3]

One of those who defected was 28-year-old Hamza Abu Zeid, who went to Abu Bakr in Tunis and said that he wanted to join him in eliminating Abu Nidal. Abu Bakr turned him over to the PLO. Abu Zeid said that he was a fighter ready to use his talents to help the Palestinian people, offering to tell the PLO everything he knew about the Abu Nidal group. Abu Hol (Hayel Abd al-Hamid), the PLO's chief of security, bought the story and took him under his wing, eventually making him a driver and bodyguard.

After the assassination of Abu Jihad, the two most well-guarded officials in Tunis were Arafat and Abu Iyad. Arafat's security included escorted armored cars and an array of guards inside and outside his villa in a suburb of Tunis. Abu Iyad had a fortress in the embassy district, with several guards outside and more behind the wall to his house. Israel repeatedly tried to kill both Arafat and Abu Iyad, including during the commando attack on Beirut in April 1973 and during the 1982 Lebanon invasion when Israel dropped bombs on buildings in a desperate attempt to kill leaders. In April 1980 an FRC member named Samir Najib threw a bomb at a Mercedes in which Abu Iyad was riding in Belgrade[4] (Najib left the FRC during the 1989 split, escaping to Jordan). I asked Abu Iyad once what kept him alive all these years. He had once said that Arafat had a sixth sense sensitive to danger, and I expected a similar esoteric answer.

"I'm well guarded," he said pragmatically. "I have many guards around me."

What Abu Iyad did not know was that Abu Zeid had not amended his ways. According to several sources, Abu Zeid was actually with the Mossad and had been instructed to leave the FRC by his Mossad handlers in a meeting in Cyprus. He flew to Cyprus from Tripoli and was told to go to the PLO and give them the line about wanting to repent and help the PLO in its struggle against Israel. He apparently met a Mossad officer in Cyprus on at least one other occasion.[5] The story seems true, and the fact that security chief Abu Hol made him his guard is another indication of PLO immaturity. Abu Hol was a gentle and sensitive man. He should never have been the organization's security chief, but the PLO were hopeless about matching the person to the job. The timing of the killing was important—January 15, 1991, the eve of the Gulf War.[6]

Abu Iyad and his aide Abu Mohammed al-Omari were driven with the usual security to Abu Hol's house for an emergency late-night meeting. Abu Hol had just returned from Baghdad, and diplomatic activity was frantic. The Italian embassy had delivered a last-minute peace message to Abu Iyad from the Pope. Abu Zeid walked into the meeting and began shooting, killing Abu Iyad, Abu Hol, and al-Omari. Then he took Abu Hol's wife as hostage and tried to bargain for a plane. Arafat was in Baghdad trying to convince Saddam Hussein to withdraw from Kuwait. The PLO issued their usual blame on Israel, but had no proof at first. Abu Nidal, informers claim, knew nothing of Abu Zeid.

Although Abu Nidal had left Libya the year before, the group maintained its secretariat in Tripoli in what used to be Abu Nidal's home, where his two armored cars sat on the property. The secretariat looks like an ordinary mansion in the Quasim al-Shatik section, a quiet residential area, one block from the white, sandy beach. It would have been easy to invade. When Abu Nidal was there, he kept at night only two men with automatics guarding (his guards and closest aides are fanatically, even unnaturally, loyal). The group also kept its training camp in the Ghergan Yivin area about 150 kilometers southeast of Tripoli. They reopened an office in Baghdad and moved their men from Lebanon to Yemen and Sudan.[7]

Abu Nidal's family is grossly dysfunctional. His wife lives with him, but in a different section of the house. After Abu Nidal had her brother killed in 1986, they never slept together. Nidal lives with his father as a scared hostage, while his younger sister, born in 1977, reads the Koran and mouses about the house, hardly having contact with anyone. All family members have bank accounts in their names.

At the beginning of the Gulf Crisis Abu Nidal was said to have been in Baghdad, and he apparently crossed the border into Jordan overland at the onset of the crisis. He visited Prague after that, but since the fall of communism he no longer enjoys a safe haven. His most knowledgeable people have been killed or have left. At one time he had student cells in Pakistan, Turkey, Yugoslavia, Spain, England, Hungry, Poland, and Bulgaria, but all have collapsed. After Arafat shook Rabin's hand in Washington, the group remained silent.

Chapter 21
Conclusions

After Arafat spoke at the United Nations in November 1974, tacitly committing himself to negotiation and accepting territorial compromise, the face of covert violence in the Middle East changed. The Palestinians became divided between those ready to accept Israel and those who rejected negotiation, and attacks by the militant rejectionists became directed against the pro–Arafat forces as much or more than they were against Israel.[1] Conservative Israelis, feeling threatened by the possible diplomacy, sabotaged peace deals. They provoked conflict and killed moderate Palestinian leaders.

The Middle East conflict continually intensified. During the first decades of Middle East violence, thousands of people were killed and hundreds of thousands displaced. During the 1970s and 1980s warfare accelerated, especially in Lebanon, accompanied by a broader use of terrorism. However, the tone of conflict set in the first years remained static. The intensity increased, the actors changed (sometimes), the field of operations changed, but the substantive nature of the conflict and the issues remained virtually unchanged since the battle lines were drawn during the 1936 Arab revolt.

The effectiveness of terrorism—that is, whether the use of terrorism helped the Palestinians and Israelis—is a multifaceted question. Stern and Irgun terrorism convinced the British to abandon Palestine. The killings and beatings of British soldiers had run down the morale of British troops, and public opinion could neither stomach nor rationalize continuing to waste lives and resources where British interests were not paramount and conflict resolution seemed a distant prospect. Historians and researchers have shown that the Zionist militias, including the Haganah, employed systematic terror as well as forced expulsion to clear the land of Palestinians, effectively terrorizing over 750,000 Palestinians into fleeing, a necessary prerequisite to the foundation of a state with a Jewish majority.[2] However, the terror campaign, culminating in the massacre at Deir Yassin, went hand-in-hand with military victory over Arab forces, and it would be difficult to deduce what effect the terrorist activities by the Stern or Irgun might have had if the Haganah military campaign had not been such a sweeping success.

The 1965–73 Palestinian terror crusade, concentrating first on direct attacks against Israel and then on headline-grabbing international operations, was also successful, since it brought about the 1967 and 1970 wars, which Palestinians had wanted but which they lost since they had neither the foresight nor the military intelligence to know that the combined Arab armies were no match for Israel's. The wars they instigated led to further disappointment and further lost territory. Because of infighting and Israeli security measures, the Palestinians turned to terrorist attacks abroad, and it is debatable whether this helped the Arabs by keeping their cause alive or hurt them by giving them a bad reputation.

However, it would be rash to conclude that terrorists get their way. In the period leading up to Israel's statehood the British were already prepared to withdraw, and while the Israeli armies were successful in the 1948 war, they dramatically failed to create a safe state. Israel's military expenditure over the next decades drained the country's economy, not to mention the moral or spiritual costs. Had it not been for a massive and continuous infusion of foreign capital from the United States and Europe, Israel would never have been a viable state. So, while violence achieved Israel's short-term goal of territory, it did not, one can argue, fulfill the Zionist dream of a successful socialist state free from fear or persecution. They won it all, but they never enjoyed it. And of course, Palestinian terrorism did not win a square inch of land or unite the Arab countries to fight on their behalf. Radicals used terrorism for the opposite effect: enlarging divisions within the Palestinian camp and disuniting the movement.

Regarding post-1974 Arab terrorism, the principal actor has been Abu Nidal, and after studying his group and its activities, there should be no question that it was run by the Mossad. Almost every knowledgeable person acknowledges connections between Abu Nidal and the Mossad. Patrick Seale does not reach this conclusion because he believes that Jews do not kill Jews. Certainly, Israeli citizens are not responsible for the Rome and Vienna airport attacks or the Istanbul synagogue massacre any more than Irish citizens are responsible for bombing Harrod's, but whoever can bomb the ship *Patria* and kill 250 Jews, or bomb the King David and kill Jews; whoever can throw grenades at synagogues in Baghdad and place bombs at American government offices in Cairo; whoever can knowingly bomb the American ship *Liberty* and kill Americans[3]; whoever can raid Jewish settlements in the West Bank in order to launch reprisals; those whoevers are capable of anything. Many believe that FRC was infiltrated and later controlled, but that would mean that the group changed over the years. It did not, so it seems that FRC was linked to the Mossad from the beginning, and it seems no coincidence that the FRC began just as the Palestinians were becoming politically recognized.

Another certain conclusion is that reprisals, often called counter-terrorism, have been entirely ineffective in stopping terrorist operations. The British and Israeli iron fists delayed but did not destroy Palestinian nationalism, and British force was ineffective against the Stern and Irgun. Reprisals only raised the level of conflict. Perhaps if either the Jews or the Arabs had not been passionate about their cause they could have abandoned it. But history provides us too few examples of national movements being terminated by the imposition of harsh measures or reprisals.

If anything, counterterrorist measures have been the strongest force for the promotion of terrorism, since they radicalize the opposition. Reprisals are not rationally thought out; they are inspired more by revenge than by a desire to

American Embassy in Beirut after suicide bombing.

end the conflict victoriously, and they are directed at those who represent a political, not a military, threat. Reprisals appear racist: bombing Lebanese villages for the Munich Olympics or bombing Tripoli for Abu Nidal terrorism does not represent justice but increases the conflict. In the United States, if an African American shot a white man in Washington, or a Chinese man attacked a grocery store in Los Angeles, would the government bomb Chicago's South Side or Grant Avenue in San Francisco? Ludicrous. Is the bombing of Lebanon or Libya different? Clearly, justice is the key to dealing with such problems, and punishing a population is a sure way to stir more hatred. While describing the Suez Crisis, Kenneth Love observes, "The steady growth of the *fedayeen* organizations ... in the face of ever-larger and swifter Israeli reprisals is good evidence that the reprisal policy ... is a failure."[4] After the Shia bombing of the United States Marines in 1983, Israel and France bombed Islamic groups. Wilhelm Dieth notes, "It was precisely these bombardments that led to further radicalization within the Shiite commandos."[5]

West Bank woman who had part of her house sealed by the Israeli military when her son was imprisoned on security charges. The authorities claim that such collective punishment controls violence.

In 1992 Lieutenant-General Ehud Barak said that during the first five years of the Intifada 100,000 Palestinians had been through prison,[6] a remarkable statistic given that the imprisonable male population is under 500,000. Yet their revolt did not evaporate.

In the Middle East, terrorism became a form of war for the less powerful, and it cannot be properly discussed without considering the military actions of the enemy. Gerard Chaliand notes, "The weaker the guerrilla movement is, the stronger the temptation to turn to urban terrorism." Regarding the late 1960s, Chaliand observes, "For the Palestinians ... the use of transnational terrorism was also an admission of powerlessness."[7] The low level of violence characteristic of Palestinian terrorism is dwarfed by Israeli bombings and mass arrests, even though such actions by a country have an air of legitimacy. As a cheap form of war, terrorists have concentrated on easy targets such as unguarded leaders. Countries with the weakest defenses were the first targets for Israeli reprisals, even if they had nothing to do with the original attack.[8] The Palestinians abandoned attacks on Israel because they were too hard and concentrated on easier targets in Europe.

When a people firmly believe in a political or social cause but do not have an army, cannot mobilize tanks and squadrons of jet fighters, do not have the money, space, or political liberty to build armored units, they will fight in any way they can. Hijacking planes, taking hostages, planting bombs, or launching cross-border raids with a half-dozen men are the forms of war open to them, and during the past decades we have seen many such activities from groups fighting for their causes: the Basques, Kurds, Northern Irish, Corsicans, and Sikhs, to mention only a few of the parties to conflicts which have ethnic origins. It would be unrealistic to think that these groups would abandon their cause because their opposition is more powerful. Human nature does not work that way.

Political violence does not seem to be successful unless it has a mass following behind it. Isolated acts of violence do not change policy, but a mass movement such as Zionism in the 1940s seems to be far more effective in bringing about political change. But we have to be careful not to consider all terrorism equal. The 1973 Palestinian attack on Rome's airport, in which all victims were innocents who had nothing to do with the Middle East conflict, cannot be considered in the same category as a 1969 Fatah attack on an Israeli army base. Equally, military attacks by legitimate armies cannot be considered in the same light as terrorist actions. Bombing villages as revenge is clearly not the same as defending a border against armed attack. Physicians for Human Rights claims that in a conventional war involving air bombardment, 70 to 80 percent of the victims are civilians. Killing the enemy, even the civilian enemy, is justified by those who wage war, but random killing is not justified by any sane person.

Commando operations against those who are holding hostages fail more often than they succeed, often with dreadful consequences. The successes are remembered and glamorized while the failures fade into forgotten misfortune. Countries who refuse to negotiate in hostage situations are ready to deal a death penalty to innocents. Refusing to negotiate has not diminished the amount of violence, and there is no evidence that "giving in" in hostage situations encourages more terrorism. It can also be concluded that America's belligerent policy accelerated terrorism.[9]

Concentrating on terrorism is a way of avoiding larger issues. In the first six months of 1993 there were 11 violent deaths in Belfast, a city synonymous with terrorism, while Washington, D.C., during the same time experienced 230 murders. The *Economist* notes, "By comparison with anywhere else in the developed world, America is an astonishingly violent place... The real, everyday terror of violent crime continues unabated."[10] A society embroiled in such violence has no business counseling others on dealing with violence, and by concentrating attention on events like the *Achille Lauro* hijacking America avoids dealing with its serious problems such as crime.

The war against Middle East terrorism did not work. So much human tragedy might have been avoided if serious negotiations had begun in 1953 instead of 1993. The United States government estimated the direct cost to its taxpayers for the first four Middle East wars at $55 to $70 billion, with indirect costs much greater.[11] The Arab Monetary Fund estimated the Persian Gulf crisis and war cost Arab countries $676 billion.[12] In the end, it did not matter how many bombs were dropped or by whom; as long as the outstanding political questions remain unsolved, there remained unrest, and since one side was militarily weaker than the other, it led to a terror war where on both sides of the conflict the radicals were given power to control events. Israeli leaders should not have allowed hawks like Sharon and Palestinians should have never allowed men of violence like Haddad to force events and mold policy. Extremists are either immature (and therefore dangerous), or they are saboteurs, and events in the Middle East were run by the immature and the saboteurs.

The glorification of thugs encourages more thuggery. Both sides of this conflict are guilty, but the glorification seems to be a universal trait. The United States is full of shrines and statues to killers of native Americans. London's St. Paul Cathedral is crammed with the glorification of war leaders of dubious integrity. I have not met one gunman in the Middle East whom I would consider worthy of the slightest recognition for the advancement of society. If we want the world to turn from violence, we have to refuse to glorify its heroes.

The best security system for the world is not a bomb detector but a world body where groups can take grievances, have a just hearing, and be assured of a mechanism for enforcing the justice. Security comes from dealing fairly with the problems in Palestine, Northern Ireland, Kurdistan, and wherever else there is an unsettled political question. The current world body for justice, the World Court which sits in the Haag, is impotent.[13] To defeat terrorism we need a real court of justice, just as countries have internal civil courts where grieved parties can take come forward and argue their case. Such a court makes its decision, which can then be enforced by the police. This system is never satisfactory, but it is our closest form of justice. Currently our world is ruled not by justice but by strength, and since groups such as the Shia or the Palestinians cannot match the military strength of their adversaries, their only weapon becomes terrorism.

Another point to remember in any attempt to eliminate terrorism is that some government secret services have been involved in terrorist operations. Such governments certainly do not contribute to world stability and should be controlled. Furthermore, countries such as Switzerland, the Cayman Islands, and the Bahamas help terrorists and criminals by their secret banking practices. Switzerland kept Abu Nidal in business. If we are serious about fighting crime and terror, we should not deal with these countries until they change their policies.

Recently, much of the conflict in the Middle East arises from Islamic nationalists—though the Muslim struggle against European and other outside influences, dating back at least to the Crusades, can hardly be considered of recent origin. In 1885 General Charles "Chinese" Gordan was hacked to death in Khartoum by followers of the Mahdi in the first successful Islamic uprising against a European power since the Crusades. Islamic nationalism again surfaced in Egypt on March 23, 1928, with the founding of the Brotherhood by Hassan al-Banna (no relation to Abu Nidal). Since then the increasing popularity of Islamic nationalism has worried both Arab and Western governments. Banna was assassinated in 1949 by the Egyptian government, and thousands of followers of similar movement in Syria, Algeria, Tunisia, Iraq, and other Arab countries have been arrested or killed. After the 1979 Iranian revolution, this force was perceived as a major obstacle to world stability. Islamic nationalists—a more correct phrase than fundamentalists, which seems to belong to conservative Christians—are the new terrorists. Among Palestinians, Hamas has evolved into a potent force,[14] and Islam has become the second religion for many Western countries. Perhaps we can learn from the years of terrorist conflict between Israelis and Palestinians and apply our insight into this new terrorism.

There is a familiar ring to the rhetoric surrounding acts of Islamic terrorism. We are told that we cannot negotiate with such people since they are undemocratic, violent, terrorist, and fanatic. The same accusation was made against the PLO in the early 1970s, but 20 years later Israel ended up negotiating with them—20 bitter years and 30,000 lives later. The issues did not change in between. Are we going to waste another 20 years, or will we have the wisdom to sit down with these people and deal with the real economic and social issues of the day? Islam has a long tradition of negotiation, and there is no reason the West cannot work with them.

One of the West's closest allies is Saudi Arabia, a tremendously conservative Islamic country. The Pakistani government, which tends to be more rigid in following Islam than Arab countries, has good relations with America. The West helped Islamic militants in the 1950s as an anticommunist force and formed an alliance with them in the 1980s to fight the Soviet Union in Afghanistan. Many of those fighters went back to their countries, especially Egypt, and became the core of national Islamic movements. Having been our allies, there is no reason that they should now be our enemies. Certainly, radicals are propelled by the West's fear of them, but we are dealing with a mass movement, millions of people, especially strong among the poor and uneducated, the sector of society which governments ignored and are now trying to repress, a strategy unlikely to stop this mass movement. If we think that by bombing them and repressing they will turn around and say, "Ah yes, now we see the light of day, the error of our ways, and we are going to change our beliefs and become docile," we are living in unreality.

I have spoken about terrorism without taking into account its potential for creating human tragedy, especially among innocent people. Terrorism is a crime against human beings, civilians, and many would argue that no cause, no political ideal, no territorial dispute can justify the actions that were committed by both sides during the Middle East conflict. Two armies willing to fight each other is a different story than having mothers, fathers, children, people with no ideological prejudice killed or mutilated. Such violence is not an acceptable method for creating a better world or a better country, bringing justice, or whatever the romantic stated goal of the terrorist group.

Once in Jerusalem a religious Jew was stabbed in the back as he was returning from the Wailing Wall. I worked on a local newspaper at the time, and we reported the not-too-uncommon story. Several of the Palestinians I worked with, although they believed in peace and were what most people called moderates, could not personally condemn the attack. It was, they said, the fruit of Israeli repression. The victim was a faceless figure, a statistic, a news story, a Jew probably from Europe or the United States who had come to Palestine and may have taken away the land of the Palestinians. However, it turned out that the man was a kindly old rabbi who opposed Zionism and helped Palestinians in his own small way. There are hundreds of such people. The people in the office had an entire different perspective about the attack when they heard who it was. The victim had a name, a family, a life. He was not simply one of the obscure mass called Zionists. He was not just "an Israeli." He was a human being with whom they might have some connection. Fortunately, he was only lightly injured, and lived to walk among us again. We have lost too many others.

Notes

Introduction

1. The clearest example of this phenomenon came after a major 1968 Israeli reprisal attack on the Jordanian village of Karameh. Recruits came in by the thousands, transforming the guerrillas from a marginal group of agitators to a powerful movement.

2. February 1993, p. 10. Israel encouraged Hamas in the 1980s as an alternative to the PLO.

3. Paul Wilkinson, "Terrorism: International Dimensions," in *The New Terrorism*, William Gutteridge, ed., Institute for the Study of Conflict (London: Mansell, 1986). The League of Nations met in Geneva in 1937 to discuss the issue and drafted the first conventions against terrorism.

4. Edward S. Herman and Gerry O'Sullivan, "'Terrorism' as Ideology and Cultural Industry," in *Western State Terrorism*, Alexander George, ed. (London: Polity, 1991), p. 53. James Rusbridger, *The Intelligence Game* (London: Bodley Head, 1989), p. 3.

5. Frederick J. Hacker adds: "The terms 'criminal' and 'crazy' are labels that pretend to be descriptive but often merely express disapproval. The criminal is loathed; the crazy is pitied; both are feared. Punishment is legitimate only when the offender can be blamed." *Crusaders, Criminals, Crazies* (New Tirj: Norton, 1976), p. 9.

6. Robert O. Slater and Michael Stohl say that "terrorism is a purposeful act which is intended to influence an audience directly or indirectly." *Current Perspectives on International Terrorism* (New York: St. Martin's, 1988, p. 4). In the same volume (p. 49), Alex Schmid argues that the majority of terrorist attacks are "based on a rational choice and therefore remain open to rational analysis."

7. Edmund Ghareeb, ed., *Split Vision: The Portrayal of Arabs in the American Media* (Washington: American-Arab Affairs Council, 1983), discusses this topic.

8. The pogroms came after the 1881 assassination of Tsar Alexander II, for which Jews were blamed. In 1882 a group of youths called Hoveve Zion, lovers of Zion, formed by Leo Pinsker, began actively calling for Jewish immigration to

215

Palestine. *See* Simla Flapan, *Zionism and the Palestinians* (New York: Barnes and Noble), 1979; David Vital, *The Origins of Zionism* (Oxford University Press, 1975); Michael J. Cohen, *The Origins and Evolution of the Arab-Zionist Conflict* (Berkeley: University of California Press, 1987), p. 34.

    9. Amos Elon, *Herzl* (New York: Holt, Rinehart and Winston, 1975), p. 129. This history is detailed by many scholars. Herzl died in 1904.

    10. Israel Shahak, "The Jewish Religion and Its Attitude to Non-Jews," *Khamsin: Journal of Revolutionary Socialists of the Middle East*, no. 9, 1981; Lenni Brenner, *The Iron Wall: Zionist Revisionism from Jabotinsky to Shamir* (London: Zed, 1984), p. 9. The count instigated the pogrom after a Jew tried to kill a newspaper editor.

    11. Colin Chapman, *Whose Promised Land* (Ann Arbor, MI: Lion, 1983), p. 19. Of the 480,000 inhabitants of Palestine in 1880, the Jewish community numbered approximately 24,000. By 1914, following another wave of immigration, the community grew to 60,000.

    12. The Sykes-Picot Agreement, made public on the eve of World War II, divided the Middle East into French and British territory.

    13. T.E. Lawrence, *The Seven Pillars of Wisdom* (New York: Doubleday, 1926). Izzat Tannous, *The Palestinians: A Detailed Documented Eyewitness History of Palestine Under British Mandate* (New York: I.G.T., 1988, p. 60, describes the 1916 treaty between Sir Henry McMahon, representing the British government, and Sherif Hussein Ibn Ali, Sherif of Mecca, a recognized Arab leader, promising Arab independence. Churchill visited Palestine in March 1921 with Lawrence.

    14. Ruth W. Mouly, *The Religious Right and Israel* (Chicago: Midwest), p. 17.

    15. For example, relevant chapters in Walid Khalidi, ed., *From Haven to Conquest: Readings in Zionism and the Palestine Problem until 1948* (Beirut: Institute for Palestinian Studies, 1971).

    16. For example, Walter Laqueur, *A History of Zionism* (New York: Schocken, 1976); Mordechai Chertoff, ed., *Zionism: A Basic Reader* (Herzl, 1975); Leonard Stein, *The Balfour Declaration* (New York: Simon and Schuster, 1961).

    17. Nur Masalha in the study *Expulsion of the Palestinians* (Washington: Institute of Palestine Studies, 1992), p. 208, concludes that the 1948 Palestinian exodus was the result of "painstaking planning and an unswerving vision."

    18. The League of Nations confirmed the British Mandate on July 24, 1922, including the intention to create a national home for the Jewish people.

    19. Many studies discuss this incident. *See also* Philip Mattar, *The Mufti of Jerusalem* (Columbia University, 1988), p.27.

    20. This riot is discussed in all histories, including Cohen, *Origins*, pp. 80–81; Barnet Litvinoff, *To the House of Their Fathers: A History of Zionism* (New York: Praeger, 1965), p. 91; and George Antonias, *The Arab Awakening: The Story of the Arab National Movement* (Beirut: Librairie du Liban, 1969). Plans of the World Zionist Organization for control of Palestine from al-Arish in the South to Sidon in the North and covering both sides of the Jordan River were discussed in the Arab press, raising sensitivities.

    21. Laqueur, *History of Zionism*, p. 343; Trevor Dupuy, *Elusive Victory: The Arab-Israeli Wars 1947–74* (New York: Harper and Row, 1978), p. 4; Ze'ev Schiff,

A History of the Israeli Army: 1874 to the Present (New York: Macmillan, 1985), pp. 1–6.

22. Interim Report on the Civil Administration of Palestine, Presented to Parliament August 1921, p. 6. Y. Porath, *The Emergence of the Palestinian-Arab National Movement 1918–1929* (London: Frank Cass, 1974), p. 53, adds: "In general the Arabs made no distinction when presenting their case between official Zionist positions and the private utterances of the spokesmen for the more extreme Zionist factions."

23. He arrived in Palestine on June 30, 1920, and granted amnesty to those arrested in the riots earlier that year. W.F. Stirling, "Palestine: 1920-23," in Khalidi, pp. 227-35.

Chapter 1

1. The screen was put up on September 24 and left overnight, the rabbi arguing that to remove it would violate religious rules prohibiting work. Some archaeologists argue that the current position of the Temple Mount was not the site of the Temple of Solomon. Extensive excavation has been inconclusive.

2. There are many accounts of this incident, the most extensive being Esco Foundation for Palestine, Inc., *Palestine: A Study of Jewish, Arab, and British Policies* (New Haven, CT: Yale University Press, 1947), pp. 598–624.

3. J. Bowyer Bell, *Terror Out of Zion: Irgun, Zvai Leumi, LEHI, and the Palestine Underground, 1929-1949* (New York: St. Martin's, 1977), pp. 1–7.

4. Cohen, *Origins*, p. 84.

5. The actual number of killed and injured varies slightly from source to source. *See* Michael Bar-Zohar, *Ben Gurion: The Armed Prophet* (New York: Prentice Hall, 1968), p. 14; and Thomas Kiernan, *Yasir Arafat* (London: Abacus, 1976), p. 11.

6. Vincent Sheean, "Holy Land 1929," in Khalidi, pp. 273–331 has a detailed account of the riots.

7. The Shaw Commission, which issued its report in 1930, upheld the Arab view against a Jewish national home.

8. In his 1923 essay entitled "The Iron Wall," Jabotinsky wrote, "All colonization, even the most restricted, must continue in defiance of the will of the native population. Therefore, it can continue and develop only under the shield of force which comprises an *Iron Wall* through which the local population can never break through. This is our Arab policy." *See also* Joseph B. Schechtman, *The Life and Times of Vladimir Jabotinsky: Rebel and Statesman*, with foreword by Menachem Begin (Maryland: Eshel, no date, pp. 399–400. During the period 1917 to 1920 there were 897 pogroms in Ukraine, and the author states that this affected Jabotinsky's attitude during the Jerusalem and Jaffa pogroms. In another strange alliance, Jabotinsky sided with Petlyura, an anti–Semitic Ukrainian leader responsible for pogroms which killed 80,000 Jews after World War I.

9. Named after Brit Trumpeldor, who was killed in 1920 at the Galilee community of Tel Hai, probably by Arab bandits. Brenner, *Iron Wall*, p. 78.

10. Muhammad Y. Muslih, *The Origins of Palestinian Nationalism* (New York: Columbia University Press, 1988), p. 218; Mattar, p. 50.

11. "Middle East Terrorism and the American Ideological System," *Blaming the Victims: Spurious Scholarship and the Palestinian Question*, in Edward Said and Christopher Hitchens, eds. (London: Verso, 1988), p. 157.

12. Rosemary Sayigh, *Palestinians: from Peasants to Revolutionaries* (London: Zed, 1979), pp. 11–13.

13. Christopher Sykes, *Crossroads to Israel* (Bloomington: Indiana University Press, 1965), pp. 132–33, adds that details of the forgery were revealed in a 1934-35 trial in Switzerland. Morris Kominsky, *The Hoaxers: Plain Liars, Fancy Liars, and Damned Liars* (Boston: Branden, 1970), p. 205, says that the South African Supreme Court in August 1934 found the book "an impudent forgery."

14. Esco Foundation, p. 617.

15. Robert I. Friedman, *Zealots for Zion: Inside Israel's West Bank Settlement Movement* (New York: Random House, 1992), p. 66.

16. Ghassan Kanafani, "The 1936–39 Revolt in Palestine," first published in *Sho'un Falastinia* and reprinted by the PFLP in Beirut, no date, adds, "The death of al-Qassam aroused a wave of powerful feelings in political and other circles in the country, and the Arabic newspapers agreed in calling him a martyr in the articles they wrote about him."

17. *Palestine Royal Commission Report*, presented by Secretary of State for the Colonies, July 1937, pp. 88–89.

18. Sources describe the group as including Faran al-Saudi and Mahmud Dairawi, two members of the "Qassamiyoun."

19. Porath, p. 271.

20. It is usually alleged that the mufti called for the strike, but he was keen on keeping good relations with the British and was forced to support the strike, which was actively instigated by his political rivals, the Nashashibi clan.

21. Khalidi, Appendix 4.

22. David Ben-Gurion, "Britain's Contribution to Arming the Hagana" in Khalidi, p. 372, states that these police "provided an excellent framework for training the Hagana." The British began allowing them to take their arms for defense of Jewish settlements, and in 1938, 3,000 special constables and volunteers were added to the force. Ralph Schoenman, *The Hidden History of Zionism* (San Francisco: Veritas, 1988), p. 29.

23. Robert John and Sami Hadawi, *The Palestine Diary* (New York: New World, 1970), p. 265.

24. Dupuy, p. 6.

25. Christopher Sykes, *Orde Wingate* (London: Collins, 1959), p. 111.

26. Leonard Mosley, "Orde Wingate and Moshe Dayan," in Khalidi, pp. 377–78.

27. Ronald Payne, *Mossad: Israel's Most Secret Service* (New York: Bantam, 1990), p. 32. Dan Raviv and Yossi Melman, *Every Spy a Prince* (Boston: Houghton Mifflin, 1991), pp. 247, 412. Unit 101 used the same tactics as the Night Squads.

28. Michael J. Cohen, *Churchill and the Jews* (London: Frank Class, 1985), Chapter 2.

29. This report, issued in March 1937, is discussed by all Middle East historical studies. Reginald Coupland, a member of the commission, came up with the partition idea, then went to India and applied the same principle. Punyapriya Dasgupta, *Cheated by the World* (India: Irient Longman, 1988), p. 93.

30. Mossad, which means "institution," was headquartered in Europe until statehood. Its history is discussed by studies such as Richard Deacon, *The Israeli Secret Service* (London: Sphere, 1979). Golda Meir, *My Life* (New York: Putnam's, 1975), p. 171, states that Shaul Avigur, an in-law of Moshe Sharett, created the Mossad.

31. Esco Foundation, p. 861.

32. He was arrested November 22, 1937, and killed during Ramadan; some sources have his age as over 80. Neville Barbour, "The Dark Path of Repression 1937-38," in Khalidi, pp. 335-42. Tannous, p. 233. John and Hadawi, p. 279.

33. John and Hadawi, p. 261. Michael F.J. McDonell and R.J. Manning, "The 'Town Planning' of Jaffa, 1936," in Khalidi, pp. 343-36. The British air-dropped leaflets saying that they intended to beautify the city.

34. Tannous, p. 272.

35. John and Hadawi, p. 264; Tannous, p. 190.

36. *New York Times*, October 15, 1938 has an exaggerated story about Arabs killing collaborators.

37. Mattar, p. 83.

38. *The Angry Arabs* (Pennsylvania: Westminster, 1974), p. 128.

39. Khalidi, Appendix 4.

40. James Zogby, *The Palestinians* (Washington: ADC, 1981), p. 19.

Chapter 2

1. Menachim Begin, *The Revolt: Story of the Irgun* (Tel-Aviv: Hadar, 1964).

2. Benny Morris, *The Birth of the Palestinian Refugee Problem, 1947-49*, (Cambridge University Press, 1988),

3. Edgar O'Ballance, *Terrorism in the 1980s* (1989), pp. 24-28.

4. Shabtai Teveth, *Ben-Gurion and the Palestinian Arabs* (Oxford University Press, 1985), p. 110; Joseph Gorny, *The British Labour Movement and Zionism 1917-1948* (London: Frank Cass, 1983), p. 95. Sir John Hope Simpson, "On the Employment of Arab Labour," in Khalidi, pp. 303-07.

5. David Ben-Gurion, *Israel: Years of Challenge* (New York: Holt, Rinehart and Winston, 1963), p. 17.

6. Brenner, *Iron Wall*, p. 97.

7. Itzhak Gurion, *Triumph on the Gallows* (New York: Brit Trumpeldor of America, 1950), p. 26.

8. Nicholas Bethell, *The Palestine Triangle: The Struggle Between the British, the Jews and the Arabs, 1935-48* (London: Andre Deutsch, 1979), p. 298.

9. Cohen, *Origins*, p. 113.

10. Bethell, p. 41.

11. The extremist groups had so much hatred for the British that they tried

to make deals with the Nazis to increase Jewish immigration. Adolph Eichmann was invited to Haifa, and Stern actively tried to enlist Nazi support. Lenni Brenner, *Zionism in the Age of the Dictators* (Westport, CT: Lawrence Hill, 1983); Deacon, p. 25.

12. *London Times*, 9 August 1944, p. 4.

13. There are conflicting reports on Moyne's attitude to Zionism, with many Jews claiming he was anti–Semitic. In James G. McDonald, *My Mission in Israel 1948-51* (New York: Simon and Schuster, 1951), pp. 69–70, the author claims that Moyne was sympathetic to Zionist aspirations.

14. *London Times*, 7 November 1944, p. 4. This was the day of the United States presidential election.

15. Cohen, *Churchill and the Jews*, pp. 257–59, discusses this in more detail. Churchill called Weizmann to see him November 11, the day after the identities of the two men were known.

16. Bethell, p. 187; Sami Hadawi, *Bitter Harvest: A Modern History of Palestine*, rev. ed. (New York: Olive Branch, 1989), p. 190; David Hirst, *The Gun and the Olive Branch* (Harcourt Brace Jovanovich, 1977), p. 155.

17. *Sunday Times*, 24 September 1972, p. 8.

18. *Ibid.* A bomb intended for the War Department exploded in the General Post Office.

19. Israeli military historian Uri Milshtein in *Hadashot* 31 (December 1987), who refers to Eliav's 1983 book *Hamevukash*, cited by Noam Chomsky, *The Culture of Terrorism* (Boston: South End, 1988).

20. Begin, p. 220. The blast occurred July 22, 1946.

21. Abu Iyad and Eric Rouleau, *My Home, My Land* (New York: Times Books, 1981).

22. *By Blood and Fire: The Attack on the King David Hotel* (New York: Putnam; London: Hutchinson, 1981). The book contains an in-depth account of the bombing.

23. Hirst, p. 315.

24. *London Times*, 6 June 1949, p. 4. The bombing was a mistake; they thought the hotel was a headquarters for an Arab militia, according to Tannous, p. 474.

25. *London Times*, 14 July 1947, p. 4. The officers were freed on July 3, 1946.

26. *London Times*, 14 July 1947, p. 4, and 1 August 1947, p. 4. The unarmed sergeants, Clifford Martin and Mervin Paice, were seized June 18; the three Irgun members executed July 28, and the Sergeants hanged July 31. Many sources describe the Zionist campaign against the British, such as Michael J. Cohen, ed., *Jewish Resistance to British Rule in Palestine 1944-47* (New York: Garland, 1987).

27. Tannous, 1988, p. 358. The flogging is covered on p. 354. Bethell, pp. 339, 358; Jewish militias killed 338 Britons between 1945 and 1948.

28. Bethell, p. 337.

29. Brenner, *Iron Wall*, p. 135.

30. A list of these incidents is available in *Who Are the Terrorists: Aspects of Zionist and Israeli Terrorism*, by the Institute for Palestine Studies (Beirut: 1972).

31. Hirst, pp. 124–28.

32. Dupuy, p. 34.

33. Larry Collins and Dominque Lapierre, *O Jerusalem* (New York: Grafton, 1988), p. 273. Harry Levin recalls that three truckloads of villagers were paraded around King George V Avenue in Jerusalem. Sayigh, p. 76.

34. Sayed Noful, *Israel's Crime Record* (Cairo: Information Department, 1965), p. 19.

35. Sayigh, p. 76.

36. *Al-Fajr* (Jerusalem), 10 October 1986, p. 4; 17 October 1986. p. 4. Naomi Shepherd, *Teddy Kollek, Mayor of Jerusalem* (New York: Harper & Row, 1988), p. 40.

37. Meir, p. 182.

38. Munya M. Mandor, *Strictly Illegal*, trans. from 1957 Hebrew edition by H.A.G. Shucklev (London: Robert Hale, 1964), p. 75. The British announced on 20 November 1940 that they would deport the immigrants to Mauritius, and Mandor claims that the Haganah only wanted to cripple the ship.

39. Sykes, *Crossroads to Israel*, p. 237. The Jewish Agency called the sinking an act of "mass-protest and mass-suicide." The *Struma* sank February 24, 1942.

40. Bethell, p. 276.

41. Shlomo Hillel, *Operation Babylon: The Story of the Rescue of the Jews of Iraq* (New York: Doubleday, 1987, pp. 8–9, claims that the *Struma* was probably sunk by a torpedo from a Soviet submarine, and in the case of the *Patria*, "someone miscalculated" the amount of explosives. Menachem Begin, p. 35: "the direct cause [of the explosion of the *Struma*] has never been discovered." Notice the use of the word "direct."

42. Kiernan, p. 11.

43. Avi Shlaim, *Collusion Across the Jordan: King Abdullah, the Zionist Movement, and the Partition of Palestine* (Oxford University Press, 1988), p. 81. Raviv and Melman, p. 81, claim that Zionist contacts paid the king $10,000, which sounds like a small sum for a large chunk of his kingdom. Israeli leaders met Abdullah a few times but never formalized an agreement.

44. Dupuy, pp. 19, 121.

45. James Lunt, *Hussein of Jordan* (London: Macmillan, 1989), p. 5. *London Times*, 23 July 1951, p. 6, states that Israeli leaders had crossed to Jordan for secret meetings with Abdullah.

46. Ben-Gurion, p. 36. On p. 32 he says that the Arabs withdrew, and "many villages were entirely emptied."

47. Begin, p. 51. The Intifada nullified this intimidation factor. In 1988 Shamir urged soldiers to "put the fear back into the Arabs." *Newsweek*, 8 February 1988.

48. Livia Rokach, *Israel's Secret Terrorism: A Study Based on Moshe Sharett's Personal Diary and Other Documents* (Belmont MA: AAUG, 1980), pp. 46–47.

49. General Sir John Glubb, *A Soldier With the Arabs* (London: Hodder and Stoughton, 1957). Hirst, pp. 147–48.

50. Bernadotte wrote in *To Jerusalem*, trans. from the Swedish by Joan Bulman (London: Hodder and Stoughton, 1951), p. 208: "The Arabs are still Enemy No. 1. But I and the United Nations Observers ran them a close second." Hirst, pp. 151–52; Howard M. Suchar, *A History of Israel: From the Rise of Zionism to Our Time* (Oxford: Basil Blackwell, 1976), pp. 336–38.

51. Institute for Palestine Studies 1968 pamphlet "Death of a Mediator," containing eyewitness accounts of Bernadotte and the United Nations mission. George Kirke, "The Middle East, 1945-50" in *Survey of International Affairs, 1936-46*, Arnold Toynbee, ed. (Oxford University Press, 1954), pp. 184–86.

52. O'Ballance, Terrorism, p. 28. Ben-Gurion told the United States ambassador after Bernadotte's death, "What we have won on the battlefield, we will not yield at the council table." Rinna Samuel, *A History of Israel* (London: Weidenfeld and Nicolson, 1989), p. 77. AFP received a letter from the Fatherland Front taking responsibility for the action and admitting the killing of Serot was a mistake. *London Times*, 29 May 1950, p. 6: Israel agreed to pay the United Nations $54,628 for the assassination of Bernadotte and to continue looking for the assassins. In Andrew and Leslie Cockburn, *Dangerous Liaison: The Inside Story of the U.S.-Israeli Covert Relationship* (New York: HarperCollins, 1991), p. 36, the authors claim the killers were given exit visas for Czechoslovakia and that Ben-Gurion became close friends with one of the assassins.

53. Jon Kimche, *Seven Fallen Pillars: The Middle East, 1915–50* (London: Secker and Warburg, 1950), pp. 261–62.

54. McDonald, p. 108. McDonald, the United States' first ambassador to Israel, referred to Arabs as the enemy. When he arrived in Israel, he said he had come home in the biblical sense, p. 38.

55. An in-depth report is contained in *News from Within* (Jerusalem) 2, no. 37, 23 October 1986.

Chapter 3

1. *Guardian*, 8 December 1992, p. 11.

2. *New Statesman and Society*, 4 September 1992, pp. 18–20, claims that at least 97 Palestinians died at the hands of Israelis disguised as Palestinians. In July 1988 Reuters described such a unit, code-named "Samson" in Gaza, and three months later another unit operating in the West Bank (Israel withdrew the journalists' credentials). On May 21, 1991, Israel television showed undercover Israelis operating in the West Bank, sometimes in drag.

3. Raviv and Melman, pp. 247, 412. The authors add that Unit 101 often posed as Arab guerrillas.

4. 22 June 1991, p. 1. Also *San Francisco Chronicle*, 29 March 1994, p. 8.

5. *Guardian*, 9 July 1975; Deacon, p. 281.

6. Ian Black and Benny Morris, *Israel's Secret Wars: The Untold History of Israeli Intelligence* (London: Hamish Hamilton, 1991), p. 9.

7. *Al-Yom al-Saba'* (Paris), 24 July 1989; *Jerusalem Post*, 2 August 1989, p. 7. *See also* Raviv and Melman, p. 400, where the authors add that the fake leaflets called for more extreme action.

8. Black and Morris, p. 358; also reported in Raviv and Melman, p. 249, but with a different date.

9. *London Times*, 5 January 1948. Nine people were killed and 71 wounded in the explosion.

10. Meir, pp. 215–21.

11. Gurion, p. 194.

12. Bethell, p. 156; Geula Cohen, *Woman of Violence: Memoirs of a Young Terrorist 1943–1948*, trans. from the Hebrew (New York: Holt, Rinehart and Winston, 1966), p. 116; Gurion, pp. 65, 87, 137.

13. Dupuy, p. 22.

14. Tannous, p. 489.

15. Many studies discuss this episode, but the most thorough is Abbas Shiblak, *The Lure of Zion: The Case of the Iraqi Jews* (London: Saqi, 1986). *See also* Hillel, pp. 276–80, and Hirst, pp. 155–64. At least three Jews were killed and dozens injured by the bombs thrown at Masoda Shemtob Synagogue on 14 January 1951. A bomb was also thrown at the American Information Office, injuring four (*London Times* 20 March 1951, p. 3). Shiblak (pp. 74–75) adds that the U.S. State Department believed the Zionists agitated "a) to assist fund-raising in the United States [and] b) to create favorable sentiments in the United Nations Assembly to offset the bad impression caused by the Jewish attitudes to Arab refugees." Dr. Elath, an Israeli diplomat, added that most Iraqi Jews have no wish to leave. Researchers say that a Palestinian recognized one of the agents and informed the police.

16. Munya M. Mandor, p. 96. The group had a large cache of arms, including 425 grenades.

17. *London Times*, 4 March 1950, p. 5. Anyone leaving had to renounce Iraqi citizenship and make his intention known before March 1951. Richard Nyrop, ed., *Iraq: A Country Study*, (Washington: American University, 1979), p. 46: Iraq was having an economically hard time because of bad harvests, but the bombs were the Jewish community's greatest concern since they had been victims of a riot 1 June 1941 when the British moved into Baghdad. Elias Chacour, *Blood Brothers* (Grand Rapids MI: Chosen, 1984), pp. 125–26).

18. *London Times*, 16 and 20 May 1950, p. 3. Shlomo Hillel, posing as Charles Armstrong, negotiated the Mid East Air deal with Iraqi officials including Prime Minister Tufiq al-Suwaidi, probably with bribes. Black and Morris, pp. 88–91, cite CIA advisor in Baghdad Wilbur Crane Eveland, who said that the Zionists planted the bombs to terrorize Jews and to portray Iraqis as anti–American.

19. Raviv and Melman, p. 36; Tareq Y. Ismael, *The Arab Left* (Syracuse University Press, 1976), p. 163. Donald Neff, "The U.S., Iraq, Israel, and Iran: Backdrop to War," *Journal of Palestine* 20, no. 4, Summer 1991, p. 24.

20. Tad Szulc, *The Secret Alliance: The Extraordinary Story of the Rescue of the Jews Since World War II* (New York: Farrar, Straus, and Giroux, 1991). The backward corrupt Imman Ahmed li-din Allah of Yemen, who would send his army to stop a school from opening before he would defend his palace, almost certainly received money from Israel, and all emigrants' property was confiscated.

21. Shiblak, p. 74.

22. *Chicago Tribune*, 14 May 1990, p. 3, and 15 May 1990, p. 3. *New York Times*, 28 May 1990, p. 2. A court in Haifa found David Goldner and Gershon Tannenbaum guilty of the desecrations. Goldner, who was sentenced for three years, said that he wanted to unite Jews against Arabs.

23. *Jerusalem Post*, 22 December 1987, p. 1.

24. *New York Review of Books*, 23 November 1989, p. 60.

25. Raviv and Melman, p. 245.

26. Just about every historical study discusses this operation. Aviezer Golan, *Operation Suzannah*, as told by Marcelle Ninio *et al.*, trans. by Peretz Kidron (New York: Harper and Row, 1978). Payne, p. 32. Max Bennet, one of their friends involved in another espionage operation, was also caught, and he later committed suicide in prison (we should always be suspicious of prison suicides, but in this case it seems that Bennet did take his own life by thrusting an old nail into his wrists).

27. Deacon, p. 66.

28. Deacon, p. 74. Stewart Steven, *The Spymasters of Israel* (New York: Macmillan, 1980), p. 103f, adds that the affair was kept "out of the comprehension of the ordinary person." Meir, p. 289, adds, "the public was unaware of the entire top-secret episode," calling it a security blunder. The press was forbidden to mention their release.

29. James Rusbridger, *The Intelligence Game* (London: Bodley Head, 1989), p. 134.

30. *Sunday Telegraph*, 24 July 1988, p. A7; *Jerusalem Post*, 24 July 1988, p. 1; *London Times*, 25 July 1988, p. 1; *Intelligence Newsletter*, 18 January 1989, p. 7. This affair has been widely discussed but just as widely misrepresented in the literature of the Israeli-Arab covert war. But the bare fact that Israeli diplomats ran Arab agents and had access to weapons connected to the killing of Naji are beyond dispute, and three Israeli diplomats were told to leave the U.K.

31. Shiblak, p. 120, quotes a report saying that 300 young Jewish men received military training.

32. Black and Morris, p. 177.

33. Raviv and Melman, p. 109.

34. Szulc, p. 209. In January 1961 a boat carrying Moroccan Jews sank, killing 44 people, breaking the secrecy. The study also describes how Operation Magic Carpet ferried the Yemeni Jews by air, including Near East Air Transport. Ben-Gurion, p. 58, says that the Jews of Yemen "braved the perils of an uncharted desert."

35. Raviv and Melman, p. 121.

36. Raviv and Melman, p. 238. The authors allege that President Gaafar Numeiri was paid bribes for his cooperation. *See* Tudor Parfitt, *Operation Moses* (London: Weidenfeld and Nicolson, 1985), p. 97.

37. *Independent*, 31 May 1991, p. 12. American officials played a key role in the deal.

38. 24 September 1972, p. 8.

39. Noam Chomsky, "International Terrorism: Image and Reality," p. 25. Many histories discuss these killings.

40. Samuel M. Katz, *Guards Without Frontiers* (London: Arms and Armour, 1990), p. 15; Kenneth Love, *Suez: The Twice-Forgot War* (New York: McGraw-Hill, 1969), p. 124; *Davar* claimed that Hafez was killed by revenge-seeking Palestinians.

41. Steven, p. 89. *See also* Deacon, p. 246.

42. 9–10 December 1972, p. 3.

43. 9 December 1972, cited in Vincent Monteil, *Dossier Secret sur Israel: Le Terrorisme* (Paris: Guy Authier, 1978), p. 262. In almost all the Mossad assassinations during the 1972-73 period there were press stories about Arabs killing Arabs.

44. For example, Payne, p. 26. It should be pointed out that this book, like many others on the subject, has serious flaws.

45. *Intelligence Newsletter* no. 111, 14 December 1988, p. 7.

46. Stephen Green, *Living by the Sword: America and Israel in the Middle East* (London: Faber and Faber, 1988), pp. 42–43. Green points out that such misrepresentation violates the Hague Conventions on warfare. *See also The Middle East Record, vol. 5, 1969–70* (Jerusalem: Israel University Press, 1977), pp. 134–36: On 22 October 1972 Maj-Gen Avraham Adan, who was in command in 1969, confirmed this story.

47. Alan Hart, *Arafat: Terrorist or Peacemaker?* (London: Sidgwick & Jackson, 1984), p. 306; David Yallop, *Tracking the Jackal: The Search for Carlos, the World's Most Wanted Man*, (New York: Random House, 1993), p.38. Israel also bombed an American-funded irrigation project, threatening the Jordanians with more bombings unless they stopped the fedayeen.

48. Bean Grosscup, *The Explosion of Terrorism* (New York: New Horizon, 1987), p. 249.

49. Jonathan Randal, *Going All the Way: Christian Warlords, Israeli Adventurers, and the War in Lebanon* (New York: Viking, 1983), p. 237.

50. *Chicago Tribune*, 30 July 1993, p. 2. Those attacks sent 500,000–800,000 people fleeing north.

51. Both quotes cited in Noam Chomsky, "Middle East Terrorism and the American Ideological System," in Said and Hitchens, p. 106.

52. *London Times*, 10 April 1973, p. 1; *New York Times*, 10 April 1972, p. 1; George Jonas, *Vengeance: The True Story of an Israeli Counter-Terrorist Mission* (London: Collins, 1984), p. 357. The Arabs killed a Cypriot policeman, and an Israeli guard killed one of the plane attackers.

53. Abdullah Frangi, *The PLO and Palestine* (London: Zed, 1983), p. 126.

54. Many authors believe the operation was precise and accurate: Raviv and Melman, p. 188. Steven, p. 274, states, "More than a hundred Palestinians, all terrorists, lost their lives in the action."

55. Details of this operation are in almost every history of the Palestine-Israel conflict. *See New York Times*, 10 April 1973, pp. 1, 17, or other dailies and weeklies of that date. In the *New York Times* 11 April 1973, p. 13, Israeli General Elazer said the raid had been planned in advance and did not hinge on the Cyprus attack.

56. The incident happened August 5, 1973, and was reported in all newspapers the next day. The three gunmen, at first trying to pass themselves off as members of Black September, were sentenced to death on January 24, 1974, but were later released after another terror attack.

57. 17 December 1973, reported in all newspapers the next day. Thirty-two people died and over forty were injured.

58. 21 November 1974. The plane was taken to Tunis.

59. *New York Times*, 6 November 1973, pp. 1, 22.
60. *Guardian*, 18 December 1992, p. 8; Friedman, p. 66.
61. Suchar, pp. 479–80, observes that Israel's hard-hitting offensive tactics were used to break Arab morale and boost Israel's.

Chapter 4

1. William B. Quandt, Fuad Jabber, Ann Mosely Lesch, *The Politics of Palestinian Nationalism* (Berkeley: University of California Press, 1973), p. 160.
2. Former ambassador Sir James Craig in *Foreign Service* (London), January 1991, p. 6.
3. Hart, p. 175.
4. Kiernan, pp. 163–64.
5. Steven, p. 238. The engineer was Ayre Chizik.
6. Edgar O'Ballance, *Arab Guerilla Power 1967–1972* (London: Faber and Faber, 1974), p. 18.
7. Steve Posner, *Israel Undercover* (Syracuse NY: Syracuse University Press, 1987), p. 33. Chief of Staff Mordechai Makleff established the army camp 101, and Sharon was asked to command about 50 men.
8. Uzi Benziman, *Sharon: An Israeli Caesar* (New York: Adama, 1985), pp. 51–56.
9. John K. Cooley, *Green March, Black September* (London: Frank Cass, 1973), p. 93.
10. Benziman, p. 65.
11. Rokach, p. 45.
12. Hart, p. 107.
13. Love, pp. 5–20.
14. Dupuy, p. 131.
15. Fred J. Khouri, *The Arab-Israeli Dilemma*, 3d ed. (Syracuse NY: University Press, 1985), p. 190.
16. Terence Robertson, *Crisis: The Inside Story of the Suez Conspiracy* (New York: Atheneum, 1965), p. 20.
17. Ariel Sharon with David Chanoff, *Warrior* (New York: Simon and Schuster, 1989), p. 121.
18. Rokach, p. 45. Sharett added that military leaders believe, "Israel may— no must—behave ... according to the laws of the jungle."
19. Benziman, pp. 65–66: Unit 101 "perceived themselves as partners in the secret effort to motivate the political leadership to take some concrete action.... Every action conducted by Sharon somehow exceeded the proportions expected by the General Staff."
20. Sharon, pp. 124–26.
21. Geoffrey Regan, *Someone Had Blundered: A Historical Survey of Military Incompetence* (London: Batsford, 1987, p. 278). Steven, p. 94, says that bad Israeli intelligence and overestimating the Egyptian army "had the effect of placing Israeli armored divisions very frequently at the wrong place at the wrong time."

22. Ben-Gurion, pp. 81, 148.

23. Cockburn and Cockburn, p. 68.

24. Lauri A. Brand, *Palestinians in the Arab World: Institution Building and the Search for State* (New York: Columbia University Press, 1988), p. 5.

25. Cooley, p. 91. Arafat became personal friends with Mohammed Khidder, an FLN leader, who helped Fatah open an office in Algiers and allowed a few Palestinians to receive training at a military academy.

26. O'Ballance, *Arab Guerilla Power*, p. 28, notes that although the Syrians helped the group, they would not permit the attackers to use Syria as a base.

27. Rex Brynen, *Sanctuary and Survival: The PLO in Lebanon* (London: Pinter, 1990), p. 22.

28. Hart, p. 100.

29. Cooley, p. 45.

30. Brynen, pp. 21–24.

31. Green, p. 27.

32. A military analysis of the battle is contained in Dupuy, pp. 350–56, and *Middle East Record 1969–70*, pp. 365–73.

33. Hirst, p. 296; David Downing and Gary Herman, *War Without End, Peace Without Hope* (London: New English Library, 1978), say that by late 1968 Jordan hosted 20,000–25,000 *fedayeen*; *New York Times*, 15 August 1970, said Fatah had 10,000 men under arms, including 20 per cent non–Palestinians.

34. John Laffin, *Fedayeen: The Arab-Israeli Dilemma* (New York: Free Press, 1977), p. 39, adds that by mid–1972 Fatah's strength was down to 4000.

35. Laffin, p. 37, notes that after Karameh only 8 percent of recruits were college graduates, while 54 percent had only a primary school education.

36. Laffin, p. 101. Payne, p. 81, says that between 1967 and 1970 wars there were 5840 raids launched from Jordan, resulting in the killing of 141 Israelis and the wounding of 800.

37. Fard O'Neil, *Revolutionary Warfare in the Middle East: The Israelis vs. the Fedayeen* (Boulder CO: Paladin Press, 1974), p. 5.

Chapter 5

1. Mitchell G. Bard, "The Turning Point in United States Relations with Israel: The 1968 Sale of Phantom Jets," *Middle East Review* Vol. 20, no. 4, Summer 1988; pp.50–58, supports the claim made in the title. The sale had become an elections issue. Green, Chapter 2.

2. William Turner and John Christian, *The Assassination of Robert F. Kennedy: The Conspiracy and Coverup* (New York: Thunder's Mouth, 1978, 1993).

3. Rokach, 1980. The hijack occurred December 12, 1954, and Sharret wrote about it in his diary on December 22, adding that the U.S. State Department said the "action was without precedent."

4. *New York Times*, 5 May 1982.

5. O'Neill, p. 41.

6. This event received more coverage. *See* Michael Curtis *et al.*, *The Palestinians: People, History, Politics* (New Jersey: Transaction, 1975), p. 255.

7. Downing and Herman, p. 188.

8. Georges Corm, *Fragmentation of the Middle East*, trans. from 1983 French edition (London: Hutchinson, 1988), p. 158.

9. O'Ballance, *Arab Guerilla Power*, p. 69.

10. John Bullock, *The Making of a War: The Middle East from 1967 to 1973* (London: Longman, 1974), p. 130.

11. One Palestinian was killed during the raid, and the other three captured and tried (*London Times*, 28 November 1969). They were released after a Swissair was hijacked June 9, 1970.

12. Her story is related in Leila Khaled and George Hajjar, *My People Shall Live: An Autobiography of a Revolutionary* (Toronto: NC Press, 1975). She had been in Haddad's Beirut home when six katyushas were fired at it, injuring Haddad's son Hani and another person. Khaled carried him around the corner to the AUB hospital where Haddad graduated. This, I believe, is the only time Israel, who is thought to have been responsible, targeted a radical Palestinian. Haddad intensified security and began operating from South Yemen.

13. Christopher Dobson, *Black September* (New York: Macmillan, 1974), p. 308.

14. Brian Jenkins and Janera A. Johnson, *International Terrorism: Chronology 1968–74* Santa Monica CA: Rand, 1976).

15. *London Times*, 28 November 1969, pp. 1, 6: Two Palestinians were arrested; all casualties, including three Americans, were non–Israeli.

16. *London Times*, 23 February 1970, p. 1.

17. Bullock, p. 192. The author says that the PFLP had $1,500 in the bank on the eve of the September 1970 hijackings and had to turn to Arafat to help them cover expenses.

18. Michael Curtis *et al.*, *The Palestinians: People, History, Politics* (New Jersey: Transaction, 1975), Appendix, has a list of Palestinian attacks against airlines and El Al offices.

19. 14 September 1970; *The Middle East Record 1969–1970*, vol. 5, p. 839.

20. *Guardian*, 7 September 1970, p. 2. The front pages of most newspapers were dedicated to the hijackings.

21. Iraq kept three divisions in Jordan after the 1967 war and began extolling the guerrillas after Cairo accepted the Rogers Plan. The PLO published *Black September* in 1970, blaming Hussein for a war. Bullock, p. 133. Yallop, pp. 41–42, claims the Iraqi defense minister was bribed with two suitcases of dollars.

22. Israel had threatened to intervene in the fighting if the Palestinians gained control, and Iraq used that threat to justify its inaction in the civil war. If the Baath party was ruined, they argued, all hope for the Arab nation would vanish.

23. Don McCullin, *Unreasonable Behavior* (London: Johnathan Cape, 1990), p. 155.

24. Peter Snow and David Phillips, *The Arab Hijack War* (New York: Ballantine, 1970), pp. 75–100, deals with this subject in more detail.

25. O'Ballance, *Terrorism in the 1980s*, p. 93.

26. Yallop, *Tracking the Jackal,* discusses Carlos and the work he did for Haddad.

27. *Panorama* (Rome), 9 July 1989, pp. 68–75.

28. Geraldine Brooks, *Nine Parts of Desire: The Hidden World of Islamic Women* (New York: Anchor, 1995), Chapter 6.

29. O'Ballance, *Arab Guerilla Power,* pp. 57, 59.

30. Noah Lucas, *Modern History of Israel,* p. 437, cited in Chomsky, *The Fateful Triangle: The United States, Israel and the Palestinians* (Boston: South End, 1983).

31. Meir, p. 174.

Chapter 6

1. William B. Quandt, *Decade of Decisions: American Policy Toward the Arab-Israeli Conflict 1967-76* (Berkeley: University of California Press, 1977), p. 248.

2. Cooley, p. 124.

3. *See* Jonas.

4. Payne, p. 84, claims Mossad chief Zwi Zamir was dispatched to Munich. Colonel Livnat Liberman was also there.

5. Hart, p. 351.

6. Hirst, p. 313.

7. Dobson, p. 315. It was widely assumed that Abu Daoud or Abu Iyad helped prepare the operation, Abu Daoud traveling to Germany on a false passport (*Time* 24 January 1977, p. 30). Since 1970 Abu Daoud had used an Iraqi passport under the name Tariq Nehdi, and at the time of Munich he was in southern Lebanon. Abu Iyad claimed that he had nothing to do with the action. Laffin, p. 155, gives the identities of the freed gunmen.

8. David Gilmour, *Dispossessed: The Ordeal of the Palestinians* (London: Sphere, 1980), p. 160; Sandra Mackey, *Lebanon: Death of a Nation* (New York: Congdon and Weed, 1989), p. 150; Hart, p. 353.

9. Hart, p. 353.

10. Cooley, p. 125.

11. Frangi, p. 121.

12. Seymour M. Hersh, *The Samson Option: Israel, America and the Bomb* (London: Faber & Faber, 1991), p. 218. Posner, p. 66.

13. William R. Farrell, *Blood and Rage: The Story of the Japanese Red Army* (Massachusetts: 1990), pp. 130-35. The Red Army was partly a family business. Komoto's older brother participated in another hijack, and his wife, Okudaira, and another man named Maruoka Osamu were on the Tel Aviv attack.

14. The story was carried in all papers during the first days of March. John Richard Thackray, *Encyclopedia of Terrorism and Political Violence* (London: Routledge and Kegan Paul, 1987), p. 37. *New York Times,* 15 March 1973. Shortly after the Khartoum tragedy King Hussein commuted the sentences of Abu Daoud and 16 other Palestinians arrested with him. *New York Times,* 8 September 1973, p. 1.

15. Abraham H. Miller, *Terrorism and Hostage Negotiations* (Boulder CO: Westview, 1980), p. 26.

16. Meir, pp. 370-71.

17. Deacon, p. 255; *The Washington Post*, 29 December 1972, pp. 1, A5. Eight Thais, including two cabinet ministers, went on the plane to guarantee safe conduct.

18. Bullock, p. 5.

19. This story is carried by all the papers. It was not the first time Israel shot down a civilian plane. In October 1956, following the Suez War, Israeli jets downed an Egyptian plane in an attempt to kill Defense Minister Adal Hakim Amar.

20. O'Ballance, *Terrorism*, p. 189.

21. Posner, p. 83; Green, Chapter 5; Larry Ekin, *Enduring Witness: The Churches and the Palestinians* (Geneva: World Council of Churches, 1985), p. 68, cites telegram of protest by church leaders sent February 27, 1973.

22. 12 March 1973, p. 18. Hart, p. 361, adds, "After the Khartoum killings the Israelis could do no wrong." The gunmen were tried in Cairo and given eighty-year sentences, after which they disappeared into the Arab world.

23. Quote cited in Paul Findley, *They Dare to Speak Out* (Westport CT: Lawrence Hill, 1985), pp. 307-08. The CBS switchboards were jammed for hours as a result of Pierpoint's comment.

24. *New York Times*, 16 January 1977, p. E4.

25. *Washington Post*, 17 April 1973, p. C1. The afternoon before, United States Secretary of State Will Rogers held a meeting with three Arab-American leaders.

26. *Washington Post*, 2 July 1973, pp. 1, 16.

27. Seymour Hersh, *The Price of Power* (New York: Summit, 1983), p. 214f.

28. This program against German scientists was stopped after Mossad agents Yosef Ben-Gal and Otto Joklik were arrested in Switzerland. The head of the Mossad, Isser Harel, was forced to resign over the affair. *See* Raymond Palmer, *The Making of a Spy* (Crescent, 1977), p. 121; Deacon, pp. 162-67; *Intelligence Newsletter* no. 122, 7 June 1989, p. 6. *See also* Dobson, p. 135, for Israeli letter-bomb campaign from Belgrade in October 1972.

29. Michael Bar-Zohar and Eitan Haber, *Quest for the Red Prince* (New York: William Morrow, 1983); Deacon; Dennis Eisenberg, Uri Dan and Eli Landau, *Mossad: Inside Stories* (London: Paddington, 1978); Jonas; Payne; Steven, 1980; David Tinnin and Dag Christensen, *The Hit Team* (Boston: Little, Brown, 1976).

30. Stephen E. Atkins, *Terrorism: A Reference Handbook* (Santa Barbara CA: ABC-CLIO, 1992), p. 134.

31. *Middle East Newsletter* (Beirut), 6, no. 4, July-August 1972, p. 2.

32. As'ad Abu Khalil, "Internal Contradictions in the PFLP: Decision Making and Policy Orientation," *The Middle East Journal* 41, no. 3, Summer 1987, p. 368.

33. Abu Iyad and Eric Rouleau, *My Home, My Land* (New York: Times Books, 1981), p. 104.

34. Monteil, p. 246; *New Outlook* (Tel Aviv), Nov/Dec 1972, p. 127.

35. *Wall Street Journal*, 15 April 1982, cited in Henry Cattan, *The Palestine Question* (London: Croom Helm, 1988), p. 127.

36. *Le Monde*, 5 October 1972, p. 9.

37. Deacon, p. 254.

38. *Le Monde*, 5 October 1972, p. 9.

39. *France-Soir*, 9 December 1972, p. 3; *L'Aurore*, 9-10 December 1973, p. 3, says Hamshari was a victim of his bomb.

40. *Le Monde*, 12 December 1972.

41. *Guardian*, 29 January 1973, p. 4.

42. *New York Times*, 26 January 1973, p. 26.

43. *New York Times*, 10 April 1973, p. 1.

44. *New York Times*, 11 April 1973, p. 14. Najjar became "liaison between Fatah...and the [Lebanese] government," a friend of many ambassadors. Saeb Salam, the Lebanese premier who temporarily resigned over the raid, was a close friend of Najjar.

45. *Sunday Times*, 26 September 1976, letters.

46. Frangi, p. 126.

47. Miles Copeland, *Without Cloak or Dagger* (New York: Simon and Schuster, 1974), p. 219.

48. *Le Monde*, 24 July 1982.

49. *London Times*, 10 April 1973, p. 1; *New York Times*, 10 April 1973, p. 1.

50. *Le Monde*, 24 July 1982.

51. Monteil, p. 279.

52. Deacon, p. 260; Meir, pp. 347-52.

53. Tinnin and Christensen discuss this operation in detail.

54. Elaine Davenport, Paul Eddy, and Peter Gillman, *The Plumbat Affair* (New York: J.B. Lippincott, 1978), discusses this affair in detail. *The Observer*, 5 March 1978, claims the ship carried 200 tons of enriched uranium, enough for 20 bombs. Israeli agents were on the ship as it loaded in Antwerp.

55. Deacon, p. 273.

56. *Intelligence Newsletter*, 17 January 1990, p. 8. This information is also contained in many other sources.

57. *Intelligence Newsletter*, no. 127, 30 August 1989, p. 5.

58. Tinnin and Christensen, p. 169.

59. *Time*, 6 August 1973, pp. 31-32. The previous issue also discusses the affair.

60. *Newsweek*, 20 August 1973, pp. 37-38.

61. *Los Angeles Times*, 15 April 1974.

62. Cattan, p. 123, states, "There is little doubt that the school children were shot by the Israeli army"; Chomsky, *Culture of Terrorism* p. 122.; Hirst, pp. 328-30.

63. Patrick Seale, *Assad: The Struggle for the Middle East* (Berkeley: University of California Press, 1988), p. 274.

Chapter 7

1. Yossi Melman, *The Master Terrorist: The True Story of Abu-Nidal* (London: Adama, 1986), p. 59. This study has several errors. Neil Livingstone and

David Halevy, *Inside the PLO* (London: Robert Hale, 1990), p. 235, also a book with many errors.

2. Norman Rose, *Chaim Weizmann* (New York: Elisabeth Sifton Books, 1986, p. 193; after a meeting with Arab leaders in Jerusalem, Weizmann said, "I feel that I do not need to concern myself with the Arabs any more."

3. Livingstone & Halevy, pp. 236, 241; *Time*, 13 January 1986, p. 31.

Chapter 8

1. Pamela Ann Smith, *Palestine and the Palestinians 1976–83* (London: Croom Helm, 1984), argues that the division over territorial compromise was also a product of class differences.

2. Tariq Ismael, *The Arab Left* (Syracuse, NY: Syracuse University Press, 1976), pp. 41–42.

3. Ghassan Ahmed al-Haithi, born in Baghdad; Gabrial Khouri, born in Damascus; Amin Elhendi, from Algeria; and Tayeb Ali al-Gergani, a Libyan. The story is also contained in the *Guardian*, 6 September 1973, and *New York Times*, same day.

4. *New York Times*, 5 September 1973, p. 1.

5. *New York Times*, 18 December 1973, p. 1, 18.

6. The story of the Argo 16 was extensively covered in the Italian press on February 25, 1989, following a television program on RAI 3 about the incident. *See also Panorama* (Rome), October 1974; *Manifesto*, 24 February 1989; *La Stampa*, 21 January 1989.

7. Robert C Meade, Jr., *Red Brigades: The Story of Italian Terrorism* (London: Macmillan, 1990), p. 224.

8. David Hirst and Irene Beeson, *Sadat* (London: Faber and Faber, 1981), p. 181.

9. *Guardian* and *New York Times*, 6 and 7 September 1973, p. 1.

Chapter 9

1. Dilip Hiro, *The Longest War: The Iran-Iraq Military Conflict* (London: Grafton, 1989), p. 147.

2. James Adams, *The Financing of Terror* (New York: Simon and Schuster, 1986), p. 61, claims Abu Nidal trained in China and North Korea. These reports are untrue.

3. Hart, pp. 394–95, according to Abu Iyad's account, which he confirmed to me.

4. Shiblak, p. 86, 91.

5. *Jerusalem Post*, 5 January 1977, p. 4; Victor Ostrovsky and Claire Hoy, *By Way of Deception: The Making and Unmaking of a Mossad Officer* (New York: St. Martin's, 1990), pp. 291–92, claim that Israel armed militant Jewish groups.

6. *Time*, 24 January 1977, p. 30. He was released January 11.

7. *Commentary*, March 1977, p. 70.

8. *New York Times*, 18 November 1976, p. 1, 4; *Jordan Times*, 18 November 1976, p. 1.

9. Seale, *Assad*, p. 313.

10. *New York Times*, 26 October 1977, p. 1, 27 October p. 10; *London Times*, 26 October 1977, p. 1.

11. *New York Times*, 17 November 1977, p. A13.

12. *Jerusalem Post*, 6 August 1981, p. 1, 4. He was wounded on August 1 at close range by an Arab who fled in a waiting car.

13. *London Times*, 14 August 1978, p. 1.

Chapter 10

1. Cited in *Dictionary of War Quotations*, Justine Wintle, ed. (London: Hodder and Stoughton, 1989, p. 206).

2. Saad el Shazly, *The Crossing of the Suez* (San Francisco: American Mideast Research, 1980), discusses war preparations.

3. Hersh, *Samson Option*, p. 168n.

4. Kameel Nasr and Dina Lawrence, *Children of Palestinian Refugees vs. the Israeli Military* (California: BIP, 1987).

5. Archie Roosevelt, *For Lust of Knowing: Memoirs of an Intelligence Officer* (Boston: Little, Brown, 1988), p. 447. Roosevelt and Miles Copeland were the principal CIA officers in the Middle East.

6. Nigel West, *Games of Intelligence* (London: Coronet, 1989), p. 192. False-flagging means claiming to belong to a different country.

7. *Independent*, 21 February 1991, p. 2.

8. Roosevelt, p. 448.

9. Hart, p. 248. After the Iranian revolution the American and Israeli embassies were sacked; sequestered documents showed the European intelligence supplied information on Palestinian students in their countries.

10. Copeland, p. 221.

11. An estimated 40 percent of border guards and prison guards are Arab.

12. After the 1988 PNC that recognized Israel, spokesman Abu Sharif said PLO intelligence found that the Mossad was planning a series of attacks against synagogues and other Jewish targets, and they passed the information to European authorities. *The Middle East* (London), no. 173, March 1989, p. 16.

Chapter 11

1. Christopher Hitchens, *Prepared for the Worst: Selected Essays and Minority Reports* (New York: Hill and Wang, 1988), p. 193.

2. Hart, pp. 396–97.

3. *London Times*, 5 January 1978, p. 1; *Chicago Tribune*, 5 January 1978, p. 1.

4. *Israel and Palestine Report* no. 127, September 1987, p. 3.

5. *Jerusalem Post*, 23 June 1979, p. 1.

6. *Time*, 31 January 1986, p. 31; 5 February 1979.

7. *Israel and Palestine Report* no. 127, September 1986, p. 20. Rizk and Salameh had just been married, and she was pregnant at the time of her husband's assassination. After the baby was born, Arafat held up the baby to a crowd, calling him a child of Palestine.

8. Stephen Segaller, *Invisible Armies: Terrorism into the 1990s* (New York: Harcourt Brace Jovanovich, 1986), p. 194. Hassan was protagonist in David Ignatius's novel *Agents of Innocence* (New York: Norton, 1987).

9. Shaul Mishall, *The PLO Under Arafat: Between Gun and Olive Branch* (New Haven CT: Yale University Press, 1986), p. 12.

10. *New York Times*, 29 September 1973; Golda Meir, pp. 414–19. The train came from Czechoslovakia to Schönau Castle near Vienna, which the Jewish Agency rented; from there they tried to convince people to go to Israel.

11. *Nice-Matin*, 26 July 1979, p. 13; *Jerusalem Post*, 26 July 1979, p. 1; *New York Times*, 26 July 1979, p. 2.

12. Michael B Jenkins, *Embassies Under Siege: A Review of 48 Embassy Takeovers, 1971–1980* (California: Rand, 1981), p. 35; *Chicago Tribune*, 15 July 1979, p. 1; 16 July 1979, p. 2.

13. Gilmour, pp. 152–53. Patrick Seale, *Abu Nidal: A Gun for Hire* (New York: Random House, 1992), p. 293, claims that Abu Nidal killed Mohsin, but that does not seem likely.

14. Hirst and Beeson, p. 267. The authors also point out (p. 285) that in late 1977 Arafat offered to accept a modified version of Resolution 242, but Israel pressured the U.S. to decline. Gilmour, pp. 152–53. *Chicago Tribune*, 27 July 1979, p. 14. On December 23, 1981, Turkey sentenced the four gunmen to death.

15. *New York Times*, 19 February 1978, p. 1.

16. *New York Times* 20 February 1978, p. 1.

17. Hirst and Beeson, p. 291.

18. *Le Monde*, 20 February 1978, p. 1.

19. *Washington Post*, 28 February 1978, p. 1.

20. *Jerusalem Post*, 26 February 1978, p. 1.

21. *Jerusalem Post*, 2 June 1981, p. 1.

22. *Corriera della Sera*, 2 June 1981, p. 5.

23. Ostrovsky and Hoy, pp. 251–53. The author acknowledges that the Mossad killed Khader, although the dates given are inaccurate.

24. Naim Khader, Fouzi al-Asmar, and Uri Davis, *Towards a Socialist Republic of Palestine* (London: Ithaca, 1978).

25. *Il Secolo XIX*, 10 October 1981, pp. 1, 2; *New York Times*, 10 October 1981, p. 5.

26. *Corriera della Sera*, 10 October 1981, p. 1.

27. *Journal of Palestine Studies*, October 1982, pp. 153–54, cited in Mishall, pp. 122–23.

28. Hart, p. 398.

29. *New York Times*, 16 June 1978, p. A4.

30. *New York Times*, 1 August 1978, pp. 1, 9.

31. *Chicago Tribune*, 2 August 1978, p. 12.

32. *Le Monde*, 4 August 1978, p. 1; *New York Times*, 4 August 1978, p. 1; *Jerusalem Post*, 4 August 1978, p. 1; *Washington Post*, 6 August 1978, p. 21.

33. *Karachi Dawn*, 6 August 1978, p. 1; *Washington Post*, 6 August 1978, p. 1.

Chapter 12

1. *Chicago Tribune*, 21 May 1978, p. 4.

2. O'Ballance, p. 212.

3. *Washington Post*, 17 April 1979, pp. 1, 13. On 17 September 1982 two men from Black March again tossed a grenade at Zaventem Airport, wounding six. It seems to have been a locally organized group. *Le Soir* (Brussels), 20 September 1982, p. 4.

4. *New York Times*, 14 November 1979, p. 5.

5. *Jerusalem Post*, 14 November 1979, p. 1.

6. *Jerusalem Post*, 15 November 1979, p. 1.

7. *El País*, 4 March 1980, p. 1; *New York Times*, 4 March 1980, p. 5; *Jerusalem Post*, 4 March 1980, p. 1.

8. *New York Times*, 28 January 1973, p. 7; *Guardian*, 29 January 1973. Initially identified as Moshe Hanan Yshia. Black September took responsibility. A few recruiters were killed during this period, including (March 12, 1973) Simha Gilzer in Nicosia in front of the Palace Hotel. Richard Deacon (1979) and others make the mistaken assumption that Mohammed Boudia killed Cohen.

9. *New York Times*, 29 July 1980, p. 5; *Jerusalem Post*, 28 July 1980, p. 1.

10. *Jerusalem Post*, 29 July 1980, p. 1; *Le Soir*, 20 September 1982, p. 4, reports that he was condemned to death in March 1981.

11. *Jerusalem Post*, 9 October 1981, p. 2; Brian Jenkins, *International Terrorism: A New Mode of Conflict*, (Los Angeles: Crescent, 1975), p. 154. Husham Mohammed Rajih was sentenced on October 22, 1982, to life for the killing of Nittal and the synagogue attack, and Bahij Mohammed Younis was sentenced to life for killing Nittal. Marwan Hassan was the third person involved in the synagogue attack.

12. *Jerusalem Post*, 3 May 1981, p. 1. This was the first political killing in Austria since 1945; *Washington Post*, 8 October 1981, p. 26.

13. *Sunday Times*, 30 August 1981, p. 1; *London Times*, 31 August 1981, p. 1; *Jerusalem Post*, 30 August 1981, pp. 1, 2. Israel claimed that Austria was too friendly with the PLO. The three gunmen were trained in Iraq. Younis was a resident of Salzburg.

14. *Jerusalem Post*, 12 October 1981, p. 1.

15. Ostrosvsky and Hoy, p. 266.

16. *Chicago Tribune*, 31 August 1981, p. 8.

17. *Le Monde*, 10 August 1982, pp. 1, 4; *Jerusalem Post*, 10 August 1982, pp. 1, 2.

18. *Le Soir*, 20 September 1982, p. 1; three men were seriously wounded. *New York Times*, 19 September 1982, p. 12; *Washington Post*, 19 September 1982, p. 21; Israel blamed the PLO.

19. *Il Secolo XIX*, 10 October 1982, p. 1; *Corriera della Sera*, 10 October 1982, p. 1. Israel called on Italy to renounce Arafat, claiming he was the author of the attack.

20. Reuters (Rome), 23 May 1989; *Reader's Digest*, October 1986, p. 156.

21. Yeshayahu Ben-Porat, Eitan Haber, and Zeev Schiff, *Entebbe Rescue* (New York: Delacorte, 1977). Among the killed was Jonathan Netanayahu, group leader, in whose memory was created the Jonathan Institute for the Study of Terrorism. Edward S. Herman and Noam Chomsky, *Manufacturing Consent: The Political Economy of the Mass Media* (New York: Pantheon, 1988), p. 144, adds that the first meeting of the Jonathan Institute in Jerusalem in July 1979 included George Bush and influential journalists. Menachem Begin expanded the theme of linking the Soviet Union and the PLO to terrorism. Abeed Dawisha, *The Arab Radicals* (New York: Council of Foreign Relations, 1986), p. 120.

22. Dobson, p. 328.

Chapter 13

1. Green, p. 164; Seale, *Assad*, p. 371. Sharon became defense minister ten days after the accord.

2. *New York Times*, 18 July 1981, p. 1.

3. *New York Times*, 3 December 1975, p. 1.

4. "The Palestinian Factor in the Lebanese Civil War," in *Middle East Journal* vol. 32, no. 3, Summer 1978, cited in Seale, *Assad*, p. 275.

5. Katz, *Guards*, p. 75.

6. David Martin, *Wilderness of Mirrors* (New York: Harper and Row, 1980), p. 217; *see also Jerusalem Post*, 29 November 1986, p. 5.

7. 3 April 1978.

8. Brynen, p 120.

9. Randal, pp. 208–10, 237, 286.

10. *Jerusalem Post*, 21 August 1978, p. 1.

11. *London Times*, 21 August 1978, p. 1; *Jerusalem Post*, 10 June 1979.

12. Hart, p. 438.

13. William Polk, *The Arab World Today* (Cambridge MA: Harvard University Press, 1991), pp. 350–51.

14. Laurent Gally, *The Black Agent: Traitor to an Unjust Cause*, trans. by Victoria Reiter (London: Andre Deutsch, 1988), p. 194.

15. *Washington Post*, 4 April 1982, p. 16; *New York Times*, 4 April 1982, p. 3.

16. Randal, p. 246.

17. *Washington Post*, 26 February 1982.

18. Walter Laqueur, *A World of Secrets: The Uses and Limits of Intelligence* (New York: Basic, 1985), p. 221.

19. Sharon with Chanoff, pp. 432–33; George W. Ball, *Error and Betrayal in Lebanon* (Washington: Foundation for Middle East Peace [1522 K street NW, Washington DC 20005], 1984), pp. 34–35. Alexander M. Haig, Jr., *Caveat: Realism, Reagan, and Foreign Policy* (London: Weidenfeld and Nicolson, 1984), pp. 326–27: Haig

talked with Begin during Sadat's funeral [he was killed October 6, 1981] and told Begin regarding the invasion, "If you move you move alone," adding and reiterating at a later time that Israel needed "an internationally recognized provocation."

20. Ronald Reagan, *An American Life* (New York: Simon and Schuster, 1990), p. 421; Uzi Benziman, p. 234.

21. *London Times*, 4 June 1982, p. 1.

22. *London Times*, 5 June 1982, p. 2.

23. Maxwell probably helped the Mossad in clandestine activities such as the sequester of turncoat nuclear technician Vanunu.

24. Simpson claimed that during the chase Said tried to shoot him, but that was not proved in court. Simpson may have said that to make an excuse for shooting since he was supposed to shoot only if shot at. Said's lack of memory was augmented by his nervous state of mind.

25. *London Times*, 7 March 1983, p. 4.

26. *Time*, 31 January 1986, p. 31.

27. *Guardian*, 7 March 1983, p. 1, back page; *Washington Post*, 8 March 1983, p. 10.

28. John C. Cambell, "The Reagan Plan and the Western Alliance" (Center for Middle East Policy, 1983): Israel showed "no concern for American objectives and no fear of American penalties" during the Lebanon invasion.

29. Sean MacBride, *Israel in Lebanon* (London: International Commission, 1983).

30. Mackey, p. 178; Israel destroyed many buildings while aiming for Arafat.

31. Hart, pp. 453–55, discusses this in more detail.

32. *Yehoshua Porath*, cited by Chomsky, "Middle East Terrorism…" in Said and Hitchens, eds., p. 115. Chomsky adds, "It threatened the policy of evading a political settlement."

33. The accounts of these killings were on the front pages of all Italian newspapers. *Corriera della Sera*, 18 June 1981, p. 1, describes the Palestinians as capable, efficient, and honest.

34. *Israel and Palestine Report* no. 142, May 1988, and all newspapers, 18 June, including *New York Times*, p. 7.

35. *Le Monde*, 24 July 1982, pp. 1, 22; *London Times*, 24 July 1982, p. 1; *New York Times*, 24 July 1982, calls him a "Palestinian guerrilla leader"; *Jerusalem Post*, 25 and 26 July 1982, p. 4.

36. *London Times*, 7 March 1983, p. 8.

37. Hitchens, p. 194. Sartawi knew Bruno Kreisky, Willy Brandt, Andreas Papandreaou, and other world leaders, and he set up one of the first meetings between Arafat and Israeli peace activists. He was also ready to meet Sharon, but Sharon backed down.

38. Mishall, pp. 69–72, discusses Sartawi's proposal.

39. Gilles Perrault, *Un Homme à Part* (Paris: Editions Bernard Barrault, 1994), p. 26. Curiel's assassination remains unsolved.

40. Benziman, p. 194, says the meeting was arranged by Amos Kenan.

41. *Washington Post*, 11 May 1985, p. 19.

Chapter 14

1. Noam Chomsky, "International Terrorism: Image and Reality," in George.

2. Abu Nidal topped the January 1989 U.S. Defense Department's list of 52 terror groups.

3. D.A. Pluchinsky, "Middle Eastern Terrorist Activity in Western Europe in 1985: A Diagnosis and Prognosis" in Wilkinson and Stewart, p. 174, counts 233 terrorist incidents between 1980 and 1985 and finds 62 percent were against Arabs/Palestinians, 17 percent against Israel/Jews, and 5 percent against the United States. A deeper analysis will show that attacks against Jews or Israelis were almost all against European Jews in targets such as synagogues and Jewish schools.

Chapter 15

1. *Washington Post*, 19 October 1985, pp. 2, 18.

2. Jaffee Center for Strategic Studies, Tel Aviv, was very active in this. See *New York Times* June 24, 1985, p. 8. Also *New York Times*, May 16, 1986, p. 81, article by United Nations ambassador Benjamin Netanyahu.

3. Edward Said, "The Essential Terrorist" in Said and Hitchens, p. 157. Noam Chomsky, "International Terrorism: Image and Reality," in George, claims that Claire Sterling's *The Terror Network* became the founding document of the Reagan government, even though it "was soon exposed as a worthless propaganda tract." These pseudostudies on terrorism linked the Soviet Union with Palestinians. In reality their relationship was cold, but in a 1985 *Der Spiegel* interview Abu Nidal follows this line, claiming that the USSR was a true friend of the Arabs. Mossad chief Isser Harel said, "The PLO is organizing terrorism all over the world.... They are at the heart of international terrorism, a thing that will destroy civilization if it is not stopped." From Mike Evans, *Israel: America's Key to Survival* (New Jersey: Logos, 1981).

4. Herman and Chomsky: Rand Corporation hosted a conference chaired by Brian Jenkins on March 24, 1984, and the Jonathan Institute held several conferences attended by Bush, Schultz, Edward Teller, Ray Cline, Jack Kemp, George Will, Norman Podhoretz, Richard Pipes, Henry Jackson, and other prominent journalists.

5. Nir was the contact in the Iran-Contra affair and was wanted for questioning in the United States. He supposedly died in a plane crash in Mexico under a false name.

6. *New York Times*, 27 October 1983, p. 7. The gunman escaped.

7. *Secolo XIX*, 27 October 1983, p. 5.

8. *El País*, 30 December 1983, pp. 1, 13.

9. Jenkins, p. 475.

10. *New York Times*, 5 December 1985, p. 6.

11. *Il Manifesto*, 22 March 1985, p. 2.

12. *Il Manifesto*, 4 April 1985, p. 1; Reuters (Rome), 15 April 1988, says his prison sentence was reduced from 15 to 8 years.

13. AP (Athens), 5 April 1985.

14. *El País*, 2 July 1985, pp. 1, 14, 15.

15. *London Times*, 2 July 1985.

16. AP and Reuters (Athens), 29 March 1984.

17. *Times of India* (Bombay), 28 November 1984, p. 1; *New York Times*, 28 November 1984, p. 4.

18. *Sout al-Shark* (London), 9 August 1985, p. 1.

19. AP (Athens), 3 September 1985; *Sout al-Shark* (London), 9 August 1985, p. 1. A story in *Newsweek* about the second bombing erroneously said two people were killed.

20. All Italian newspapers and *New York Times*, 18 September 1985, p. 3.

21. *New York Times*, 16 September 1985, p. 2.

22. *Il Manifesto*, 18 September 1985, p. 1; Reuters (Rome), 11 July 1987, says he was sentenced to 17 years.

23. Reuters (Rome), 25 September 1985.

24. Reuters (Rome), 30 June 1986.

25. *Economist*, 19 October 1985, p. 31.

26. *Il Manifesto*, 26 September 1985, pp. 1, 3.

27. *Jerusalem Post*, 26 September 1985, p. 1.

28. *Cyprus Mail*, 27 September 1985, p. 1.

29. *Jerusalem Post*, 1 October 1985, p. 2.

30. *Cyprus Mail*, 27 September 1985, p. 1.

31. 3 October 1985. Posner, p. 213, says a Norwegian newspaper broke the story citing an Israeli government source, but Posner claims to have had a lettert from Rafael since then.

32. *Israel and Palestine Report* no. 127, September 1986, gives a long account of the Larnaca episode.

33. Thomas B. Allen and Norman Pollmar, *Merchants of Treason* (New York: Delacorte, 1988), p. 290.

34. *Guardian*, 2 October 1985, pp. 1, 30.

35. Chomsky, "Middle East Terrorism…," in Said and Hitchens, p. 100.

36. Asaf Hussain, *Political Terrorism and the State in the Middle East* (London: Mansell, 1988, p. 128), says the cruise was advertised in the *New York Times* with the slogan, "Come for a cruise with Maureen Reagan in the fall," but the United States president's eldest daughter was not on the ship. This book suffers from strong anti–Israeli propaganda.

37. *Guardian*, 18 December 1990, p. 17, has an interview with Abu Abbas.

38. Almost every terrorism book discusses this event; the *New York Times* had exhaustive coverage. Gally, p. 109, says that the hijackers demanded the release of Josephine Abdo and Mohammed al-Mansuri, FARL members in France, the only specific prisoners mentioned.

39. *Middle East International*, no. 387, 9 November 1990, p. 13.

40. Bob Woodward, *Veil: The Secret Wars of the CIA 1981–87* (New York: Simon and Schuster, 1987), p. 476.

41. Reagan, p. 508. The F-14s came from the *Saratoga*.

42. *Economist*, 19 October 1985, pp. 45–46.

43. The Italian national police respond to all internal matters, which is why the army was not called out, even though it was a military base.

44. Richard Clutterbuck, *Terrorism, Drugs and Crime in Europe After 1992* (London: Routledge, 1990), p. 18.

45. *New York Times*, 12 October 1985.

46. *Washington Post*, 12 January 1986, p. 23.

47. *Jerusalem Post*, 6 February 1987, p. 3.

48. All European and United States newspapers carried the story on page one. *Jerusalem Post*, 11 March 1986, said Abu Nidal was indicted *in absentia* in Rome along with the group's controller, Rashid al-Hamieda, and the sole survivor and leader, Ibrahim Mahmood Khaled.

49. *London Times*, 22 April 1986, p. 7.

50. *London Times*, 5 May 1986, p. 1.

51. *Jerusalem Post*, 5 December 1986, p. 1.

52. Fadlallah, author of the 1976 book *Islam and the Logic of Force*, supports armed force but believes that spiritual power is more important. Hussain, p. 99.

53. Woodward, p. 396; *Nation*, 19 June 1989, p. 851; *Washington Post*, 12 May 1985, pp. 1, 23; 14 May, pp. 2, 18; 23 June, p. 4; *Washington Post Weekly*, 14 March 1988.

Chapter 16

1. *Jerusalem Post*, 31 March 1986, p. 4.; *Washington Post*, 11 January 1988, pp. 13, 17.

2. *Sunday Times*, 6 April 1986, p. 1; *Corriera della Sera*, 6 April 1986, p. 1.

3. George Schultz, *Turmoil and Triumph*, p. 684.

4. *Covert Action*, no. 30, Summer 1986.

5. John F. Devlin, "Syria and Its Neighbors," in Friedman, p. 317.

6. Mary Kaldor and Paul Anderson, *Mad Dogs: The U.S. Raid on Libya* (London: Pluto, 1986), p. 12.

7. Wolf Blitzer in *Jerusalem Post*, 26 September 1986, p. 17, adds that the bombing had important political benefits for Israel since it demonstrated Israeli use of "legitimate self-defense" in its bombings of Arab countries.

8. Donald Haule, *Terrorism: The Newest Face of Warfare*, Yonah Alexander, general ed. (New York: Pergamon-Brassey, 1989), p. 218.

9. Here again terrorism experts were saying that Syria used Ahmed Jabril for the attack and that the U.S. should bomb Syria as revenge. Fortunately, the U.S. did not attack Syria, avoiding more retaliation. A.M. Rosenthal in *New York Times*, 3 November 1989, p. 27. For erroneous terrorist studies of the incident, see Steve Emerson and Brian Duffy, *The Fall of Pan Am 103* (New York: Putnam, 1990).

10. *Corriera della Sera*, 6 April 1986, p. 2.

11. CBS News, 28 April 1986; *Chicago Tribune*, 29 April 1986, p. 5.

12. *Washington Times*, 10 November 1986, p. 8. Although the paper is not always credible, it seems that the interview was accurate.

13. Seale, *Assad*, pp. 475–81; Seale, *Abu Nidal*, pp. 247–52, discusses the Hindawi affair in more detail.

14. Chris Ryan, *Tourism, Terrorism and Violence* (London: Research Institute for the Study of Conflict and Terrorism, 1991), pp. 1, 2: 17 Americans were killed abroad by terrorists that year.

15. Roy L. Cleveland, *The Middle East and South Asia 1984* (Washington: Skye), p. 63 "Next to armaments, [Israel's] second largest industry earning foreign currency is tourism."

16. *Al-Zahf al-Akhdar* (Tripoli), 11 March 1985; CIA "FBIS Trends," 8 January 1986, p. 9.

17. *Al Qabas* (Kuwait), 7 May 1987, *Al-Tadamun* (London), 9 May 1987; *see also* CIA "FBIS Trends," 20 May 1987.

18. *London Times*, 13 April 1987, p. 7.

19. *Israel and Palestine Report*, no. 132, April 1987, p. 4.

20. The incident happened April 22, 1980, in Belgrade.

21. Payne, devotes a chapter to the affair.

22. *Guardian*, 30 January 1985, p. 9.

23. Rusbridger, p. 134.

24. Ostrovsky and Hoy explain in the first section of their book how Mossad cells function.

25. *Times of India* (Bombay), 6 September 1986, p. 1; London *Times*, 6 September 1986, pp. 1, 7.

26. *Times of India*, 7 September 1986, p. 1; 9 September 1986, p. 1; *New York Times*, 7 September 1986, p. 1.

27. *The Middle East*, #142, August 1986, p. 36, adding that the 20,000 strong community are the "most contented [Jewish] community in the Islamic World." Aron Rodrigue, "The Sephardim in the Ottoman Empire" in *Spain and the Jews*, Elie Kedourie, ed., London: Themes and Hudson, 1992.

28. *Jerusalem Post*, 7 November 1986, p. 1; London *Times*, 8 September 1986, p. 1.

29. *Al-Fajr*, 12 September 1986, p. 7, the news conference held 7 September.

30. Reuters 13 June 1987.

31. *London Times*, 23 July 1987.

32. *Sunday Telegraph*, 24 January 1988.

33. *Jerusalem Post*, 24 July 1988, p. 1; *London Times*, 25 July 1988, p. 1. "Terrorist Group Profiles" (U.S. Government Printing Office, 1988), p. 14, says only that Force 17 was implicated in the attack.

34. *Yediot Ahronot*, 16 March 1987; *Sunday Times*, 15 March 1987, p. 1; *New York Times*, 16 March 1987, p. 10.

35. This incident is discussed in many Mossad books; *see Israeli Foreign Affairs*, August 1988, p. 3, which also discusses the death of Naji al-Ali. Julius Emeka Okolo, "Nigerian Politics and the Dikko Affair," in *Terrorism* (Washington), vol. 9, no. 4, 1987, pp. 327–34.

36. *Sunday Telegraph*, 16 December 1988; *Intelligence Newsletter*, 18 January 1988, p. 7.

37. *London Times*, 15 February 1988, p. 6; *Jerusalem Post*, 15 February 1988, p. 1.

38. *San Francisco Chronicle*, 18 February 1988, p. 15.

39. *Times of India*, 26 March 1986, p. 1.

40. The story is detailed in many sources. A U.S. Deputy Secretary of State said the killing of Abu Jihad was, "A reprehensible act on the part of Israel," *Washington Post*, 13 May 1988, p. 27.

41. *Christian Science Monitor*, 6 June 1988, p. 1. Five FRC members were convicted but released after only 3 years in prison, the U.S. State Department calling the release reprehensible and an insult (14 January 1991 dispatch, p. 32).

42. *Jerusalem Post*, 12 May 1988, p. 1; *Patterns of Global Terrorism, 1988*, U.S. Department of State, p. 12.

Chapter 17

1. Norman Antokol and Mayer Nudell, *No One a Neutral: Political Hostage-Taking in the Modern World* (Ohio: Alpha Publications, 1990), p. 25. "These individuals often come from middle-and upper-class families and frequently have benefited from college education." Actually, most FRC gunmen come from ignorant poverty.

2. United States, Department of State, Dispatch, 5 November 1990, p. 241.

3. ETA, Euskandi ta Askatasuna ("Freedom for a Basque Homeland"), began activities in the early 1960s. ASALA, Armenian Secret Army for Liberating Armenia, was an anti–Turkish group begun by Hagop Hagopian in 1975. He had worked for the PFLP and was a friend of Wadi Haddad. He was assassinated in 1983 by, most people believe, the CIA, since Armenian nationalism represented a threat to Turkish solidarity against the Soviet Union. The group faded shortly after his death. FRC developed relations with ASALA in the second half of the 1980s. At one time the FRC had relations with members of international revolutionary movements such as Action Directe, but they lost those, although they continued to claim otherwise; for instance, they claimed to have participated in the attempted assassination of Prime Minister Thatcher in Brighton.

4. Philip Willan, *Puppet Masters: The Political Use of Terrorism in Italy* (London: Constable, 1991), p. 203.

5. Willan, p. 347, gives the example of William Lemmer, who rose quickly to leader of Vietnam Veterans Against the War, one of the most active antiwar groups during the Nixon presidency. Lemmer advocated nationwide violence as a means of stopping the war. He shunned compromise and tried to militarize the antiwar movement, until it was discovered that he was an FBI *agent provocateur*.

6. According to Brigadista Alberto Buonavita, the Mossad approached the BR and offered weapons, money, and training, but the BR, still idealistic, refused.

7. *Corriera della Sera*, 7 September 1989, p. 8: One of Abu Nidal's men, identified by the false name Khalid Hassan Tamer Birawi, was arrested by Italian police along with members of the PCC (Fighting Communist Party), showing a link between the groups.

8. *Middle East International*, no. 377, 8 June 1990, p. 8: Rabin said that they knew about it from the beginning, which meant that they had plants in the group. This was confirmed to me by an ex-CIA agent. *Middle East International*, no. 387,

9 November 1990, p. 13, states that Gadaffi gave Abu Abbas three to four days to clear out after the May attack that left sixteen of his men dead. *Guardian*, 18 December 1990, p. 17: Abu Abbas claimed that the raid was retaliation for the killing of eight Palestinian workers ten days prior. Abu Abbas was with Jabril until 1976, when he rebelled against Syria's actions in Tal al-Zaitar camp. His secretary, Talat Yaqub, who was loyal to Syria, died of a heart attack in 1988.

9. For example, when Sandanista revolutionary Omar Cabezas went to the mountains to join the guerrillas, he almost left right away when he discovered that there were only a handful of fighters. Omar Cabezas, *Fire from the Mountain: The Making of a Sandanista* (New York: Crown, 1985), p. 48.

10. Seale, *Abu Nidal*, pp. 214–20, discusses accounts from the Abu Bakr camp of FRC collaborators killed in the late 1980s.

11. United States, Department of State, Factsheet, "Abu Nidal Organization Called One of the Most Dangerous," 14 February 1989, p. 5.

12. *Reader's Digest*, October 1986, p. 204.

13. Livingstone and Halevy, p. 243.

14. *Private Eye*, 9 December 1988.

15. *Private Eye*, 9 December 1988, cited in *Intelligence Newsletter*, no. 114, 1 February 1989, p. 7.

16. Much has been written about Abu Nidal and BCCI. On July 5, 1991, *Time* and the *Guardian* broke the story. *See also* Jonathan Beaty and S.C. Gwynne, *The Outlaw Bank: A Wild Ride into the Secret Heart of BCCI* (New York: Random House, 1993), p. 113; James Ring Adams and Douglas Frantz, *A Full Service Bank* (New York: Pocket, 1992), p. 6.

17. Seale, *Abu Nidal*, Chapter 9. The structure of the Mossad is described by Black and Morris, p. 331; Raviv and Melman, p. 134; and Laqueur, *World of Secrets*, p. 220.

18. Samuel Katz, *Israel versus Jabril: The Thirty-Year War Against a Master Terrorist* (New York: Paragon, 1993), p. 88.

Chapter 18

1. Reagan, p. 508.

2. Defense Minister Giovanni Spadolini agreed with the Americans. Angered at not being consulted, he withdrew his support for the government, bringing it to an end.

3. James J. Kilpatrick in *Washington Post*, 20 June 1985, p. 21. He also suggests, quoting Exodus 21:23, that Israel kills Muslim and Palestinian prisoners.

4. *Newsweek*, 5 July 1993, pp. 22–23. Warren Christopher downgraded the office and reassigned 80 percent of its staff. David E. Long, deputy director of the Office of Counter Terrorism, wrote *The Anatomy of Terrorism* (New York: Free Press, 1990), which shows a limited and inaccurate knowledge of the Arab World and of conflict, reflecting poorly on the department's ability.

5. Robert Fisk, *Pity the Nation* (London: Andre Deutsch, 1990), p. 127.

6. Edward Said, "The Essential Terrorist" in Said and Hitchens, p. 150. Herman and Chomsky, pp. 160–61, discuss the backgrounds of some terrorism experts. Sterling lost libel suits against her in France, while Ledeen was declared *persona non grate* in Italy.

7. Alex Schmid, in Slater and Stohl, p. 49.

8. Richard Rubenstein, *Alchemists of Revolution: Terrorism in the Modern World* (New York: Basic, 1974, revised 1987), p. 58.

9. Said, "The Essential Terrorist," p. 157.

10. George P. Schultz, *Turmoil and Triumph: My Years as Secretary of State* (New York: Scribner's, 1993). The book shows immense preoccupation with terrorism and belligerence against terrorists. P. 648: Speaking before the Park Avenue Synagogue October 25, 1984, he said, "Occasions will come when government must act before each and every fact is known."

11. *Washington Post*, 9 November 1985, p. A2. On June 7, 1991, the district court in Jerusalem ruled that Manning and his wife, Rachel, must be extradited to the United States to face charges of murdering Patricia Wilkerson, who died from a 1980 letter bomb. *Independent*, 8 June 1991, p. 11.

12. Bruce Hoffman, "Terrorism in the United States during 1985," in Wilkinson and Stewart, p. 235. The JDL is legal and tax-exempt since it is religious. Between 1977 and 1984 it committed 37 acts of terror, according to the FBI.

13. *Intelligence Newsletter*, no. 119, 12 April 1989, pp. 6–7.

14. *Intelligence Newsletter*, no. 127, 30 August 1989, p. 5.

15. United States, Department of State, "Patterns of Global Terrorism 1988," published March 1989, p. 30. The sole surviving terrorist, Omara Mohammed Ali Rezaq, was sentenced to 25 years: "The U.S. government publicly applauded the trial results." *Sout al-Shark* (London), 26 November 1985. On April 2, 1993, he was released, the U.S. condemning the action. Voice of the Mediterranean Radio (Malta). *Chicago Tribune*, 17 July 1993: Rezaq was turned over to the FBI in Nigeria and taken to Washington for trial.

16. To use an example from *International Affairs* (an English version of a Soviet magazine), April 1989, p. 22, an article by Boris Chaplin, USSR deputy minister of foreign affairs, describes an affair where criminals took a busload of 30 children hostage on December 1, 1988. The Soviets went out of their way to ensure the safety of the children, even cooperating with Tel Aviv (with whom they had no formal relations), until the drama ended peacefully. Miller, p. 38, quotes Richard Klapp, police specialist in negotiations: "Negotiation is the most compassionate, most human and most professional way to handle these things."

17. This is described in Meade.

18. Willan, p. 245.

19. Leonardo Sciascia, *The Moro Affair*, trans. by Sacha Rubinovitch (Manchester: Carcanet, 1987), p. 76.

20. Christopher Hewitt, *The Effectiveness of Anti-Terrorist Policies*, (Lanham MD: University Press of America, 1984), pp. 88–89.

21. The United States criticized the deal, saying that the hijackers evaded justice which will lead to more terrorism, but they offered no alternative, *San Francisco Examiner*, 21 April 1988, p. A11; *La Repubblica*, 16 April and 21 April 1988,

have in-depth articles on the negotiations. The bombings were the work of al-Dawa al-Islamiya, a right-wing religious group.

22. Schultz, p. 644.

23. One of the Shia hijackers, Mohammed Ali Hamade, was arrested January 13, 1987, in Frankfurt with 12 liters of the liquid explosive nitromethane. Subsequently, two Germans were kidnapped, and Syria helped obtain their release, enabling it to climb out of its isolation caused by the Hindawi affair. *Intelligence Newsletter*, no. 121, 10 May 1989, p. 6. Noam Chomsky, "Middle East Terrorism and the American Ideological System" in Said and Hitchins, p. 127.

24. Hart, p. 309; Robin Wright, *Sacred Rage* (New York: Simon and Schuster, 1985), p. 78.

25. *New York Times*, 11 March 1984, p. 20E, signed by Marianne Buckley and Harry Stokes.

26. Ostrovsky and Hoy, pp. 320–22.

27. *I&P Report*, October-November 1983; Posner, p. 286; Segaller, p. 197.

28. Wright, p. 66.

29. Green, Chapter 11; Michael Petit, *Peacekeepers at War: A Marine's Account of the Beirut Catastrophe* (London: Faber and Faber, 1986), pp. 94–95.

30. Wright, p. 73; Cockburn and Cockburn, p. 334. The loss left the U.S. dependent on Israel for intelligence. Seale, *Assad*, p. 406.

31. *New York Times*, 19 June 1986.

Chapter 19

1. *Sunday Times*, 24 July 1988, claims there were two Mossad agents on the ship.

2. *La Repubblica*, 27 February 1989.

3. Nathan M. Adams in *Reader's Digest*, June 1989, p. 204. Abu Nidal was supposed to have met Vassilis Konstantineas, Kosta Tsimas, and other Greek officials.

4. *Sout al-Shark* (London), 10 June 1986, p. 1.

Chapter 20

1. *Al-Fajr*, 6 November 1989, p. 4.

2. *New York Times*, 12 November 1989, pp. 1, 16.

3. On July 30, 1988, police in Lima, Peru, broke up a small FRC that was trying to form. One of those arrested had ties to the Rome and Vienna attacks and the 1985 Egypt Air plane hijacked to Malta. *Washington Post*, 31 July 1988, p. 24; *Christian Science Monitor*, 1 August 1988, p. 2.

4. *San Francisco Chronicle*, 23 April 1980, p. 39.

5. Seale, *Abu Nidal*, pp. 36–38, gives a summary of Abu Zeid's life.

6. All newspapers on 16 January 1991 carry the story. *Jordan Times* and *Independent* give a brief Abu Iyad biography.

7. *Chicago Tribune,* 18 August 1993, p. 6, 26 September 1993, p. 14: The U.S. placed Sudan on its list of terrorist states, citing National Islamic Front leader Hannan Turabi's welcome to Abu Nidal and radical Islamic groups.

Chapter 21

1. D.A. Pluchinsky, "Middle East Terrorist Activity in Western Europe in 1985: A Diagnosis and Prognosis" in Wilkinson and Stewart, p. 174, counts 233 terrorist incidents between 1980 and 1985 and finds 62 percent were against Arabs/Palestinians, 17 percent against Israel/Jews, and 5 percent against the U.S.
2. Masalha (1992) presents this point clearly.
3. The ship was attacked June 8, 1967, during the war, by four Mirage fighters and three torpedo boats. Israel claimed it was a mistake, but it was probably deliberately hit in international waters. *See* James M. Ennes, Jr., *Assault on the Liberty: The True Story of the Israeli Attack on an American Intelligence Ship* (New York: Random House, 1979); Anthony Pearson, *Conspiracy of Silence* (London: Quartet, 1978). President Johnson wanted to launch a counter-attack on the port of Haifa, but Walt Rostow, NSA advisor, advised him against it.
4. Love, p. 694.
5. Wilhelm Dieth, *Holy War,* (New York: Macmillan, 1984).
6. *Guardian,* 18 December 1992, p. 1.
7. Chaliand, p. 55.
8. Chomsky, "Middle East Terrorism and the American Ideological System," in Said and Hitchens, p. 102, adds, "Retaliation is directed against those who are vulnerable, not the perpetrators of atrocities."
9. Gally, p. 142, gives the example of the U.S. protesting the light sentences French courts gave to FARL members, for which the U.S. had no business, which the FARL interpreted as "an act of war" and went on a bombing spree.
10. 10 July 1993, p. 24.
11. House Committee on Foreign Affairs hearing, 26 April 1979, report by Harold H. Saunders, Assistant Secretary of State for Near East and South Asian Affairs.
12. *San Francisco Chronicle,* 11 May 1993, p. 8.
13. In September 1993 a U.S. panel urged the U.N. to form a commission of an international court for dictators. Conservatives, including the Heritage Foundation and Jeane Kirkpatrick, former U.N. ambassador, opposed such a move, wanting less cooperation with the U.N. *Chicago Tribune,* 11 September 1993, p. 2.
14. Ahmad J. Rashed, "Hamas: The History of the Islamic Opposition Movement in Palestine," *Washington Report on Middle Eastern Affairs* 6, no. 8, March 1993, pp. 37–38, The U.S. put Hamas on its terrorist list, but Hamas claims that they are struggling against occupation and hence their military activities are justified.

Bibliography

Abboushi, W.F. *The Angry Arabs*. Philadelphia: Westminster, 1974.

Abu Iyad and Eric Rouleau. *My Home, My Land*. New York: Times Books, 1981.

Abu-Lughod, Ibrahim. *Palestinian Rights: Affirmation and Denial*. Wilmette IL: Media, 1982.

Adams, James. *The Financing of Terror*. New York: Simon & Schuster, London: New English Library, 1986.

Alexander, Yonah, and Joshua Sinai. *Terrorism: The PLO Connection*. New York: Taylor and Francis, 1989.

Allen, Thomas B., and Norman Polmar. *Merchants of Treason*. New York: Delacorte, 1988.

Antokol, Norman, and Mayer Nudell. *No One a Neutral: Political Hostage-Taking in the Modern World*. Ohio: Alpha, 1990.

Antonias, George. *The Arab Awakening: The Story of the Arab National Movement*. Beirut: Librairie du Liban, 1969.

Atkins, Stephen E. *Terrorism: A Reference Handbook*. Santa Barbara CA: ABC-CLIO, 1992.

Ball, George W. *Error and Betrayal in Lebanon*. Foundation for Middle East Peace, 1984.

Bar-Zohar, Michael. *Ben Gurion: The Armed Prophet*. New York: Prentice Hall, 1968.

_____, and Eitan Haber. *Quest for the Red Prince*. New York: William Morrow, 1983.

Becker, Julian. *The Rise and Fall of the Palestinian Liberation Organization*. New York: St. Martin's, 1984.

_____. *The Soviet Connection: State Sponsorship of Terrorism*. London: Institute for European Defense and Strategic Studies, 1985

Begin, Menachem. *The Revolt: The Story of the Irgun*. Tel-Aviv: Hadar, 1964.

Bell, J. Bowyer. *Terror Out of Zion: Irgun, Zvai Leumi, LEHI, and the Palestine Underground, 1929–49*. New York: St. Martin's, 1977.

Ben-Gurion, David. *Israel: Years of Challenge*. New York: Holt, Rinehart and Winston, 1963.

Ben-Porat, Yeshayahu, Eitan Haber, and Zeev Schiff. *Entebbe Rescue*. Tel-Aviv: Zmora, Bitan, Modan, 1976; reprint, New York: Delacorte, 1977.

Benziman, Uzi. *Sharon: An Israeli Caesar*. New York: Adama, 1985.

Bernadotte, Folke. *To Jerusalem*. Trans. from Swedish by Joan Bulman. London: Hodder and Stoughton, 1951.

Bethell, Nicholas. *The Palestine Triangle: The Struggle Between the British, the Jews and the Arabs, 1935-48*. London: Andre Deutsch, 1979.

Black, Edwin. *The Transfer Agreement: The Untold Story of the Secret Pact Between the Third Reich and Jewish Palestine*. New York: Macmillan, 1984.

Black, Ian, and Benny Morris. *Israel's Secret Wars: The Untold History of Israeli Intelligence*. London: Hamish Hamilton, 1991.

Blitzer, Wolf. *Territory of Lies*. New York: Harper and Row, 1989.

Blumberg, Stanley A., and Gwinn Owens. *The Survival Factor*. New York: Putnam's, 1981.

Brand, Lauri A. *Palestinians in the Arab World: Institution Building and the Search for State*. New York: Columbia University, 1988.

Brenner, Lenni, *The Iron Wall: Zionist Revisionism from Jabotinsky to Shamir*. London: Zed, 1984.

_____. *Zionism in the Age of Dictators*. Westport CT: Lawrence Hill, 1983.

Brooks, Geraldine. *Nine Parts of Desire: The Hidden World of Islamic Women*. New York: Anchor, 1995.

Brynen, Rex. *Sanctuary and Survival: The PLO in Lebanon*. London: Pinter, 1990.

Bullock, John. *The Making of a War: The Middle East from 1967 to 1973*. London: Longman, 1974.

Cattan, Henry. *The Palestine Question*. London: Croom Helm, 1988.

Chacour, Elias. *Blood Brothers*. Grand Rapids MI: Chosen Books, 1984.

Chaliand, Gerard. *Terrorism: From Popular Struggle to Media Spectacle*. Trans. from French. London: Saqi, 1987.

Chapman, Colin. *Whose Promised Land*. Ann Arbor MI: Lion, 1983.

Chertoff, Mordechai, ed. *Zionism: A Basic Reader*. Herzl, 1975.

Chomsky, Noam. *The Culture of Terrorism*. Boston: South End, 1988.

_____. *The Fateful Triangle: The United States, Israel and the Palestinians*. Boston: South End, 1983.

Clarke, Thurston. *By Blood and Fire: The Attack on the King David Hotel*. New York: Putnam; London: Hutchinson, 1981.

Cleveland, Roy L. *The Middle East and South Asia 1984*. Washington: Skye.

Clutterbuck, Richard. *Terrorism, Drugs and Crime in Europe After 1992*. London: Routledge, 1990.

Cobban, Helena. *The Palestine Liberation Organization*. Cambridge University, 1984.

Cockburn, Andrew, and Cockburn, Leslie. *Dangerous Liaison: The Inside Story of the U.S.–Israeli Covert Relationship*. New York: HarperCollins, 1991.

Cohen, Geula. *Woman of Violence: Memoirs of a Young Terrorist 1943–1948*. Trans. from Hebrew. New York: Holt, Rinehart and Winston, 1966

Cohen, Michael J., *Churchill and the Jews*. London: Frank Class, 1985.

_____. *The Origins and Evolution of the Arab-Zionist Conflict*. Berkeley: University of California Press, 1987.

_____, ed. *Jewish Resistance to British Rule in Palestine 1944–47*. New York: Garland, 1987.

Collins, Larry, and Dominique Lapierre. *O Jerusalem*. New York: Grafton Books, 1988.

Cooley, John K. *Green March, Black September*. London: Frank Cass, 1973.

Copeland, Miles. *Without Cloak or Dagger*. New York: Simon and Schuster, 1974.

Corm, Georges. *Fragmentation of the Middle East*. London: Hutchinson, 1988.

Curtis, Michael, *et al*. *The Palestinians: People, History, Politics*. New Brunswick, NJ: Transaction, 1975.

Dasgupta, Punyapriya. *Cheated by the World*. India: Irient Longman, 1988.

Davenport, Elaine, Paul Eddy, and Peter Gillman. *The Plumbat Affair*. New York: Lippincott, 1978.

Dawisha, Abeed. *The Arab Radicals*. New York: Council of Foreign Relations, 1986.

Deacon, Richard. *The Israeli Secret Service*. London: Sphere, 1979.

Dieth, Wilhelm. *Holy War*. Trans. from German by Martha Humphreys. New York: Macmillan, 1984.

Dobson, Christopher. *Black September*. New York: Macmillan, 1974.

_____, and Ronald Payne. *The Never-Ending War: Terrorism in the 80's*. New York: Facts on File, 1987.

Downing, David, and Gary Herman. *War Without End, Peace Without Hope*. London: New English Library, 1978.

Dupuy, Trevor N. *Elusive Victory: The Arab-Israeli Wars 1947–74*. New York: Harper and Row, 1978.

Dyan, Moshe. *The Story of My Life*. New York: Morrow, 1976.

Eisenberg, Dennis, Uri Dan, and Eli Landau. *Mossad: Inside Stories*. London: Paddington, 1978.

Ekin, Larry. *Enduring Witness: The Churches and the Palestinians*. Geneva: World Council of Churches, 1985.

Elon, Amos. *Herzl*. New York: Holt, Rinehart and Winston, 1975.

Ennes, James M., Jr. *Assault on the Liberty: The True Story of the Israeli Attack on an American Intelligence Ship*. New York: Random House, 1979.

Esco Foundation for Palestine. *Palestine: A Study of Jewish, Arab, and British Policies*. New Haven CT: Yale University Press, 1947.

Evans, Mike. *Israel: America's Key to Survival*. New Jersey: Logos, 1981.

Farrell, William R. *Blood and Rage: The Story of the Japanese Red Army*. Massachusetts: 1990.

Findley, Paul. *They Dare to Speak Out*. Westport CT: Lawrence Hill, 1985.

Fisk, Robert. *Pity the Nation*. London: Andre Deutsch, 1990.

Flapan, Simla. *Zionism and the Palestinians*. New York: Barnes and Noble, 1979.

Frangi, Abdullah. *The PLO and Palestine*. London: Zed, 1983.

Freedman, Lawrence Zelic, and Yonah Alexander, eds. *Perspectives on Terrorism*. Delhi: Hindustan, 1985.

Freedman, Robert O., ed. *The Middle East from the Iran-Contra Affair to the Intifada*. Syracuse NY: Syracuse University Press, 1991.

Friedman, Robert I. *Zealots for Zion: Inside Israel's West Bank Settlement Movement*. New York: Random House, 1992.

Gally, Laurent. *The Black Agent: Traitor to an Unjust Cause*. Trans. by Victoria Reiter. London: Andre Deutsch, 1988.

George, Alexander, ed. *Western State Terrorism*. London: Polity, 1991.

Ghareeb, Edmund, ed. *Split Vision: The Portrayal of Arabs in the American Media*. Washington DC: American-Arab Affairs Council, 1983.

Gilmour, David. *Dispossessed: The Ordeal of the Palestinians*. London: Sphere, 1980.

Glubb, Sir John. *A Soldier with the Arabs*. London: Hodder and Stoughton, 1957.

Golan, Aviezer, as told by Marcelle Ninio, Victor Levy, Robert Dassa and Philip Natansar. *Operation Suzannah*. Trans by Peretz Kidron, with Foreword by Golda Meir. New York: Harper and Row, 1978.

Gorny, Joseph. *The British Labour Movement and Zionism 1917–48*. London: Frank Cass, 1983.

Green, Stephen. *Living by the Sword: America and Israel in the Middle East 1968–87*. London: Faber and Faber, 1988.

Gresh, Alain. *The PLO: The Struggle Within*. London: Zed, 1985.

Grosscup, Bean. *The Explosion of Terrorism*. New York: New Horizon, 1987.

Gurion, Itzhak. *Triumph on the Gallows*. New York: Brit Trumpldor of America, 1950.

Gutteridge, William, ed., for the Institute for the Study of Conflict. *The New Terrorism*. London: Mansell, 1986.

Hacker, Frederick J. *Crusaders, Criminals, Crazies*. New York: Norton, 1976.

Hadawi, Sami. *Bitter Harvest: A Modern History of Palestine*. Rev. ed. New York: Olive Branch, 1989.

Haig, Alexander M., Jr. *Caveat: Realism, Reagan, and Foreign Policy*. London: Weidenfeld and Nicolson, 1984.

Handerson, Bernard R. *Pollard: The Spy's Story*. New York: Alpha, 1988.

Hart, Alan. *Arafat: Terrorist or Peacemaker?* London: Sidgwick and Jackson, 1984.

Haule, Donald. *Terrorism: The Newest Face of Warfare*. New York: Pergamon-Brassey, 1989.

Herman, Edward S., and Gerry O'Sullivan. *The Terrorism Industry*. New York: Pantheon, 1990.

Herman, Edward S., and Noam Chomsky. *Manufacturing Consent: The Political Economy of the Mass Media*. New York: Pantheon, 1988.

Hersh, Seymour M. *The Price of Power*. New York: Summit, 1983.

_____. *The Samson Option: Israel, America and the Bomb*. London: Faber and Faber, 1991.

Hewitt, Christopher. *The Effectiveness of Anti-Terrorist Policies*. Lanham MD: University Press of America, 1984.

Hillel, Shlomo. *Operation Babylon: The Story of the Rescue of the Jews of Iraq*. New York: Doubleday, 1987.

Hiro, David. *The Longest War: The Iran-Iraq Military Conflict*. London: Grafton, 1989.

Hirst, David. *The Gun and the Olive Branch*. Harcourt Brace Jovanovich, 1977.

_____, and Irene Beeson. *Sadat*. London: Faber and Faber, 1981.

Hitchens, Christopher. *Prepared for the Worst: Selected Essays and Minority Reports*. New York: Hill and Wang, 1988.

Hoffman, Bruce. *Recent Trends in Palestinian Terrorism*. Santa Monica CA: Rand, 1985.

Hussain, Asaf. *Political Terrorism and the State in the Middle East*. London: Mansell, 1988.

Institute for Palestine Studies. *Who Are the Terrorists: Aspects of Zionist and Israeli Terrorism*. Beirut, 1972.

Ismael, Tareq Y. *The Arab Left*. Syracuse NY: Syracuse University Press, 1976.

Jansen, Michael. *The Battle of Beirut: Why Israel Invaded Lebanon*. London: Zed, 1982.

_____. *The United States and the Palestinian People*. Beirut: Institute for Palestinian Studies, 1970.

Jenkins, Brian M. *International Terrorism: A New Mode of Conflict*. Los Angeles: Crescent, 1975.

_____, and Janera A. Johnson. *International Terrorism: Chronology 1968–74*. Santa Monica CA: Rand, 1975.

Jenkins, Michael B. *Embassies Under Siege: A Review of 48 Embassy Takeovers, 1971–1980*. Santa Monica CA: Rand, 1981.

John, Robert, and Sami Hadawi. *The Palestine Diary*. New York: New World, 1970.

Johnston, David. *Lockerbie: The Real Story*. London: Bloomsberg, 1989.

Jonas, George. *Vengeance: The True Story of an Israeli Counter-Terrorist Mission*. London: Collins, 1984.

Kaldor, Mary, and Paul Anderson. *Mad Dogs: The U.S. Raid on Libya*. London: Pluto, 1986.

Kanafani, Ghassan. *The 1936–39 Revolt in Palestine*. First published in *Sho'un Falastinia*; reprint, Beirut: PFLP, no date.

Katz, Samuel M. *Guards Without Frontiers*. London: Arms and Armour, 1990.

_____. *Israel Versus Jabril: The Thirty-Year War Against a Master Terrorist*. New York: Paragon, 1993.

Kedourie, Elie, ed. *Spain and the Jews*. London: Thames and Hudson, 1992.

Khader, Naim, Fouzi al-Asmar, and Uri Davis. *Towards a Socialist Republic of Palestine*. London: Ithaca, 1978.

Khaled, Leila, and George Hajjar. *My People Shall Live: An Autobiography of a Revolutionary*. Toronto: NC, 1975.

Khalidi, Walid, ed. *From Haven to Conquest: Readings in Zionism and the Palestine Problem until 1948*. Beirut: Institute for Palestinian Studies, 1971.

el-Khawas, Mohamed, and Samir Abed-Rabbo. *American Aid to Israel: Nature and Impact*. Vermont: Amana, 1984.

Khouri, Fred J. *The Arab-Israeli Dilemma*. 3d ed. Syracuse NY: Syracuse University Press, 1985.

Kiernan, Thomas. *Yasir Arafat*. London: ACACUS, 1976.

Kimche, Jon. *Seven Fallen Pillars: The Middle East, 1915–50*. London: Secker and Warburg, 1950.

Kimche, Jon, and Kimche, David. *The Secret Roads: The Illegal Migration of a People, 1938–48*. London, 1954.

Kominsky, Morris. *The Hoaxers: Plain Liars, Fancy Liars, and Damned Liars*. Boston: Branden, 1970.

Kurz, Anat, ed. *Contemporary Trends in World Terrorism*. New York: Praeger, 1987.

Laffin, John. *Fedayeen: The Arab-Israeli Dilemma*. New York: Free Press, 1977.

Laqueur, Walter. *The Age of Terrorism*. Boston: Little, Brown, 1987.

_____. *A History of Zionism*. New York: Schocken, 1976.

_____. *A World of Secrets: The Uses and Limits of Intelligence*. New York: Basic, 1985.

Lawrence, T.E. *The Seven Pillars of Wisdom*. New York: Doubleday, 1926.

Litvinoff, Barnet. *To the House of Their Fathers: A History of Zionism*. New York: Praeger, 1965.

Livingston, Marius, ed. *International Terrorism in the Contemporary World*. Westport, CT: Greenwood, 1976.

Livingstone, Neil, and David Halevy. *Inside the PLO*. London: Robert Hale, 1990.

Long, David E. *The Anatomy of Terrorism*. New York: Free Press, 1990.

Love, Kenneth. *Suez: The Twice-Forgot War*. New York: McGraw-Hill, 1969.

Lunt, James. *Hussein of Jordan*. London: Macmillan, 1989.

MacBride, Sean. *Israel in Lebanon*. London: International Commission, 1983.

McCullin, Don. *Unreasonable Behavior*. London: Johnathan Cape, 1990.

McDonald, James G. *My Mission in Israel 1948–51*. New York: Simon and Schuster, 1951.

Mackey, Sandra. *Lebanon: Death of a Nation*. New York: Congdon and Weed, 1989.

Mandor, Munya. *Strictly Illegal*. Trans. from 1957 Hebrew edition by H.A.G. Shucklev. London: Robert Hale, 1964.

Martin, David. *Wilderness of Mirrors*. Harper and Row, 1980.

Martin, David, and John Walcott. *Best Laid Plans: The Inside Story of America's War Against Terrorism*. New York: Harper and Row, 1988.

Masalha, Nur. *Expulsion of the Palestinians*. Washington DC: Institute for Palestine Studies, 1992.

Mattar, Philip. *The Mufti of Jerusalem*. New York: Columbia University Press, 1988.

Meade, Robert C., Jr. *Red Brigades: The Story of Italian Terrorism*. London: Macmillan, 1990.

Meir, Golda. *My Life*. London: Futura, 1976; New York: Putnam's, 1975.

Melman, Yossi. *The Master Terrorist: The True Story Behind Abu Nidal*. London: Adama, 1986.

Menuhin, Moshe. *Count Folke Bernadotte*. New York: Arab Information Center, no date.

Mickolus, Edward F. *International Terrorism: Attributes of Terrorist Events, 1968–77*. Ann Arbor MI: Inter-University Consortium for Political and Social Research, 1982.

_____. *Transnational Terrorism: A Chronology 1968–79*. New York: Greenwood, 1980.

_____, Todd Sandler, and Jean Murdock. *International Terrorism in the 1980s: A Chronology of Events*. Ames: Iowa State University Press, 1989.

The Middle East Record. Jerusalem: Israel University Press, 1977.

Miller, Abraham H. *Terrorism and Hostage Negotiations*. Boulder CO: Westview, 1980.

Mishall, Shaul. *The PLO Under Arafat: Between Gun and Olive Branch*. New Haven CT: Yale University Press, 1986.

Monteil, Vincent. *Dossier Secret sur Israel: Le Terrorisme.* Paris: Guy Authier, 1978.

Morris, Benny. *The Birth of the Palestinian Refugee Problem 1947-49.* New York: Cambridge University Press, 1987.

_____. *1948 and After: Israel and the Palestinians.* Oxford: Clarendon, 1991.

Mouly, Ruth W. *The Religious Right and Israel.* Chicago: Midwest Research.

Muslih, Muhammad Y. *The Origins of Palestinian Nationalism.* New York: Columbia University Press, 1988.

Nasr, Kameel, and Dina Lawrence. *Children of Palestinian Refugees vs. the Israeli Military.* California: BIP, 1987.

Netanyahu, Benjamin. *Terrorism: How the West Can Win.* New York: Avon, 1987

Nicosia, Francis R. *The Third Reich and the Palestine Question.* London: I.B. Tauris, 1985.

Noful, Sayed. *Israel's Crime Record.* Cairo: Information Department, 1965.

Nyrop, Richard, ed. for Foreign Area Studies. *Iraq: A Country Study.* Washington DC: American University, 1979.

O'Ballance, Edgar. *Arab Guerilla Power 1967–1972.* London: Faber and Faber, 1974.

_____. *Terrorism in the 1980s.* 1989.

O'Neil, Fard. *Revolutionary Warfare in the Middle East: The Israelis vs. the Fadayeen.* Boulder CO: Paladin, 1974.

Oots, Kent Layne. *A Political Organization Approach to Transnational Terrorism.* New York: Greenwood, 1986.

Ostrovsky, Victor, and Claire Hoy. *By Way of Deception: The Making and Unmaking of a Mossad Officer.* New York: St. Martin's, 1990.

Palestine Liberation Organization Research Center. *Black September.* Beirut: PLORC, 1970.

Palestine Royal Commision Report. Presented by Secretary of State for the Colonies, July 1937.

Palmer, Raymond. *The Making of a Spy.* London: Crescent, 1977.

Parfitt, Tudor. *Operation Moses: The Story of the Exodus of the Falasha Jews from Ethiopia.* London: Weidenfeld and Nicolson, 1985.

Payne, Ronald. *Mossad: Israel's Most Secret Service.* London: Bantam, 1990.

Pearson, Anthony. *Conspiracy of Silence.* London: Quartet, 1978.

Perdue, William D. *Terrorism and the State.* New York: Praeger, 1989.

Perrault, Gilles. *Un Homme à Part.* Paris: Editions Bernard Barrault, 1994.

Petit, Michael. *Peacekeepers at War: A Marine's Account of the Beirut Catastrophe.* London: Faber and Faber, 1986.

Polk, William. *The Arab World Today.* Cambridge: Harvard University Press, 1991.

Porath, Y. *The Emergence of the Palestinian-Arab National Movement 1918–1929.* London: Frank Cass, 1974.

Posner, Steve. *Israel Undercover.* Syracuse NY: Syracuse University Press, 1987.

Powers, Thomas. *The Man Who Kept the Secrets: Richard Helms and the CIA.* Alfred A. Knopf, 1979.

Quandt, William B. *Decade of Decisions: American Policy Toward the Arab-Israeli Conflict 1967–76.* Berkeley: University of California Press, 1977.

_____, Fuad Jabber, and Ann Mosely Lesch. *The Politics of Palestinian Nationalism.* Berkeley: University of California Press, 1973.

Ra'anan, Uri, et al., *Hydra of Carnage: International Linkages of Terrorism*. Lexington MA: Lexington, 1986.

Randal, Jonathan. *Going All the Way: Christian Warlords, Israeli Adventurers, and the War in Lebanon*. New York: Viking, 1983.

Raviv, Dan, and Yossi Melman. *Every Spy a Prince*. Boston: Houghton Mifflin Company, 1991. New edition of *The Imperfect Spies: The History of Israeli Intelligence*. London: Sidgwick and Jakcson, 1989.

Raynor, Thomas P. *Terrorism: Past, Present, Future*. New York: Franklin Watts, 1982.

Reagan, Ronald. *An American Life*. New York: Simon and Schuster, 1990.

Regan, Geoffrey. *Someone Had Blundered: A Historical Survey of Military Incompetence*. London: B.T. Batsford, 1987.

Rivers, Gayle. *The War Against the Terrorists*. New York: Stein and Day, 1986.

Robertson, Terence. *Crisis: The Inside Story of the Suez Conspiracy*. New York: Atheneum, 1965.

Rokach, Livia. *Israel's Secret Terrorism: A Study Based on Moshe Sharett's Personal Diary and Other Documents*. Belmont MA: AAUG, 1980.

Roosevelt, Archie. *For Lust of Knowing: Memoirs of an Intelligence Officer*. Boston: Little, Brown, 1988.

Rose, Norman. *Chaim Weizmann*. New York: Elisabeth Sifton Books, 1986.

Rubenstein, Richard. *Alchemists of Revolution: Terrorism in the Modern World*. New York: Basic, 1974 (revised 1987).

Rudolph, Harold. *Security, Terrorism, and Torture: Detainees' Rights in South Africa and Israel: A Comparative Study*. Cape Town: Juta, 1984.

Rusbridger, James. *The Intelligence Game*. London: Bodley Head, 1989.

Ryan, Chris. *Tourism, Terrorism and Violence*. London: Research Institute for the Study of Conflict and Terrorism, 1991.

Sachar, H. *From the Ends of the Earth*. New York: Dell, 1970.

Said, Edward W., and Christopher Hitchens, eds. *Blaming the Victims: Spurious Scholarship and the Palestinian Question*. London: Verso, 1988.

Samuel, Rinna. *A History of Israel*. London: Weidenfeld and Nicolson, 1989.

Sayigh, Rosemary. *Palestinians: From Peasants to Revolutionaries*. London: Zed, 1979.

Schechtman, Joseph B. *The Life and Times of Vladimir Jabotinsky: Rebel and Statesman*. Foreword by Menachem Begin. Maryland: Eshel, no date.

Schiff, Ze'ev. *A History of the Israeli Army: 1874 to the Present*. New York: Macmillan, 1985.

Schlagheck, Donna M. *International Terrorism*. Lexington MA: Lexington, 1988.

Schoenman, Ralph. *The Hidden History of Zionism*, California: Veritas, 1988.

Sciascia, Leonardo. *The Moro Affair* Trans. by Sacha Rubinovitch. Manchester: Carcanet, 1987; first published in Palermo, 1978.

Seale, Patrick. *Abu Nidal: A Gun for Hire*. New York: Random House, 1992.

_____. *Assad: The Struggle for the Middle East*. Berkeley: University of California Press, 1988.

Segaller, Stephen. *Invisible Armies: Terrorism into the 1990s*. New York: Harcourt Brace Jovanovich, 1986.

Sharon, Ariel, with David Chanoff. *Warrior.* New York: Simon and Schuster, 1989.

el Shazly, Saad. *The Crossing of the Suez.* San Francisco: American Mideast Research, 1980.

Shepherd, Naomi. *Teddy Kollek, Mayor of Jerusalem,* New York: Harper and Row, 1988.

Shiblak, Abbas. *The Lure of Zion: The Case of the Iraqi Jews.* London: Saqi Books, 1986.

Shlaim, Avi. *Collusion Across the Jordan: King Abdullah, the Zionist Movement, and the Partition of Palestine.* New York: Columbia University Press, 1988.

Shultz, George P. *Turmoil and Triumph: My Years as Secretary of State.* New York: Scribner's, 1993.

Slater, Robert O., and Michael Stohl, eds. *Current Perspectives on International Terrorism.* New York: St. Martin's, 1988.

Smith, Colin. *Carlos, Portrait of a Terrorist.* New York: Holt, Rinehart and Winston, 1976.

Smith, Pamela Ann. *Palestine and the Palestinians 1976–83.* London: Croom Helm, 1984.

Snow, Peter, and David Phillips. *The Arab Hijack War.* New York: Ballantine, 1970.

Souresrafil, Behrouz. *Khomeini and Israel.* England: I. Researchers. 1988.

Stein, Leonard. *The Balfour Declaration.* New York: Simon and Schuster, 1961.

Sterling, Claire. *The Terror Network.* Holt, Rinehart and Winston and Reader's Digest Press, 1981.

Steven, Stewart. *The Spymasters of Israel.* New York: Macmillan, 1980.

Suchar, Howard M. *A History of Israel: From the Rise of Zionism to Our Time.* Oxford: Basil Backwell, 1976.

Sykes, Christopher. *Crossroads to Israel.* Bloomington: Indiana University Press (London: Mentor), 1965.

_____. *Orde Wingate.* London: Collins, 1959.

Szulc, Tad. *The Secret Alliance: The Extraordinary Story of the Rescue of the Jews Since World War II.* New York: Farrar, Straus, and Giroux, 1991.

Taheri, Amir. *Holy Terror.* Maryland: Adler and Adler, 1987.

Tannous, Izzat. *The Palestinians: A Detailed Documented Eyewitness History of Palestine under British Mandate.* New York: I.G.T., 1988.

Teveth, Shabtai. *Ben-Gurion and the Palestinian Arabs.* New York: Oxford University Press, 1985.

Thackray, John Richard. *Encyclopedia of Terrorism and Political Violence.* London: Routledge and Kegan Paul, 1987.

Tinnin, David, and Dag Christensen. *The Hit Team.* Boston: Little, Brown, 1976.

Tivan, Edward. *The Lobby: Jewish Political Power and American Foreign Policy.* New York: Simon and Schuster, 1987.

Villeneuv, Charles, and Jean Pierre Peret. *Histoire Secrete du Terrorisme.* Paris: Plon, 1987.

Vital, David. *The Origins of Zionism.* New York: Oxford University Press, 1975.

West, Nigel. *Games of Intelligence,* London: Coronet, 1989.

Wilkinson, Paul, and A.M. Stewart, eds. *Contemporary Research on Terrorism.* Aberdeen University Press, 1987.

Willan, Phillip. *Puppet Masters: The Political Use of Terrorism in Italy.* London: Constable, 1991.

Wilson, Harold. *The Chariot of Israel: Britain, America and the State of Israel.* London: Weidenfeld and Nicolson, 1981.

Wise, David, and Thomas B. Ross. *The Invisible Government.* New York: Random House, 1964.

Woodward, Bob. *Veil: The Secret Wars of the CIA 1981–87.* New York: Simon and Schuster, 1987.

Wright, Robin. *Sacred Rage.* New York: Simon and Schuster, 1985.

Yahalom, Dan. *File on Arab Terrorism.* Jerusalem: Carta, 1973.

Yallop, David. *Tracking the Jackal: The Search for Carlos, the World's Most Wanted Man.* New York: Random House, 1993.

Zogby, James. *The Palestinians.* Washington DC: ADC, 1981.

Index

257